THE RISE AND FALL
OF AMERICAN LUTHERAN PIETISM

THE RISE
AND FALL
OF AMERICAN
LUTHERAN PIETISM

The Rejection
of an Activist Heritage

Paul P. Kuenning

· MERCER ·

ISBN 0-86554-306-2

Library of Congress Cataloging-in-Publication Data
Kuenning, Paul P.
    The rise and fall of American Lutheran pietism :
    the rejection of an activist heritage / Paul P. Kuenning.
        p. 271   15 cm. x 23 cm.   (6" x 9").

    Bibliography: p. 237
    Includes Index.
    ISBN 0-86554-306-2 (alk. paper)
        1. Lutheran Church—United States—History—19th
century.   2. Pietism—United States—History—19th
century.   3. Abolitionists—United States—History—
19th century.   4. Schmucker, S. S. (Samuel Simon),
1799–1873.   5. Franckean Evangelic Lutheran Synod—
History.
    I. Title.
BX8041.K84   1988   88-20933
284.1'3—dc19   CIP

Contents

To

Mary Jo

partner, friend,
and inspirer.

ACKNOWLEDGMENTS

Many people have greatly assisted me in the course of this study, whom I wish to thank. Foremost among them is Patrick Carey, of Marquette University, whose careful and critical reading of my rough manuscripts and insightful suggestions for revision were of invaluable assistance. Special thanks go to the Lutheran Theological Seminary at Gettysburg and Gettysburg College for generous publication subsidy grants as well as access to their archives, and for the kind assistance of the Abdel Ross Wentz Memorial Library's director of Special Collections, Elaine Matthews. I am also indebted to the Metropolitan-Upper New York Synod of the Lutheran Church in America and to its genial and gracious archivist, Helen Kneubel, for making available valuable source materials from its archives located in the Hormann Library at Wagner College, Staten Island, New York. Thanks are also extended to pastors and laypersons of former Franckean parishes who hosted me and offered valuable information from their parish records and to Milton Sernett of Syracuse University, who encouraged my research and discovered several articles of critical importance to this study. Neither would I forget the Trustees of the Smith Family Scholarship, whose stipend enabled me to spend most of one summer in travel and research, or Marquette University and the Lutheran Church in America, whose scholarships facilitated my studies.

Finally I must add my appreciation to a good friend, George Joosten, who urged me to persevere during difficult times, and above all to my wife, Mary Jo, without whose confidence and love I would never have begun this endeavor, let alone finished it.

INTRODUCTION

For nearly a century and a half previous to the Civil War, Pietism was the primary tradition of Lutheranism in North America. During the antebellum period a more conservative and strictly confessionalist theology gradually gained the ascendancy. The struggle for supremacy was carried on mainly within a loosely organized federation of synodical groups formed in 1820 and known as the General Synod. Pietists were called American Lutherans, since their aim was to adapt language, historical confessions, and liturgical practices of the German Lutheran Church to meet the changed conditions of the North American cultural scene. Strict confessionalists were called Old Lutherans because they were dedicated to conserving the orthodox theology, confessions, and traditions of the Reformation era. These popular labels are only partial and imprecise descriptions of the differences that separated these two groups. Old Lutherans were willing to adjust to the American scene in some degree, and the American Lutherans were by no stretch of the imagination wholly opposed to the confessional writings or the theology of Luther. It is more accurate to refer to the former as strict confessionalists and the latter as moderate confessionalists.

Philip Schaff's attempt to place Lutherans of this period into three categories, which he designated as Old, New, and Moderate or Melanchthonian, was also muddled and inaccurate. It was flawed in several respects. First, it confined the term *Old Lutheran* pretty much to the ultraconservative Missouri and Buffalo synods. Second, it considered the strict confessionalist party within the General Synod (which later broke off and became the General Council) as true heirs of the German Pietism of Spener and Francke. Third, it divorced the New Lutherans, under the leadership of Samuel Schmucker, from their Pietistic roots and associated them far too heavily with Methodist and Puritan elements, even insisting that they had given up all the points that distinguished Lutheran theology from the Reformed.[1] It is my belief that the differences between the Lutheran groups can be most accurately understood in terms of a repetition in America of the late seventeenth-century conflict waged in Germany between Lutheran Orthodoxy and Pietism. Therefore my preference is to refer to the contending parties as American Lutheran Pietists on the one hand and Orthodox on the other. This too has its drawbacks, since these two major groups displayed several gradations of more moderate or strict subdivisions.

The American controversy between these Lutheran theological traditions reached its climax in the decade just preceding the outbreak of the Civil War. The event, a major one in the history of American Lutheranism, received its classical description in the title of Vergilius Ferm's well-documented account, *The Crisis in American Lutheran Theology.*[2] The result of this historic confrontation was the defeat and nearly complete rejection of American Lutheran Pietism along with its leadership.

The dean of American Lutheran historians, Abdel Ross Wentz, considered the victory of the conservative type of Lutheranism fortuitous and final, and he was sure that the experiment of "American Lutheranism" would "never be seriously undertaken again."[3] Virgilius Ferm was not so certain. Only the passing of time, he believed, would tell.[4]

One result of the defeat of American Lutheran Pietism was predictable, for losers rarely fare well in the eyes of history. Pietism has remained one of the "most misunderstood and maligned movements within the Church of the Reformation,"[5] especially in North America. It became the whipping boy, upon which Lutheran theologians and historians of every persuasion heaped uninhibited diatribes. It was occasionally paid the compliment of having contributed a warmth of feeling, depth of devotion, and charitable concern to the Lutheran heritage. These positive aspects, however, were buried under an avalanche of negative attributes. Pietism was accused of

---

[1]Philip Schaff, *America*, part 2, ed. Perry Miller (New York: C. Scribner, 1855; reprint, Cambridge: Harvard University Press, 1961) 150-55.

[2]Vergilius Ferm, *The Crisis in American Lutheran Theology: A Study of the Issue between American Lutheranism and Old Lutheranism*, foreword by Luther Allen Weigle (New York: Century, 1927).

[3]Abdel Ross Wentz, *A Basic History of Lutheranism in America* (Philadelphia: Muhlenberg Press, 1955) 143-44.

[4]Ferm, *Crisis in American Lutheran Theology*, 344.

[5]Trygve R. Skarsten, "The Doctrine of Justification in Classical Lutheran Pietism: A Revisionist Perspective," *Trinity Seminary Review* 2 (Fall 1981): 20.

having been not only anticonfessional but anti-intellectual, antisacramental, legalistic, subjective, and otherworldly. In a word, it was condemned as an aberration from authentic Lutheranism and as a deviation from historic Lutheran traditions. Obviously this view was exaggerated, and it is gradually being questioned, reexamined, and reevaluated.

The past two decades have witnessed a revival of interest, particularly in Germany, in the study of Pietism. This resurgence of scholarship was stimulated by the appointment of a "Historical Commission for Research in Pietism," which has at the present time already published sixteen volumes on the subject.[6] The renewed interest in Pietist studies has to some extent expressed itself on the North American scene, particularly in the works of F. Ernest Stoeffler and Dale W. Brown.[7] These and other scholars have discovered in what has been called the classical form of German Pietism a Lutheranism that was nonseparatist, churchly, and reforming in nature.[8] They have concluded that many of the previous questionable assessments of Pietism resulted from a failure to distinguish this classical, churchly form from its more radical and separatist manifestations. Relying heavily on contemporary continental research, these historians have presented positive aspects of German Lutheran Pietism indicating that its passion for personal holiness was closely connected to a corresponding social concern.

This study traces the roots of American Lutheranism to its German Pietist sources. It maintains that the so-called American Lutheranism under the leadership of Samuel Schmucker during the antebellum years did not

---

[6]Some of the most significant studies of Pietism by German historians today are those of Kurt Aland, Martin Schmidt, and Martin Brecht. Other authors who have made contributions of merit are E. Peschke, G. Malzer, H. Obst, F. deBoor, A. Molnar, J. Wallman, and H. Weigelt. For an excellent survey article, see H. Weigelt, "Interpretations of Pietism in the Research of Contemporary German Church Historians," *Church History* 39 (June 1970): 236-41.

[7]F. Ernest Stoeffler, *German Pietism during the Eighteenth Century* (Leiden: E. J. Brill, 1973) and *The Rise of Evangelical Pietism* (Leiden: E. J. Brill, 1965). Brown's contributions include a doctoral thesis, "The Problem of Subjectivism in Pietism: A Redefinition with Special Reference to the Theology of Philipp Jakob Spener and August Hermann Francke" (Ph.D. diss., Garrett Theological Seminary and Northwestern University, 1962), and his book *Understanding Pietism* (Grand Rapids MI: Wm. B. Eerdmans Publishing, 1978). Among other North American contributors to this research are T. Tappert, E. Gerdes, A. Deeter, and D. Bloesch.

[8]Egon Gerdes, "Pietism: Classical and Modern," *Concordia Theological Monthly* 39 (April 1968): 257-68.

drastically depart from this basic heritage. It argues that the charges that have repeatedly been directed against it by American Lutheran historians, to the effect that it was a desertion of valid Lutheran theology and a capitulation to Puritanism, Methodism, evangelicalism, and Americanism in general,[9] have been both exaggerated and inaccurate. For well over a century the precise nature of this antebellum American Lutheran Pietism and its proper place in the history of Lutheranism has been so shrouded in clouds of controversy as to make it nearly impossible to discern. When the question has on occasion been addressed, the discussion has been so animated with animosity and distorted by caricature that any sort of objective answer was all but impossible. Enough time has elapsed for the effort to be made once again, with some hope of at least a partial success. It is important for the Lutheran Church that this attempt be made, and it is a primary purpose of this history. Because of the overwhelming negative connotations that have dominated the historical descriptions of so-called American Lutheranism, the accent here is directed, without apology, to those positive aspects that have for so long been ignored. I attempt to describe American Lutheran Pietism from the viewpoint of its own self-understanding, rather than from that of its antagonists. This accent on the positive is in no way intended to imply that Pietist traditions were free from negative tendencies. But these faults have been fully and one-sidedly documented. This study also highlights Pietism's ethical activism, since its corresponding spirituality has been somewhat more recognized and appreciated.

History is, however, more than the attempt to document *what* happened. It also involves the inquiry into *why* it happened. This latter effort encompasses the central and crucial question to which this account seeks an answer. The question is this: was the rejection of American Lutheran Pietism based almost solely on confessional and doctrinal grounds, or did the negative reaction to its moral activism and especially the willingness of a portion of its constituency to take up the cause of abolitionism also contribute significantly to this renunciation?

In order to answer this question I briefly examine the background of American Lutheran Pietism in its seventeenth- and eighteenth-century German antecedent and trace its first hundred years of development on American soil along with its growing involvement in social and moral reform and in the crusade against slavery. Finally, I center the research in a case study of both an individual and a corporate body clearly representing the American Lutheran Pietist tradition.

---

[9]A summary of this approach is contained in Paul W. Spaude, *The Lutheran Church under American Influence* (Burlington VT: Lutheran Literary Board, 1943).

The individual is Samuel S. Schmucker (1799-1873), the acknowledged leader of the American Pietist school during the antebellum period, a guiding light in the formation and leadership of the General Synod, and the founder and longtime professor of one of the first Lutheran seminaries in this country. The corporate group is the Franckean Lutheran Synod, a small body of Lutheran parishes organized in 1837 and located in upstate New York. It was the only group of Lutherans in this country who were dedicated from the beginning to the principles of abolitionism. It is my hope that the conclusions drawn will lead to a resurgence of discussion, research, and study of this crucial era in American Lutheran Church history.

C·H·A·P·T·E·R 1

German Roots

The Pietist heritage constituted the primary influence upon the shape of the Lutheran church in North America during the entire colonial and antebellum period. Both the intense spiritual fervor and the restless activism that characterized this American Lutheran Pietism had direct roots in its German antecedents. It was profoundly influenced by the sixteenth- and seventeenth-century Pietism that developed under the leadership of Philipp J. Spener (1635-1705) and August H. Francke (1663-1727).

This so-called classical German Pietism, with its center at Halle University, remained entirely within the confessional and organizational context of the Lutheran church and was distinct from a variety of sectarian and radical forms that also received the cognomen of Pietism. It was primarily a reaction to the rigid orthodoxy that had dominated Lutheranism by the latter part of the sixteenth century. Doctrinal formulations and creedal concerns had almost totally eclipsed ethical imperatives and human needs. Pietist leaders often referred to their efforts as an attempt to extend Luther's reformation of doctrine with a reformation of life. Their reform movement was also a response to the widespread human suffering and moral deterioration left in the wake of the Thirty Years' War. Its message of holy living, love for neighbor, and moral renewal spoke directly to an existential need.

The progenitor of classical Pietism was Johann Arndt (1555-1621). He was a respected pastor and leader in the Lutheran church, whose views were widely disseminated in his *Four Books of True Christianity*. From the time of its publication (1606-1610), this work became immediately popular.[1] Outside of the Bible and Luther's *Small Catechism*, no other writing has been so read and revered by Lutherans.[2] Its impact on the lives of later German Lutheran Pietist leaders was, according to their own testimony, enormous. It contains the genius and the soul of classical Pietism. Arndt himself summed up the object of his book as an effort to "lead Christians away from a dead . . . to a living faith, and to wean (them) from a bare intellectual understanding to the real practice of faith and godliness."[3]

The pages of *True Christianity* are permeated with the conviction that love for God can be expressed in a tangible way only through love for one's neighbor. This "neighbor love" is viewed as the real test of faith that "distinguishes false Christians from true Christians."[4] The book displays a sensitive ethical concern and an amazing emphasis on practical piety, which had never to this extent been a part of the Lutheran witness. Arndt's chief contribution to the development of German Lutheran Pietism lay in a profound moral concern which proclaimed that "where one does not follow Christ in his life through faith, there is neither faith nor Christ"[5] and that neither the reading or hearing but the doing and practicing of the Word demonstrates true Christianity.[6] Arndt lamented the internecine polemics that had quickly escalated after Luther's death. He called for a halt to endless disputation over doctrine so that the emphasis could be placed on what he conceived as the true witness of Christianity: service to one's neighbor. As a result he was attacked by orthodox theologians for placing too much emphasis on sanctification. In every instance, however, he survived the challenge. His defense was centered in the Lutheran confessional writings. He referred to numerous passages such as the one in the *Smalcald Articles*, formulated by Luther himself, which states that, "if good works do not fol-

---

[1]Johann Arndt, *True Christianity*, Classics of Western Spirituality, preface by Heiko Oberman, trans. Peter Erb (New York: Paulist Press, 1979) 5.

[2]James G. Morris, *The Life of John Arndt* (Baltimore: T. Newton Kurtz, 1853) 228.

[3]John Arndt, *True Christianity: A Treatise on Sincere Repentance, True Faith, the Holy Walk of the True Christian*, trans. A. W. Boehm (London, 1712); revised, corrected, and furnished with additional material from the original German by Charles F. Schaeffer (Philadelphia: United Lutheran Publication House, 1868) 176.

[4]Ibid., 124.

[5]Arndt, *True Christianity*, trans. Erb, 60.

[6]Arndt, *True Christianity*, trans. Boehm, 179.

low [justifying grace], our faith is false and not true."[7] Had Arndt not been such a perceptive student of Luther, he might never have survived the challenges of an outraged orthodoxy. He is entitled to the honor ascribed to him as being the "first Luther scholar [to] apply Luther's vision that justification by faith alone does not preclude, but to the contrary, unleashes good Works."[8]

Arndt's disciples in the circle of younger Lutheran clergy and academicians included John Gerhard (1582-1637), Johann V. Andreae (1586-1656), George Calixtus (1586-1656), and Paul Gerhardt (1607-1676). All of these influential leaders followed in the tradition of a more irenic, or Melanchthonian approach to theology with a corresponding stress on the ethical implications of faith. John Gerhard, known as the archtheologian of Lutheranism, had a close personal relationship with Arndt; and Johann Andreae, in his brilliant description of a Utopian state, Christianopolis (1619), acknowledged that his social vision had its source in "that Jerusalem" which Arndt had built "with a mighty Spirit, against the wishes of the sophists."[9]

None of Arndt's immediate followers, however, attained the universal acknowledgment of leadership among Pietists as did Philipp Jakob Spener. He was the real founder of German Lutheran Pietism, its theologian par excellence, and by far the most important figure in its rise and development. He has been called the one man in the evangelical church history of Germany who "remains only a little behind Martin Luther himself."[10] Born in Upper Alsace, Spener earned his doctorate at the University of Strasbourg, writing his dissertation on the Book of Revelation.[11] He frequently expressed his admiration for Arndt and, like Arndt, considered himself a confessional Lutheran, less interested in doctrine than in practical piety.[12]

---

[7]The Book of Concord: Confessions of the Evangelical Lutheran Church, "Smalcald Articles," trans. and ed. Theodore G. Tappert (Philadelphia: Fortress Press, 1959) Article 13, p. 315.

[8]Heiko Oberman, preface to Arndt, True Christianity, trans. Erb, xv.

[9]Johann Valentin Andreae, Christianopolis: An Ideal State of the Seventeenth Century, trans. Felix Emil Held (New York: Oxford Univesity Press, 1916) dedication page.

[10]Martin Schmidt, "Spener und Luther," Luther Jahrbuch 24 (1957): 102 (Berlin: Lutherische Verlaghaus).

[11]K. James Stein, Philipp Jakob Spener, Pietist Patriarch (Chicago: Covenant Press, 1986) 66.

[12]Most of the biographical material on Philipp Spener was taken from the following sources: Merle E. Richard, Philipp Jacob Spener and His Work; August Hermann

In 1666, after teaching for a short time, Spener accepted a call as pastor of a large parish and superintendent of the clergy at Frankfurt am Main. Three years later one of his sermons led to the inauguration of informal meetings of the laity for discussion of Scripture, sermons, and other devotional materials. These meetings, called *collegia pietatis*, later became a pivotal feature of Lutheran Pietism.

In 1675, Spener published the most significant of all his writings as an introduction to a new edition of Arndt's popular sermons on the Gospels for the church year. Spener called it *Pia Desideria* (Pious Desires), and it became the textbook of German Lutheran Pietism, containing the essence of its theological premises as well as its practical programs. The central thrust of the book was a scathing attack on some of the evident evils existing within the church and its clergy. The gross lack of morality and spirituality was excoriated. An external or formal Christianity that accepted church attendance and reception of the sacrament as an indication of real discipleship was condemned. A simple assent to doctrine or a verbal affirmation of confessions or creeds as evidence of a true faith was likewise denounced. In spite of these deplorable conditions, Spener maintained that God had better things in store for the church. But the realization of this hope awaited certain envisioned changes. The remainder of the book was devoted to a detailed examination of these proposed reforms, with special attention given to innovations in theological education.[13]

After twenty years in Frankfurt, Spener accepted a call as the court chaplain to the elector of Saxony, Duke John George II. He took up his duties there in the summer of 1686, but his five-year stay at the duke's court in Dresden proved to be a stormy one. Spener's problems arose from his proclivity to criticize directly the questionable morality of his politically powerful patron. After being transferred to St. Nicholas church in Berlin, he lived out the rest of his days in relative tranquility under the favor and protection of King Frederick I of Prussia. One of Spener's most significant achievements was realized with the founding of the new University of Halle in 1692. The school quickly became the academic center of Lutheran Pi-

---

Francke and His Work (Philadelphia: Lutheran Publication Society, 1897); Stein, *Philipp Jakob Spener*; A. Wildenhahn, *Pictures from Life: Philipp Jacob Spener, a Historical Life Picture*, trans. G. A. Wenzel, ed. J. K. Shryock (Easton PA: M. J. Riegel, 1881); Theodore Tappert, introduction to *Pia Desideria*, by Philipp Spener (1675; reprint, Philadelphia: Fortress Press, 1964); *The New Schaff-Herzog Encyclopedia*, 1964 ed., s.v. "Pietism."

[13]Philipp Jacob Spener, *Pia Desideria*, (1675; reprint, trans. Theodore G. Tappert, Philadelphia: Fortress Press, 1964).

etism. It was at Halle, during the first half of the eighteenth century, that the major portion of the clergy who organized and guided the formation of the Lutheran Church in North America received their theological training. When Spener died on 5 February 1705, the Pietism that he had fostered was on the rise and fast approaching its zenith. He had given the movement a theological foundation, impetus, and direction. Now his disciple, August H. Francke, gave it concrete expression in the form of institutional life.

Born in Lübeck in northern Germany, Francke developed expert linguistic skills. After attending the Universities of Erfurt and Kiel, he assumed his first position as a professor of Hebrew at Leipzig University.[14] He admired Spener, and after a spiritual rebirth, which took place in Arndt's city of Lüneburg, and a short stay in Hamburg, where he became interested in the education of children, he determined to visit Spener in Dresden. He spent two months with his spiritual mentor in the winter of 1688, a period he always considered as the most happy and fruitful time of his life.[15] A year later Francke's biblical lectures at Leipzig University caused such a furor that he was obliged to leave his teaching position, accepting a call to serve a parish in Erfurt. Fifteen months later he was accused of founding a new sect of fanatics and was ordered by the elector of the province to leave the city immediately. Spener interceded on his behalf, and within a month he received an appointment as professor of Greek and Oriental languages at Halle University and as pastor of a congregation in nearby Glaucha. He took up his work in January 1692. During his thirty-five years at Halle, Francke's energetic and capable leadership brought German Lutheran Pietism to its climactic point in history. The reforms that Spener had called for were transformed into reality. Spener had involved himself to some extent in practical benevolent endeavors, taking an active role in the building of a poorhouse, orphan asylum, and workhouse at Frankfurt. But for Francke, such concerns became a driving force and lifelong endeavor.

---

[14]Most of the biographical data regarding August Francke was taken from the following sources: Henry Earnest Ferdinand Guerike, *The Life of Augustus Hermann Francke: Professor of Divinity, and Founder of the Orphan-House in Halle,* trans. Samuel Jackson, introduction by E. Bickersteth (London: R. B. Seely & W. Burnside, 1837); Richard, *Spener; Francke;* August H. Francke, *Memoirs* (Philadelphia: Committee of Publication of the American Sunday School Union, 1830); Gary R. Sattler, *God's Glory, Neighbor's Good* (Chicago: Covenant Press, 1982); *The New Schaff-Herzog Encyclopedia,* 1964 ed., s.v. "Pietism."

[15]Richard, *Spener; Francke,* 43.

In 1695, Francke invited a few poor beggar children into his home and began to provide them with a regular period of instruction. From this humble beginning there arose, within a few short years, the famed Halle complex of institutions, with its renowned orphanage and numerous other preparatory schools. By the time of Francke's death in 1727, there were over 2,200 pupils enrolled. Of these, about 150 lived in the Orphan Home, while another 250 indigent students received a daily meal at the institution free of charge.[16] This huge educational and benevolent establishment was built and, for a time, funded almost entirely from donations and charitable contributions. Later on, several business enterprises, such as an apothecary that produced medicines and a publishing house that printed Bibles and other religious materials, were established at Halle. In addition to affording students on-the-job training opportunities, they contributed to the support of the entire endeavor. The Halle Orphan Home became famous as a pioneer achievement and was copied on a smaller scale by benevolent-minded persons throughout the world for many years to come. Under Francke's leadership Pietism continued to flourish and expand, exercising an increasing influence over the entire Lutheran Church in Germany. Not until after his death in 1727 did it begin a gradual decline.

In Württemberg, where the entire development of Pietism had been influenced by Spener,[17] the Halle tradition of Pietism made an even more lasting impression under the leadership of the renowned biblical scholar Johann Albrecht Bengel (1687-1752).[18] In keeping with the Hallean emphasis on the exposition of Scripture, and in contrast to orthodoxy's stress on systematic theology, Bengel became a pioneer in the field of biblical exegesis and textual criticism. In most respects the Pietism that he fostered in Württemberg was quite similar to that initiated by Spener and Francke. Bengel also insisted on a strictly nonseparatist reform and, for that reason, also stood opposed to Count Zinzendorf's Moravianism, as well as all other more radical forms of Pietism. With certain revisions, this churchly Pietism, formulated under the leadership of Bengel, has persisted in Württemberg up to the present time.

---

[16]Stoeffler, *German Pietism during the Eighteenth Century*, 1.

[17]Kurt Aland, *A History of Christianity*, 2 vols., trans. James L. Schaaf (Philadelphia: Fortress Press, 1986) 2:257.

[18]A recent study of Bengel is contained in Charles John Weborg, "The Eschatological Ethics of Johann Albrecht Bengel " (Ph.D. diss., Garrett Theological Seminary and Northwestern University, 1983).

ETHICAL ACTIVISM

German Lutheran Pietism was directed toward a reformation of Lutheranism that would relate the Christian faith more directly to everyday life and its pressing human needs. As a result it stimulated the development of two different, yet closely connected, activities. First, a deep inner spirituality, centered in Scripture and prayer, with an experience of conversion as its hallmark. Second, an intense outward thrust of missionary and benevolent activity as the inevitable and necessary expression of the New Birth, or living faith. Historically, the tendency has been to underscore and highlight the former, while negating or neglecting the latter. As a result German Lutheran Pietism has often been characterized as quietistic or otherworldly, as fostering a subjective spirituality that retreated into its own world of mystical asceticism or private piety. [19] The inaccuracy of these descriptions when applied to the classical Lutheran Pietism of the Spener-Francke school becomes apparent through even a cursory examination of its exuberant ethical activism.

The surge of benevolent and philanthropic activities generated by this Pietism is most vividly revealed in Francke's famed Orphan House and other educational institutions. The entire prodigious enterprise had its origin in the conviction that faith, when it is real, leads to acts of personal and social benevolence directed primarily to those with the most pressing needs—the poor, the underprivileged, and the oppressed. Arndt had laid the foundations for this kind of social compassion. [20] Spener dwelt at length on the same theme of the neighbor's need and coupled it with a call for charitable giving. [21]

---

[19]Among those who have taken this position and made these or similar accusations regarding Pietism are Albrecht Ritschl, "Prolegomena to the History of Pietism," in *Three Essays*, trans. Philip Hefner (Philadelphia: Fortress Press, 1972); Ernst Troeltsch, *The Social Teaching of the Christian Churches*, trans. Olive Wyon (London: George Allen & Unwin, 1931; 4th ed., 1956); Martin Schmidt, *Encyclopedia of the Lutheran Church*, 1956 ed., s.v. "Pietism"; and Martin Marty, *A Short History of Christianity* (Philadelphia: Fortress Press, 1959). At least part of the reason for what I consider an inaccurate criticism of German Lutheran Pietism comes from the failure to distinguish this churchly Pietism of Lutheranism from its more radical and separatist expressions, or from the hesitancy to acknowledge the former as Pietism at all (as in the case of Ritschl, who saw a close correlation between medieval mysticism and Pietism).

[20]Arndt, *True Christianity*, trans. Erb, 182.

[21]Spener, *Pia Desideria*, 61.

With Francke the ethical activism of Pietism reached its apex. The cause of the needy burned deeply in his heart. In one of his books he wrote about justice being denied to the poor, the widow, and the orphan because no one would take up their cause.[22] Francke took it up with vigor and perseverance. The propagation of the Christian faith in the heart of the individual, with its resulting increase in godliness and personal behavior, remained Francke's primary goal.[23] But he was always aware that his endeavors had societal implications, which went far beyond a simple individualistic charity. For instance, a number of his institutions at Halle were intended to strike at social sources of evil by providing vocational training and employment for the poor.[24] Francke remarked, as had Spener before him, that pervasive poverty was a stain upon the church, an enigma not to be endured in the midst of those who called themselves Christian. In addition he had remarkable insight into the negative implications of poverty upon the social fabric. In this connection he even commented on the intimate relationship between unemployment and crime. He noted that, by preparing young people for gainful labor, "the country will be cleared of stubborn beggars, thieves, murderers, highwaymen." He concluded that those governments flourish best "which concern themselves most to provide for the poor."[25]

A number of Francke's sermons also had strong societal implications. He indicated that the destruction of Satan's kingdom must take place in the life of the community as well as the individual, and in a homily entitled "The Duty to the Poor," he dealt directly with corporate responsibilities.[26] This passion for human justice was carried beyond the pulpit. He proposed a new concept for the court system whereby trials would be shortened and the harshness of the law alleviated, and one of his followers instigated significant prison reforms.[27]

---

[22]August H. Francke, *Nicodemus; or, A Treatise against the Fear of Man* (London: J. Downing, 1709) 34-35.

[23]A. H. Francke, *Pietas Hallensis, a Demonstration of the Foot-Steps of a Divine Being Yet in the World: In an Historical Narration of the Orphan House, and Other Charitable Institutions, at Glaucha near Halle in Saxony* (London: J. Downing, 1705) 97. See also pp. 76-88.

[24]James O. Duke, "Pietism versus Establishment: The Halle Phase," *Covenant Quarterly* 36 (November 1978): 8.

[25]Francke, *Pietas Hallensis*, 99-100.

[26]Sattler, *God's Glory, Neighbor's Good*, 71, 155, 167.

[27]Ibid., 73-74.

Of the many communal changes that Lutheran Pietism initiated, perhaps none had a more enduring influence than those that affected the education of youth. In stressing the importance of education, Pietism followed
where Luther had led the way. But its emphasis arose directly out of a concern for the poor, which placed it more emphatically in the context of social reform. Both Spener and Francke proposed and practiced many
innovative pedagogical principles. They believed that the example of the
teacher was of vital importance to a learning process in which the goal was
to influence the character and behavior of the learner.[28] Francke was the
first educator in Germany to develop extensive education for females and
was recognized as the father of the German elementary school system.[29]
The system of education that Francke devised at Halle has been evaluated
by Kurt Aland as "one of the very great achievements of modern history."[30]

In addition to its active promotion of more universal educational opportunities, and partly because of it, Lutheran Pietism was also influential
in modifying some of the rigid class distinctions that characterized German society in the seventeenth and eighteenth centuries. Arndt had expressed an egalitarian emphasis in a number of his meditations.[31] Spener's
mode of ministry reflected the same concern, resulting in criticism from
orthodox opponents for associating too closely with persons "not of his
class."[32] The most influential factor in the breakdown of class distinction
lay in the establishment of the collegia pietatis. At these small-group meetings for study and discussion, people from all professions and trades were
brought together, regardless of rank. Masters sat at the same table with
servants, discussed the Scripture, and knelt in prayer together. This sort
of thing also occurred in the schools established at Halle. While Pietism
never overtly or officially challenged the exclusive divisions of its day, in
practice it contributed to their amelioration.[33]

The activist ethic of German Lutheran Pietism found expression not
only in the social arena but in the political as well. Pietists felt little com-

[28]Arthur Wilford Nagler, *Pietism and Methodism; or, The Significance of German Pietism in the Origin and Early Development of Methodism* (Nashville: Publishing House M.E.
Church, South, 1918) 53.

[29]Brown, "Problem of Subjectivism in Pietism," 111.

[30]Aland, *History of Christianity* 2:242.

[31]Arndt, *True Christianity*, trans. Erb, 129; and trans. Schaeffer, 476.

[32]Koppel S. Pinson, *Pietism as a Factor in the Rise of German Nationalism* (New York:
Columbia University Press, 1934) 110, quoting Carpzov.

[33]Ibid., 108-109.

punction about applying the precepts of the gospel to civil affairs as well as to community, family, and personal life. Luther's legacy of dependence on secular authority, which had left the state, through the office of its territorial ruler, in virtual control of the ecclesiastical domain, was consistently opposed. In his *Pia Desideria* Spener flatly condemned the interference of civil rulers in the affairs of the church, labeling it "Caesaro-papism."[34] His work as court chaplain to the elector of Saxony was terminated at least in part because of the personal criticism he directed at his powerful patron.[35] Late in his career, Spener and, to a greater extent, Francke became friends and favorites of the Prussian leaders, including King Frederick Wilhelm I. This political patronage was a factor in Pietism's victory over Lutheran orthodoxy and contributed to the growing influence it exerted in Germany during the first half of the eighteenth century. But the alliance was initiated by the government, primarily because of the positive contributions and tolerant character of Pietism.[36]

Francke utilized this relationship on a number of occasions to apply the corrective of the gospel to policies of the state. On a visit to Halle in 1713, the king asked Francke what he thought of war. Francke replied, "Your Majesty must protect the land, but I am called to preach 'Blessed are the peacemakers.' "[37] While Pietist leaders remained strictly confessional in their recognition of the divine institution of duly-constituted civil authority and in the rejection of the right of rebellion against it, they clearly understood that the role of the church in the political realm was to function as the prophetic conscience of the state. In summary, German Lutheran Pietism exhibited on all levels a concern for the poor and the oppressed that was advanced for its day and an ethical activism without precedent in the history of Lutheranism. From a twentieth-century perspective it may well be accused of advocating a band-aid approach to social problems, but there can be little question that it made a solid contribution to an expanding con-

---

[34]Spener, *Pia Desideria*, 44.

[35]The letter of rebuke aimed at the powerful elector, which led eventually to Spener's dismissal, is usually described as relating to the elector's personal morality, especially his excessive drinking (Theodore Tappert, introduction to *Pia Desideria*, 21). However, one author strongly suggests that Spener may have spoken out against the elector's aggressive war policies (Wildenhahn, *Pictures from Life*, 152, 280).

[36]Duke, "Pietism versus Establishment," 5-9.

[37]A. H. Francke, quoted in Sattler, *God's Glory, Neighbor's Good*, 71.

cept of social justice. [38] It contained the impetus and the biblical-theological rationale for the moral crusaders, abolitionists, and Social Gospelers of the nineteenth century, who launched a more direct attack on institutionalized forms of injustice.

THE THEOLOGY
OF ETHICAL ACTIVISM

What was the theological basis of the ethical activism, foreign to Lutheran orthodoxy, which appeared as an inherent aspect of classical German Pietism? The traditional answer has been that it was due to a departure from authentic Lutheranism and to the dominating influence of Puritan and Reformed theology on Spener and his successors. Spener's opponents accused him of being dependent on Jean Labadie, a Roman Catholic who had turned Reformed. The problem with this contention, which continues to be advocated, is that it cannot be documented with any precision. Kurt Aland calls the connection with Labadie a "far-fetched insinuation" and maintains that there is "no proof, not even fragmentary evidence," on which to base it. [39] Spener did read the works of early English Puritan reformers and Dutch Reformed Pietists, as did Francke. There can be little question that a considerable amount of cross-pollination took place between Puritanism, Dutch Pietism, and Lutheran Pietism, both on the Continent and in the New World, and that a common motif is evident in their respective theologies. However, the acknowledged dean of Pietist studies in the United States, Ernest Stoeffler, states that it is not at all clear whether classical Lutheran Pietism was much indebted to Puritan and Reformed sources or whether it is to be "attributed to impulses found in the Lutheran reformation itself." [40] Aland is more positive, insisting that "there can be no doubt that German Lutheran Pietism grew out of Lutheranism." [41]

Recent scholarship has unearthed increased evidence that classical Pietism may well have had some impact upon the development of Puritanism, at least in its North American manifestation. A recent biographer of Cotton Mather calls German Lutheran Pietism "one of the most pervasive

---

[38] Allen C. Deeter, "Pietism, Moralism, and Social Concern," *Covenant Quarterly* 33 (May 1975): 31.

[39] Aland, *History of Christianity* 2: 237.

[40] F. Ernest Stoeffler, "Can These Bones Live?" *Christian History* 5 (1986): 12.

[41] Aland, *History of Christianity* 2: 238.

spiritual and intellectual influences on his adult life."[42] Mather, whose life span precisely paralleled that of August Francke, had read many German Pietist writers, including Arndt's *True Christianity*,[43] and thoroughly identified with Pietist views.[44] The New England theologian was impressed with Francke's benevolent activities, praised them highly, and sent sums of money for their support. He initiated a correspondence with Francke that continued over a decade.[45] Mather depicted Francke as a seminal force for Christianity and characterized his own theological role as an "American Pietist" in terms of an effort to fuse the Puritans' concern for God's law with the ethical emphasis of German Pietism. He looked upon the Pietist "revival at Halle as a harbinger of the coming Kingdom."[46] The current research on Mather gives further credence to the earlier contention of Ernst Benz, namely, that the Spener-Francke school of Pietism exerted a significant force on the shape of American Protestant evangelicalism, particularly with respect to its encouragement of an intimate correspondence between spiritual revival and moral reform.[47]

The leaders of classical Pietism clearly were nurtured and educated within the Lutheran church. They considered themselves authentic Lutherans who upheld *all* of its confessional writings contained in *The Book of Concord*. Any open deviation from these symbolic books meant exposure to charges of heresy and prosecution by the civil authorities. German Pietism did openly challenge the rigid and literal interpretation of the Formula of Concord, which had come to be considered the true test of Lutheran or-

---

[42]Kenneth Silverman, *The Life and Times of Cotton Mather* (New York: Harper & Row Publishers, 1984), 230, 232.

[43]Cotton Mather, *Diary of Cotton Mather*, vol. 2, *1709-1724*, American Classics (New York: Frederick Ungar Publishing, n.d.) 346, 348, 413.

[44]Winton U. Solberg, "Science and Religion in Early America: Cotton Mather's Christian Philosopher," *Church History* 56 (March 1987): 80-81.

[45]Kuno Francke, "Cotton Mather and August Hermann Francke," in *Studies and Notes in Philology and Literature*, vol. 5 (Boston: Ginn, 1896).

[46]Richard E. Lovelace, *The American Pietism of Cotton Mather: Origins of American Evangelicalism* (Grand Rapids MI: Christian University Press, 1979) 247-49.

[47]Ernst Benz, "Ecumenical Relations between Boston Puritanism and German Pietism: Cotton Mather and August Hermann Francke," *Harvard Theological Review* 54 (1961): 159-93; and "Pietist and Puritan Sources of Early Protestant World Missions," *Church History* 20 (June 1951): 28-55. See also J. P. Hoskins, "German Influence on Religious Life and Thought in America during the Colonial Period," *Princeton Theological Review* 5 (1907): 225-27.

thodoxy. While Pietists continued to pay fullest reverence to the sacraments as "means of grace," they did not emphasize them to the point of an absolute identity with the gospel itself, as orthodoxy had come to do.[48] Spener believed that the efficacy of the sacraments was always dependent on faith. While he continued to baptize children, he believed that the biblical foundations for the assumption that infants can have faith were weak.[49] In regard to the Lord's Supper, Spener placed the accent on its spiritual benefits rather than upon intricate theological formulations in regard to the mode of Christ's presence. His stress was on how the Supper made "truly present" the promised forgiveness and blessings of the Spirit.[50] Francke was later formally charged with thirty heresies in regard to his concept of the personal union of the two natures of Christ, upon which the doctrine of a corporal presence in the Supper heavily depended.[51] Both Spener and Francke were so well versed in the theology of Luther and all of the confessional writings, however, that they were never once convicted of heresy, despite the determined efforts of their orthodox adversaries. Next to the Scriptures, they turned primarily to Luther and to the Lutheran confessions for the development of their thought.

How, then, do we account for the differences that separated Pietism from Lutheran orthodoxy and to some extent from Luther himself? More precisely, what key theological distinctions, unique to classical Pietism but still within the parameters of the Lutheran confessions, were responsible for its characteristic strain of ethical activism? Two factors appear to be of primary importance: first, its revitalization and expansion of the Lutheran doctrine of sanctification; second, its introduction of an optimistic, millennialist eschatology.

While stressing the importance of sanctification, Pietism continued to uphold the fundamental Lutheran doctrine of "justification by faith alone" with great tenacity. In the introduction to his *True Christianity*, Arndt wrote, "You must take care that you do not connect your works and virtues . . . or the gifts of the new life, with your justification before God, for none of man's works, merit, gifts or virtue, however lovely these may be, count for

---

[48]Werner Jentsch, introduction to Philipp Jakob Spener, *Schriften* vol. 2, pt. 1, ed. Erich Beyreuther (Heidesheim: Georg Olms Verlag, 1982) 46.

[49]Ibid., 47.

[50]Ibid., 46.

[51]Samuel S. Schmucker, "Vocation of the American Lutheran Church," *Evangelical Review* 2 (April 1851): 506-507.

anything."[52] Philipp Spener placed a correspondingly vigorous emphasis on this crucial reformation doctrine.[53] In a theological letter entitled "Clear Thoughts on Justification," he stoutly affirmed that "justification takes place out of pure grace for the sake of Christ and is not in the least reflected directly or indirectly by our holiness or righteousness. If anyone should endeavor to mix in anything of human worthiness I would oppose that person from the bottom of my soul."[54] He added that he would rather give up his life than yield the smallest part of this belief.[55] A recent study concludes that both "Arndt and Spener saw their life work and ministry as a support of the Lutheran doctrine of justification by grace through faith."[56] Similar strong—and orthodox Lutheran—convictions on justification were held by Francke.[57]

These views on justification were voiced not sporadically but repeatedly. The genius of classical Pietism lay not in any rejection of justification by grace alone but in the revitalization and expansion of Martin Luther's original insights into the meaning of sanctification. Luther had always maintained that practical holiness expressed in concrete deeds of love for the neighbor was the sure result of a saving faith in Jesus Christ.[58] In this sense Luther viewed justification as the basis for all Christian ethics and as the most powerful activating force for producing works of love. In his treatise *On Christian Liberty* (1520), written early in his career, Luther had repeatedly expressed this conviction. Appealing to the saying of Jesus that "a good tree does not bring forth evil fruit" and its unspoken correlate, a good tree produces good fruit, he drew the obvious conclusion that "good works do not make a good man, but a good man does good works."[59] This

---

[52]Arndt, *True Christianity*, trans. Erb, 23-24.

[53]Stein, *Philipp Jakob Spener*, 192.

[54]Philipp Jacob Spener, *Theologische Bedencken*, vol. 4 (Halle: Waysenhaus, 1712) 431.

[55]Spener, *Pia Desideria*, 63.

[56]Skarsten, "Doctrine of Justification," 27.

[57]Stoeffler, *German Pietism during the Eighteenth Century*, 6.

[58]See Martin Luther, "Preface to the Epistle of St. Paul to the Romans" (1546), in *Word and Sacrament*, vol. 35 of *Luther's Works*, ed. E. Theodore Bachman (Philadelphia: Muhlenberg Press, 1960) especially p. 370, where faith is described as a "living, busy, active, mighty thing."

[59]Martin Luther, *"Treatise on Christian Liberty,"* vol. 2 of *Works of Martin Luther*, Philadelphia Edition, 6 vols. (Philadelphia: Muhlenberg Press, 1943) 331.

basic ethical insight, from which Luther never deviated, contained explosive activist principles, both psychological and theological. Rather than expanding this concept, however, Luther modified and curtailed it, paving the way for orthodoxy to complete the work of contraction to the point where sanctification was viewed as separate from rather than complementary to the doctrine of justification.[60]

It is difficult to ascertain exactly why Luther pulled back from the more activist implications of his original insights. Certainly it had to do with the rather rigid qualitative distinctions that, in good Augustinian fashion, he drew between the secular and the sacred. Buttressed by his belief in a total human depravity and the absolute bondage of the will, and later intensified by his growing apprehension that worldly affairs were fast coming to an end, Luther viewed human and secular activity as inferior to that exercised in the spiritual and ecclesiastical domain. Thus the social and political application of his inherent activism was severely curtailed.

Beginning in 1523, Luther elaborated with greater precision and theological sophistication the exact nature of this distinction between the secular and the spiritual.[61] In his formulation of the so-called doctrine of the two kingdoms or two realms,[62] Luther maintained that God was equally at work and in control of both spheres simultaneously, but in quite different ways. It is important that this crucial revision of Luther's earlier ideas occurred at the exact time in his career when he saw his reformation of the church being threatened by the revolutionary ardor of the peasants and by the radical theology of reformers like Thomas Müntzer.[63] From the viewpoint both of its intrinsic nature and its timing, Luther's doctrine of the two kingdoms seems to have been designed in part with an eye to stabilizing the political situation by upholding the status quo. Perhaps for the first time,

---

[60]Manfred W. Kohl, "Pietism as a Movement of Revival," *Covenant Quarterly* 32 (August 1975): 5.

[61]Paul Althaus, *Ethics of Martin Luther* (Philadelphia: Fortress Press, 1965) 50-53.

[62]This controversial but fundamental aspect of Luther's social and political ethic is first presented in its fullest form in his treatise "Temporal Authority: To What Extent It Should Be Obeyed" (1523), in *Christian in Society (Part 2)*, vol. 45 of *Luther's Works*, ed. Walther I. Brandt (Philadelphia: Muhlenberg Press, 1962) 81-129.

[63]In this connection it is also important to note that, in 1525, Luther suddenly began for the first time to support the idea of a state church. See Miroslov Volf, "Interview with Jürgen Moltmann," *Christian Century* 100 (16 March 1983): 248.

Luther comprehended the degree of danger from the left, and he moved correspondingly toward the right.[64]

The two-kingdom construct was based ultimately on his interpretation of the Sermon on the Mount. It insisted that the perfectionistic ethics of Christ's teachings applied only to private persons and not to offices, the state included.[65] This aspect of his thought rested on a radical division of the individual person into a private and public being.[66] Perhaps even more important, the two-kingdom theology drew an absolute qualitative distinction between all human activity in the secular realm and the kingdom of God. Thus it stood squarely on the side of a conservative political ethic, admirably equipped (if not designed) to oppose any attempt at fundamental reform in the secular world. This position became all too clear in Luther's dreadful call for the German princes to smash the peasant revolt in 1525.[67] The Reformer could not condone any overt resistance to tyranni-

---

[64]Peter Blickle, *The Revolution of 1525: The German Peasants' War from a New Perspective*, trans. Thomas A. Brady, Jr., and H. C. Erik Midelfort (Baltimore: Johns Hopkins University Press, 1981) translator's preface, 23.

[65]Althaus, *Ethics of Martin Luther*, 145.

[66]Robert Mehl, "The Basis of Christian Social Ethics," in *Christian Social Ethics in a Changing World: An Ecumenical Theological Inquiry*, ed. John C. Bennett (New York: Association Press, 1966).

[67]Martin Luther, "Against the Robbing and Murdering Hordes of Peasants," in *Christian in Society (Part 3)*, vol. 46 of *Luther's Works*, ed. Robert Schultz (Philadelphia: Fortress Press, 1967) 50, 55. It must be stressed that Luther was never able to overcome his horror of revolution and rebellion. Even after the Diet of Augsburg of in 1530, when it seemed probable that Charles V would utilize military force to wipe out the Reformation, Luther under great pressure reluctantly gave way to the jurists' claims that the emperor could lawfully be resisted because, by his action, he forfeited his office. Luther's "Warning to His Dear German People," in *Christian in Society* (pt. 4), vol. 47 of *Luther's Works*, ed. Franklin Sherman (Philadelphia: Fortress Press, 1971) 11-55, ostensibly written to acknowledge his approval of overt resistance, is fraught with ambiguity and disclaimers. Typical is his statement that, while it may be possible under imperial law to resist unjust use of power, he is incompetent as a theologian to decide. He washes his hands of it: "Go ahead and fight confidently. . . .This was not my doing" (p. 55). See Karl Holl, who rightly maintains that Luther "never reached the point of advocating resistance to authority enthusiastically and with full inner conviction," quoted in Althaus, *Ethics of Martin Luther*, 130. The claim that the Magdeburg Confession, urging resistance to the emperor on the basis of the rights of the "lesser magistrates," has its origins in the thinking of Luther is open to serious questions. See Mark U. Edwards, Jr., *Luther's Last Battles: Politics and Polemics, 1531-1546* (Ithaca NY: Cornell University Press, 1983), chap. 2, "The Question of Resistance," 20-37.

cal political institutions, even for a just cause, since he believed they were God-given. He conceived the Christians' ultimate duty to be obedience to civil government, whether good or evil. They were to pray and leave the rest to God. Here the practical conservative implications of Luther's ethical analysis are exposed.[68]

Pietist leaders did not take direct issue with this position. To do so would have severely inhibited their movement. They were undoubtedly sincere in the unbounded admiration they expressed for the founder of Lutheranism. At the same time they viewed their own historical task as the completion of a reformation he had begun and of a goal to which he had pointed the way. Treating the rigid two-kingdom distinction with benign neglect, classical Pietism refused to draw absolute distinctions between this life and the life to come. At the same time, it greatly expanded and developed Luther's original core concept of social ethics expressed in the biblical formulation of a "faith active in love." Pietism advanced precisely in the direction toward which the great Reformer had pointed but then quickly retreated.

In regard to their views on human depravity, the freedom of the will, the sacraments, and the place and purpose of the law in relation to the gospel, Pietists chose to chart a decidedly Melanchthonian course. This orientation was most notable in their decided emphasis on the importance of the ethical. In its stress on the indivisible connection between justification and sanctification and between faith and good works, Pietism patterned itself most closely to the theology of Philip Melanchthon. It was a view that clearly went beyond Luther in its insistence that good works are not only the inevitable concomitant of a true or living faith but that they are also the fulfillment of God's will and command. Even though Luther's emphasis was often quite different on these matters, he not only refused ever to condemn Melanchthon's theology but, to the end of his life, gave it his unqualified approval.[69]

---

[68]W. D. J. Cargill Thompson, *The Political Thought of Martin Luther*, ed. Philip Broadhead (Sussex: Harvester Press, 1984) 69, 72; Roy R. Pascal, *The Social Basis of the German Reformation* (London: Watts, 1933) 177.

[69]For the assertions made with regard to Melanchthon's theology in relationship to Luther's, see Philip Melanchthon, *Loci Communes 1555*, trans. and ed. Clyde L. Manschreck, introduction by Hans Engelland (New York: Oxford University Press, 1965) 39-40, 51-85, 104-29, 181-83; idem, *Selected Writings*, trans. Charles Leander Hill (Minneapolis: Augsburg Publishing House, 1962) 96, 104-106; James William Richard, *Philip Melanchthon: The Protestant Preceptor of Germany, 1497–1560* (New

The practical effect of Lutheran Pietism's revitalization of the Lutheran doctrine of sanctification, with its corresponding emphasis on holiness of life, was to trigger its uniquely activist ethic. If the test of faith was love of neighbor, then the personal experience of justification must automatically result in deeds of service to humankind. Furthermore, the emphasis on the so-called third use of the law envisioned it as of continuing importance to those justified by grace. God commanded good works. By developing an expanded, yet confessional, doctrine of sanctification, Pietism pioneered within Lutheranism the forging of a solid link connecting dogmatics and ethics and initiated the whole subject of moral theology.[70] It carried the explosive insights of Luther on justification to their logical and uninhibited conclusion. In so doing, Pietism opened wide the windows of Lutheranism to vistas of meaningful engagement in the social and political arena, which was viewed as an integral aspect of the Christian's calling.

In addition to this expanded emphasis on sanctification, the other primary motivating theological factor in the ethical activism of Lutheran Pietism was a more hopeful eschatology. Spener's interpretation of the Book of Revelation and other apocalyptic passages of Scripture resulted in his advocating a form of postmillennial eschatology that looked forward to a gradual and progressive improvement of conditions on earth, aided by the church's proclamation of the gospel and efforts on behalf of moral reform.[71] He viewed the future with a degree of hopefulness permeated by a "note of victory."[72] He stood opposed to the more pessimistic view of his-

---

York: G. F. Putman & Sons, Knickerbocker Press, 1898) 234-50; Franz Hildebrandt, *Melanchthon: Alien or Ally?* (London: Cambridge University Press, 1946) 32-41; Nestor Beck, "Faith and Works: A Study of Articles IV-VI and XX of the Augsburg Confession (1530)" (Ph.D. diss., Concordia Seminary, St. Louis, 1973), especially 62-64, 124-26, 279-318.

[70]Stoeffler, *German Pietism during the Eighteenth Century,* 53.

[71]For descriptions of the various forms of millennialism, see Ernest Lee Tuveson, *Millennium and Utopia* (Berkeley: University of California Press, 1949), 76, 112; G. C. Berkouwer, *The Return of Christ* (Grand Rapids MI: Wm. B. Eerdmans Publishing, 1972); Norman Cohn, *The Pursuit of the Millennium* (London: Oxford University Press, 1970); D. H. Kromminga, *The Millennium in the Church: Studies in the History of Christian Chiliasm,* (Grand Rapids MI: Wm. B. Eerdmans Publishing, 1945); Karl Mannheim, *Ideology and Utopia* (London: Harcourt Brace, 1949); James P. Martin, *The Last Judgment in Protestant Theology* (Grand Rapids MI: Wm. B. Eerdmans Publishing, 1963) especially 28-86.

[72]Dale Brown, "Anabaptism and Pietism: Theological Definitions in Historical Perspective," *Covenant Quarterly* 28 (1970): 124.

tory propounded by Luther and enunciated by Lutheran orthodoxy, which envisioned a worsening of conditions on earth and the imminent return of Christ in judgment.

Precisely at this point of eschatology, the deepest cleavage existed between the views of Spener and Luther. This separation accounted for a drastically divergent emphasis on the importance of an earthly oriented ethical activity. Luther had viewed history with stolid pessimism. He believed that the Last Day was close at hand[73] and hoped, in fact, that he would live to see it.[74] In his lectures on Genesis, which were begun in 1535 and completed during the last year of his life,[75] he expressed the belief that history was divided into six parts and that the sixth and last, which began with the birth of Christ, would end shortly with his second coming.[76] He had predicted the closeness of that coming in tracts composed in 1528-1529.[77] Luther was sure that the time of the end was far too near for any serious attempt at fundamental social or political change, even though it was desperately needed. The best that could be done was to patch up what existed, to "put bandages and ointment on the smallpox."[78] As a result, he held out little if any real hope for the present world. The emphasis was on its decay and collapse. He believed that the millennium was long past.[79]

---

[73]Martin Luther, *Table Talk*, vol. 54 of *Luther's Works*, ed. Theodore G. Tappert (Philadelphia: Fortress Press, 1967) 134.

[74]Ibid., 402.

[75]Martin Luther, *Lectures on Genesis*, vol. 1 of chaps. 1-5 ed. Jaroslav Pelikan (St. Louis: Concordia Publishing House, 1958) ix.

[76]Martin Luther, "Lectures on Genesis," in *Weimar Edition of Luther's Work*, vol. 42, p. 634, quoted in George Forell, *Faith Active in Love: An Investigation of the Principles Underlying Luther's Social Ethics* (Minneapolis: Augsburg Publishing House, 1954) 158, 172, 173.

[77]Edwards, *Luther's Last Battles*, 114.

[78]Martin Luther, *Selected Psalms (Part 2)*, vol. 13 of *Luther's Works*, ed. Jaroslav Pelikan (St. Louis: Concordia Publishing House, 1956) 217.

[79]George F. Hall, "Luther's Eschatology," *Augustana Quarterly* 23 (1944): 13, 14, 18. It is difficult if not impossible to categorize Luther's millennial thought. Part of the difficulty lies in the fact, as we have noted, that it was changeable and erratic. His views were obviously influenced by those of St. Augustine. (See Kromminga, *Millennium in the Church*, 109-13; also Cohn, *Pursuit of the Millennium*, 14.) For the greater part of his life Luther adopted what could best be called Augustine's amillennial point of view, interpreting the pertinent passages in the Apocalypse as a spiritual allegory, and the millennium itself as having begun with

There was nothing for the true believers to do but steel themselves for worse trials to come, making sure they did not fall back into the fold of the Antichrist before the Judgment Day arrived.[80]

It is important to note that Luther saw no positive correlation between the improvement of human conditions in this world and the coming reign of God.[81] His viewpoint was, in fact, the exact opposite. The worse those conditions became, the closer it brought God's kingdom to fruition. Speaking of the growing immorality and lack of faith in Germany, he commented that it undermined the gospel and so helped to speed the coming of the Lord.[82] As a result, Luther had much to say about the nearness of the final judgment and a great deal that is positive in terms of personal resurrection, but he spoke very little about either the importance or possibility of any renewal of the world.[83]

In stark contrast, Spener was intensely concerned with both the promise and the possibility of an earthly renovation. He attempted to demonstrate from an exegesis of New Testament passages such as 2 Thessalonians 2:8 and Revelation 18-20 that the final judgment was not so near as commonly supposed. The core of his eschatological hope was no longer dominated by the theme of cosmic judgment as much as it was by more purely historical concerns.[84] Spener's primary focus was fastened on the millennium yet to come, with its promise of the partial realization of God's kingdom on earth.[85] He opened the second section of his *Pia Desideria* with the statement that "if we consult the Holy Scriptures we can have no doubt that God promised his church here on earth a better state than this [present one]."[86] The improved future state of things he described in a later work as

the birth of Christ and fully realized within the church in the past. Even when his interpretation of Revelation was altered, the millennium itself played little part in Luther's thinking. It was a past event, and the whole emphasis was on the coming Parousia and judgment, with no thought of a transitional period between this world and eternity.

[80]Tuveson, *Millennium and Utopia*, 25-28, also T. F. Torrance, *Kingdom and Church: A Study in the Theology of the Reformation* (Edinburgh: Oliver & Boyd, 1956) 18-19.

[81]Edwards, *Luther's Last Battles*, 15.

[82]Martin Luther, *Selected Psalms (Part 2)*, 191-92.

[83]Torrance, *Kingdom and Church*, 5.

[84]Stein, *Philipp Jakob Spener*, 181.

[85]Martin, *Last Judgment in Protestant Theology*, 67-73.

[86]Spener, *Pia Desideria*, 76.

"a hope for better times in the Church."[87] Spener was certain that, since these promises were contained in the Scriptures and came from God, they would inevitably be accomplished, with or without the help of Christian people. But it was the duty of believers, as well as their opportunity, not only to hope and pray for these things but to make sure that "as much as possible is done to convert the heathen and the Jews, . . . and to reform the Church."[88]

Spener was careful to insist that, even though God chose to utilize human means, in the final analysis the establishment of the kingdom was totally a divine work. It was grounded in both God's promise and present work, not in any human capacity.[89] On this basis he argued that his views represented a new millennialism not condemned by Article 17 of the Augsburg Confession. According to Spener, the Lutheran confessions did not forbid chiliasm as such, since to do so would, in his view, violate the clear teaching of Scripture. Therefore he was convinced that the confessional anathema applied only to certain Anabaptist or Jewish forms that would force the kingdom into being by human means.[90] Although he steadfastly affirmed his belief in some type of historical restoration of a pristine Christianity, Spener averted any affirmation of utopianism by acknowledging that sin, suffering, and death would not be fully expelled from the millennial reign.[91] Nevertheless, he was accused by orthodox leaders of teaching the heresy of a subtle chiliasm. That his actual comments on this subject remained within the confines of the Lutheran confessions is indicated by the fact that these charges never resulted in any official condemnation.

Johann Bengel carried the eschatology of Spener even further, predicting the precise time when the millennium would arrive. His interest in the Apocalypse was concerned almost exclusively with its prophetic sense, and he believed that it dealt solely with future events.[92] Joachim Lange, a Halle theologian, followed essentially the same moderate program for the

---

[87]K. James Stein, "Philipp Jakob Spener's Hope for Better Times for the Church: Contribution in Controversy" *Covenant Quarterly* 37 (August 1979), quoted from *Behauptung der Hoffnung künfftiger besserer Zeiten,* 1693. This treatise contains Spener's most precise and significant exposition of his millennialism.

[88]Spener, *Pia Desideria,* 78.

[89]Stein, *Philipp Jakob Spener,* 178.

[90]Weborg, "Eschatological Ethics of Johann Albrecht Bengel," 56.

[91]Brown, "Problem of Subjectivism in Pietism," 277.

[92]Martin, *Last Judgment in Protestant Theology,* 65, 66.

future as Spener, producing the most explicit eschatological statement of all the Lutheran Pietists. Francke, who was more practically inclined than Spener, treated the theology of the future with far greater restraint. His reticence was undoubtedly due in part to the severe criticism Spener had received and to the attacks from orthodoxy to which he had been subjected for his alleged chiliasm. The tremendous activist drive behind the entire Halle movement and its evident social concern cannot, however, be explained apart from an optimistic view of history. It is a theological assumption that lies close to the surface of all that Francke said and did. In a sermon on "saving faith," he took pains to make it clear that this faith had reference not just to the life to come but to the present state of existence and activity.[93] Francke's whole life and work bore witness to the clear and present hope that the church could be better than it was and that God intended to bring about such change.

The question about the origins of this critical shift in future expectations from the pessimism of Luther and later orthodoxy cannot at present be answered with any precision. It is not sufficient simply to attribute it to Puritan and Reformed influences, as has traditionally been done. It is true that Spener and Johann Andreae before him apparently had some knowledge of the views of Joseph Mede (1586-1638). Mede, a widely read and respected English biblical scholar of the early seventeenth century, renewed the early Christian belief in the millennium as the crowning point of human history. His revival of chiliasm "took the first step away from the idea of world transcendence to . . . world reform" and to the concept that the "destined goal of humanity . . . is not to escape from this . . . evil universe . . . but rather to achieve a happier state on earth."[94] However, a distinct difference developed between the eschatology of Lutheran Pietism and that of English Puritanism. While embracing the millennial concepts of Mede, Puritanism continued to use the immediate threat of the Last Judgment as a motivation for ethical behavior. Spener altered this approach. He interpreted Revelation as predicting a twofold coming of Christ, with an interval of time between the overthrow of the Antichrist and the Last Judgment. He then endowed this intervening period with a strong degree of optimism, leaving the traditional "last things" in the background and affording them only minor attention.[95]

---

[93]Guerike, *Life of Augustus Hermann Francke*, 43.

[94]Tuveson, *Millennium and Utopia*, vii, 76, 112. For knowledge of Mede, see Spener, *Theologische Bedenken* 3:258.

[95]Martin, *Last Judgment in Protestant Theology*, 67-69.

Some of the millennial mentality of classical Pietism perhaps originated with Thomas Müntzer, a radical reformer and early follower of Luther who formulated the first and the most incisive criticism ever made of the conservative elements in Luther's social ethic. Müntzer's views regarding the realization of God's kingdom on earth, divorced from their revolutionary context and reliance on military force, were taken up by the Anabaptism that emerged in southern Germany and that had a definite impact on the shape of Lutheran Pietism. [96] Whatever its sources, Pietist leaders unanimously asserted that the moderate chiliasm voiced in the words of Spener as a "hope for better times" was not only compatible with the confessions of the Lutheran church but grounded in Scripture and therefore anchored in the fundamental Reformation doctrine of *sola Scriptura.* This eschatological hope was a primary source of the ethical activism that asserted itself in the driving concern for renewal and reform in both church and society.

The specific forms of the activism that sprang from the eschatology of Pietism were directly conditioned by the nature of its hope. From a positive perspective, that hope envisioned two things: a mass conversion of the world to Christianity and a reform of the church. Spener's millennial hope was never fanciful or metaphysical. Its fulfillment was directly related to a reform of the existing institutional church. [97] In his *Pia Desideria,* Spener had proposed "the establishment and diligent exercise of the spiritual priesthood" as one way to correct the corrupt conditions into which the church had fallen. [98] Francke agreed, complaining of the "horrid mischief" caused by the "wicked distinction" between clergy and laity. [99] This revival of Luther's stress on the priesthood of all believers also made itself felt in the establishment of a more democratic church polity. According to Spener's program, parishioners were to choose their own pastors, judge the faithfulness of their minister's preaching, and make changes in congregational

---

[96]For a fuller explication of this view, see Paul P. Kuenning, "Thomas Müntzer: Theologian and Rebel with a Cause," *Covenant Quarterly* 44 (November 1986): 3-23; and "Luther and Müntzer: Contrasting Theologies in Regard to Secular Authority within the Context of the German Peasant Revolt," *Journal of Church and State* 29 (Spring 1987): 305-21.

[97]Stein, "Philipp Jakob Spener's Hope," 8.

[98]Spener, *Pia Desideria,* p. 92.

[99]August Hermann Francke, quoted in Brown, "Problem of Subjectivism in Pietism," 203.

ceremonies.[100] At the same time, he insisted that no one could assume the right to function as a minister in the church without a special and official call.[101] He urged that the common people should always have part in the decisions of the church and that both laity and ministers were to be represented in the synods and other legislative bodies. Spener was acutely aware of the compelling reasons for a more activist laity. He saw clearly that, when the laity were denied decision-making power, the result was eventually a loss of interest. Furthermore he believed that the common sense of pious laypersons was often of more value than the greater academic learning of the clergy.[102]

While the drive for reform centered on the revitalization of Luther's original emphasis on the role of the laity, the millennial vision of worldwide conversion led to a religious tolerance unique for its day. Pietism wished to convert others to Lutheran or Protestant Christianity, not by polemics, but by love and prayer. Spener wrote that unbelievers and even heretics should be considered as neighbors, as part of a universal family by right of human creation and the divine love that extended to all without distinction.[103] Although Pietism, like the rest of Protestantism, remained vigorously anti-Catholic, and Spener envisioned the fall of the papacy as a visible sign of the millennium,[104] yet at the same time he affirmed that true believers were to be found within the Roman church also.[105] The result was that, while Pietists carefully guarded their confessional standards, they established far more friendly relations with their Calvinist neighbors than did Lutheran orthodoxy. This tolerant attitude was also related to the fact that the restoration of the unity of the church was viewed as one of the blessings of the hoped-for messianic age.[106]

---

[100]Nagler, *Pietism and Methodism*, 49.

[101]Philipp Jakob Spener, "On the Spiritual Priesthood of Believers," appendix to *A Summary of the Christian Faith*, trans. Henry E. Jacobs (Philadelphia: General Council Publication House, 1905) 584.

[102]Richard, *Spener; Francke*, 51.

[103]Spener, *Pia Desideria*, 99.

[104]Stein, "Philip Jakob Spener's Hope," 4.

[105]Nagler, *Pietism and Methodism*, 40.

[106]Martin Schmidt, "Ecumenical Activity on the Continent of Europe in the Seventeenth and Eighteenth Centuries," in *A History of the Ecumenical Movement, 1517–1948*, ed. Ruth Rouse and Stephen Charles Neill (Philadelphia: Westminster Press, 1968) 83. See also 99-105.

In keeping with this basic theological orientation, German Pietism placed the ecumenical emphasis not on the details of doctrinal agreement but on a general consensus as to fundamental beliefs coupled with the practice of a common piety. As a result, Pietism was able to cross confessional and denominational lines with apparent ease. It did not so much engage in a search for unity as it operated with the supposition that this unity already existed and had only to be expressed in cooperative activities of a benevolent nature. Francke, for instance, envisioned a joint effort of the various communions "for the purpose of supporting missionary, educational and charitable endeavors,"[107] along with a universal seminary to train both Protestants and Eastern Orthodox for missionary work. In a word, the ecumenism of Lutheran Pietism was both spontaneous and practical.[108]

In addition the hope of the mass conversion of the heathen led to a concentration on missionary activity. Neither Luther nor Calvin had shown any particular interest in the establishment of missions. The first real Protestant missionary impulse awaited the arrival of Pietism and the influence of Spener,[109] with his conviction that God was holding back the Parousia until all the elect were brought to belief.[110] But it was Francke who put this concern of Spener into concrete action. His efforts at Halle blazed a trail of Protestant missions all the way from Greenland to India to North America.

---

[107]Stoeffler, *German Pietism during the Eighteenth Century*, 35-36.

[108]Schmidt, "Ecumenical Activity on the Continent," 101.

[109]Gustav Warneck, *Outline of a History of Protestant Missions From the Reformation to the Present Time*, trans. from the 7th German edition by George Robson (New York: Fleming H. Revell, 1903) 39-40.

[110]Stein, "Philipp Jakob Spener's Hope," 7.

The First Century in North America

THE TRANSPLANTATION TO NORTH AMERICA

Pietism's accent on missions accounted for its early arrival in colonial North America. Missionaries from the University of Halle were primarily responsible for the growth of the Lutheran church in the Western Hemisphere. For seventy-five years they continued to arrive from the center of Lutheran Pietism's activity on the Continent. Throughout the entire eighteenth century these disciples of the Spener-Francke school of theology constituted the principal source of clerical leadership for Lutherans in this country. Through their stalwart efforts Pietism became the dominant form of Lutheranism in the New World, a position it retained up until the decade previous to the Civil War.

Justus Falckner, the first Halle graduate to come to the Colonies, arrived at the beginning of the eighteenth century. He joined a group of more radical German Pietists who had settled in the vicinity of Philadelphia, Pennsylvania, near the close of the previous century. Falckner had studied under August Francke and taught in his famed orphanage. In 1703, he became the first Lutheran minister to be ordained in North America. For two decades, until his death in 1723, he carried out an arduous and faithful ministry to widely scattered parishes in New York and New Jersey. He was also an author and hymn writer. [1] Following Falckner's death, his brother

---

[1] Leonard R. Riforgiato, *Missionary of Moderation* (Lewisburg PA: Bucknell Uni-

Daniel was accepted as a pastor in the New York area, where he served for a number of years.[2] In the South, two Halle-trained pastors, John Martin Boltzius and Israel Christian Gronau, had accompanied a group of Lutheran Pietist refugees from Salzburg and the Palatinate, settling at New Ebenezer near Savannah, Georgia, in 1734.[3] Within four years after their arrival, and even before erecting a house of worship, they built an orphan house after the pattern of the one in Halle. It was the first Protestant institution of its kind in the Colonies.[4]

HENRY M. MUHLENBERG: PIETIST

The widespread diffusion of German Pietism within Lutheranism and the entire religious culture of colonial North America was chiefly due to the prodigious missionary efforts of Henry Melchoir Muhlenberg (1711-1787). Muhlenberg is universally and justly regarded as the organizer and father of the Lutheran church in North America. He earned this distinction not only by serving as a faithful parish pastor to a number of congregations in Pennsylvania and New York but by his personal visits and correspondence with shepherdless Lutherans in parishes from Nova Scotia to Georgia. He acted as arbitrator in endless disputes, sought needed financial aid for new churches from the fathers at Halle University, and organized the first Lutheran synod, or ministerium, in the New World, serving as its first president.

Because of the unique and revered position Muhlenberg held as the patriarch of Lutheranism in North America, it is understandable that Lutherans of every persuasion sought to claim him as their own. Some historians even portrayed him as an upholder of a strictly orthodox confessionalist theology. These accounts excused Muhlenberg's Pietism as a lingering and degenerate aspect of his German background, which he had,

---

versity Press, 1980) 51. The early account of the Falckner brothers is most fully recorded in Julius Friedrich Sachse, *The German Pietists of Provincial Pennsylvania* (1895; reprint, New York: AMS Press, 1970). The ordination of Justus Falckner is described in detail in pp. 353-60. His hymn "Rise Ye Children of Salvation" became a classic for all Protestants.

[2]Sachse, *German Pietists of Provincial Pennsylvania*, 344-48.

[3]See George Fenwick Jones, *The Salzburger Saga: Religious Exiles and Other Germans along the Savannah* (Athens GA: University of Georgia Press, 1984).

[4]William J. Finck, *Lutheran Landmarks and Pioneers in America* (Philadelphia: United Lutheran Publishing House, 1913) 123-28.

for the most part, allegedly discarded.[5] A more moderate revisionism tended to balance the obvious evidences of Pietism with what was viewed as equally strong indications of strict confessional convictions.[6] Thus Muhlenberg was described as a kind of Pietist-confessionalist amalgamation. But all attempts to portray the patriarch as possessing a theology similar to the conservative confessionalism that has characterized American Lutheranism since the time of the Civil War faces serious problems of documentation.

In Germany, where Muhlenberg grew to manhood, his connections with Lutheran Pietism were close, and his affirmation of its convictions, complete. Born in Einbeck, in the province of Hanover on 6 September 1711, Muhlenberg had to discontinue his education at the age of twelve because of the death of his father. He was twenty-three years old when he finally entered the University of Göttingen. There, under the influence of a Pietist professor and three fellow students who had attended the University of Halle, Muhlenberg underwent what can best be described as a gradual conversion experience. During his years at Göttingen he also helped to found a school for poor children. In the spring of 1738, he entered the University of Halle, then under the direction of Gotthilf Francke, the son of its Pietist founder. Here he instructed children in the orphan school, taught languages in the seminary, and learned something about medicine and pharmacy. When opportunities for mission work to the Jews and to the West Indies failed to materialize, he was ordained in the fall of 1739 and accepted a call to a parish near Herrnhut in Saxony.[7] This location was close to the center of activities for Count Zinzendorf's restored Church of the United Brethren. Zinzendorf himself had attended Halle but had since

---

[5]The standard biography of Muhlenberg, published on the 100th anniversary of his death, is the best example of this type of revisionism. See William J. Mann, *Life and Times of Henry Melchior Muhlenberg* (Philadelphia: 2d ed., General Council, 1911). This interpretation was extremely influential and is reflected in the writings of the distinguished Lutheran historian H. E. Jacobs, as well as in a more recent biography by Paul A. W. Wallace, *The Muhlenbergs of Pennsylvania* (Philadelphia: University of Pennsylvania Press, 1950).

[6]Examples of this approach are typified by William K. Frick, *Henry Melchior Muhlenberg, Patriarch of the Lutheran Church in America* (Philadelphia: Lutheran Publishing Society, 1902); and by the recent biography by Riforgiato, *Missionary of Moderation*. Most Lutheran historians, including Abdel Ross Wentz (*Basic History of Lutheranism in America*) and E. Clifford Nelson (editor of *The Lutherans in North America* [Philadelphia: Fortress Press, 1975]) are influenced to some extent by this traditional interpretation.

[7]Riforgiato, *Missionary of Moderation*, 21-25.

fallen into disfavor with its leaders because of his more radical and separatist tendencies. The parish that Muhlenberg served was under the jurisdiction of the Baroness Gersdorf, Zinzendorf's aunt.[8]

During his pastorate there in 1741, Muhlenberg composed an article
defending Pietism against the attack of an orthodox opponent, Balthasar
Menzer.[9] It is one of only two articles known to have been published by
Muhlenberg. In it he upheld the doctrine of sanctification as the living fruit
of justification,[10] the small-group meetings (or collegia pietatis), the importance of "awakening," or conversion,[11] and the right of the congregation as against the state to appoint its own pastors and govern its own
affairs.[12] In commenting on his opposition to any form of separatism,
Muhlenberg voiced his conviction that all ministers of the gospel should
have an official call from the church, but he made it equally clear that he
was more concerned about teaching the spirit than the letter in regard to
the symbolic books.[13] All in all, it was a remarkably faithful testimony to
the credo of the Spener-Francke school of Pietism.

In the fall of 1741, Muhlenberg received and accepted a call issued by
Gotthilf Francke to serve several parishes in Pennsylvania. For a number of
years, these parishes, located in and near Philadelphia, had pleaded with
Francke to send them a pastor. It appears that one of the reasons the Halle
leader finally decided to grant their request was that Moravian missionaries
had made deep inroads among the German Lutheran constituency, and
Count Zinzendorf himself was preparing to travel to America.[14] Upon his
arrival, Zinzendorf, with an almost indiscriminate ecumenism, had attempted to bring together all the diverse pietistic groups, including Lutherans, under the umbrella of his "Church of God in the Spirit." After
arriving in Philadelphia in November 1742, Muhlenberg wasted no time
in personally confronting the count and directly challenging his Lutheran
credentials. In this stormy interview, Muhlenberg defended his commis-

---

[8]Ibid., 25.

[9]Henry M. Muhlenberg, "Muhlenberg's Defense of Pietism," trans. C. W.
Schaeffer, *Lutheran Church Review* 12 (October 1893): 349-75.

[10]Ibid., 360.

[11]Ibid., 362.

[12]Ibid., 370.

[13]Ibid., 372.

[14]Riforgiato, *Missionary of Moderation*, 91.

sion from Halle and demanded the return of an official church record book.[15] Zinzendorf refused but two days later departed for London.[16]

This opposition to the radical Pietism and indiscriminate ecumenism of Zinzendorf has been held up as proof of Muhlenberg's confessional orthodoxy. A respected Lutheran church historian even claimed that the "great battle for a confessional foundation of the [Lutheran] Church in America was fought and decided" during the course of this confrontation.[17] It would be far more accurate to say that Muhlenberg here defended a churchly Pietism against its more radical and separatist manifestation. Muhlenberg found that sectarian forms of Pietism disassociated from their churchly connections and filled with "disorder and confusion" were a more prevalent and formidable foe in colonial America than in Germany.[18] The situation posed severe problems for a Lutheran constituency that was scattered and disorganized and without adequate pastoral leadership. From the perspective of strategy, Muhlenberg's early confrontation with Count Zinzendorf may well have influenced him in a more conservative direction than he would have been otherwise inclined.[19]

---

[15]Henry Melchior Muhlenberg, *Journals*, 3 vols. trans. and ed. Theodore G. Tappert and John W. Doberstein (Philadelphia: Muhlenberg Press, 1942-1958) 1:80. This entire interview from Muhlenberg's vantage point is described in *Journals*, 1:76-82.

[16]Riforgiato, *Missionary of Moderation*, 95.

[17]Henry E. Jacobs, "The Confessional Problems in the Lutheran Church of America in 1742," *Lutheran Church Review* 31 (April 1912): 252.

[18]Samuel S. Schmucker, *The American Lutheran Church, Historically, Doctrinally, and Practically Delineated, in Several Occasional Discourses* (Springfield OH: D. Harbaugh, 1851; reprint, New York: Arno Press and New York Times, 1969) 99, quoting Muhlenberg's *Hallishe Nachricten*, 1:17.

[19]In this connection see the article by Milton J. Coalter, Jr., "The Radical Pietism of Count Nicholas Zinzendorf as a Conservative Influence on the Awakener, Gilbert Tennent," *Church History* 49 (March 1980): 35-46. Coalter first points out how Gilbert Tennent and, through him, George Whitefield and other leaders of the Great Awakening were influenced by what he calls the 'confessional Pietism' of the Reformed and Lutheran variety. He then describes how Tennent's fervor for the awakening in general and for lay spirituality, conversion, and a converted ministry appears to have cooled considerably after a confrontation with Count Zinzendorf in December 1741, very similar to that of Muhlenberg, which took place just a year later. Coalter concludes that Tennent, after his meeting with Zinzendorf, expressed greater concern for "doctrine and denominational peace" than he had before (p. 46).

Allegiance to the Augsburg Confession and a common liturgical sub-scription, matters that German Pietism had never renounced, became a practical way to establish Lutheran identity in the face of the inadequate claims to that title so often made by Moravians and other radical Pietists.[20] Muhlenberg believed that the confessions and liturgical order were im-portant, but he remained the inveterate foe of those who coveted correct doctrine more than a converted conduct. He was outspoken in his oppo-sition to those who confessed allegiance to the "unaltered" Augsburg Confession but who lived unaltered lives. His motto was *ubi vita fulgur, ubi doctrina tonitru* (true doctrine is proclaimed where godly life is manifest).[21] He was convinced that neither the confessions of the church nor the name of Lutheran were in any way sufficient for salvation, "but only a complete change of heart and a living faith."[22]

Muhlenberg's affinity for individuals and churches with deep evangel-ical concern usually rose above denominational and doctrinal differences. Several times he attended services where the noted evangelist George Whitefield or one of the Tennent brothers was preaching and commented concerning their biblical insights and edifying powers.[23] On one occasion he invited Whitefield to preach in his Philadelphia parish and did not hes-itate himself to preach from Episcopal and German Reformed pulpits. The accent in his preaching and personal ministry to people was always on re-pentance and conversion, which he most often referred to as awakening. He embraced revivalism and spoke positively of its benefits but insisted that it be kept within a churchly or liturgical framework. He believed in the expression of emotion, as long as it was not pursued as an end in itself and good order was maintained. One of Muhlenberg's significant contribu-tions to early American Lutheranism was the synthesizing of emotional earnestness and liturgical order, a direct aspect of his Halle heritage.[24] The patriarch fully identified with the stress by Lutheran Pietists on the indis-soluble connection of justification and sanctification, along with its re-sulting accent on an active Christianity.[25] Like Spener and Francke before

---

[20]Harvey L. Nelson, "A Critical Study of Henry Melchior Muhlenberg's Means of Maintaining His Lutheranism" (Ph.D. diss., Drew University, 1980) 385, 387.

[21]Muhlenberg, *Journals* 3:667.

[22]Ibid. 1:382.

[23]Ibid. 2:574.

[24]Riforgiato, *Missionary of Moderation*, 139.

[25]Nelson, "Critical Study," 132, 312.

him, he guarded carefully the temptation to bifurcate correct belief and correct living, convinced that both were equally the equipment of the mature Christian.

MUHLENBERG'S PIETIST COLLEAGUES

Muhlenberg's earliest coworkers were all trained at Halle. In 1745, just three years after his arrival in Philadelphia, Muhlenberg was joined by three colleagues. The Reverend Peter Brunholz assisted him with pastoral activities, and two unordained theological students, John N. Kurtz and John H. Schaum, taught in the schools the patriarch had established in connection with his parishes. At the organizational meeting of the first Lutheran ministerium, or synod, in 1748, Kurtz was ordained, and Schaum one year later. The preacher at Kurtz's ordination was Rev. John C. Hartwick, another Hallean, who had come to the Colonies perhaps even earlier than Muhlenberg as a chaplain to German forces during the French and Indian Wars. [26] Hartwick also assisted Muhlenberg for a time before taking a parish in New York.

The year 1748 also marked the arrival of yet another Halle graduate who would render valuable service in the New World, Rev. John H. Handschuh. All of these associates mirrored the marks of Lutheran Pietism that characterized the ministry of Muhlenberg. Their preaching was evangelical and practical, geared toward the awakening power of conversion and the strengthening of a living faith. They organized prayer meetings and Sabbath schools for the instruction of the young. They emulated the ecumenical spirit of Muhlenberg. Like him, they were on intimate terms with Whitefield, Gilbert Tennent, Samuel Davies, and other evangelical leaders. Persons of various denominations attended their services. Handschuh was a personal friend of Tennent, for whom he expressed his highest regard, [27] and clergy from the Episcopal, Presbyterian, German Reformed, and Baptist churches all took part in his funeral service in 1764. Earlier, Samuel Davies wrote of Handschuh and his colleagues that he saw in them "the religion of Jesus appear undisguised," enabling him to forget all "national and religious differences."[28] Finally, all of these early Halle colleagues shared Muhlenberg's ethical concern. Handschuh preached against

---

[26]Martin L. Stoever, "Reminiscences of Lutheran Clergymen," *Evangelical Review* 7 (October 1855): 168.

[27]"Patriarchs of the Lutheran Church from Halle," *Evangelical Review* 15 (April 1864): 185.

[28]Ibid., 167.

the intemperate use of alcohol, which led to a division within his German-town parish. Brunholz, who never married, gave all of his surplus income to the poor. Kurtz and Hartwick were well known for their benevolent efforts. All were engaged in efforts to extend a ministry to the poor and needy.[29]

As for Muhlenberg himself, the concept of service to human need as a necessary fruit of faith had been a part of his Pietist conviction since his student days at Göttingen University. He had a genuine empathy with the poor, which he retained throughout his life. He supported the charity-schools movement even when the majority of his Lutheran constituency opposed it on political grounds.[30] He always intended to establish an orphan house in America that could also be utilized as a seminary and as a home for retired pastors and their wives, but circumstances prevented its realization.[31] He lamented the fact that the "burdensome plague" of building and organizing the Lutheran church in the midst of chaotic conditions often delayed the more vital involvement of furnishing needed assistance to "poor widows and orphans."[32] Under more settled conditions he might have become another Francke, but he gave ample indication that he had inculcated Pietism's sensitive social consciousness and concern for the poor and oppressed.

This social activism was further expressed in Muhlenberg's opposition to the system of indenture, whereby Germans were given their fares to this country by promising to work off their debt under conditions of servitude that were often barbarous. He gave his energetic support to the German Benevolent Society of Pennsylvania, a group organized to remedy this evil, which held its meetings in the schoolhouse of Muhlenberg's Philadelphia parish.[33] He was appalled and depressed by the slave trade. Upon landing in Savannah in 1742, he commented in regard to the institution of slavery, "This is a horrible state of affairs, which will entail a severe judgment."[34] It

---

[29]Material on these early associates of Muhlenberg is found in Stoever, "Reminiscences of Lutheran Clergymen," *Evangelical Review* 6 (October 1854): 261-68; 7 (April 1855): 538-44; and (October 1855): 152-73. See also William B. Sprague, *Annals of the American Pulpit*, vol. 9 (New York: Robert Carter & Bros., 1869) 21-25.

[30]Nelson, "Critical Study," 177.

[31]Mann, *The Life and Times of Muhlenberg*, 382.

[32]Muhlenberg, *Journals* 1: 121.

[33]Wentz, *A Basic History of Lutheranism in America*, 327.

[34]Muhlenberg, *Journals* 1: 58.

must be noted, however, that Muhlenberg condemned slavery in the South more severely than he did in the Northern communities where he lived and labored. He catechized, baptized, married, and received numerous blacks, both slave and free, into his congregations.[35] He was interested in conducting missions among the Indians, and his understanding and interest in the Native Americans was stimulated by his father-in-law, Conrad Weiser. As a youth, Weiser had lived with an Indian tribe, learned their language and customs, and was one of the few whites trusted by Indian leaders. However, during the French and Indian War, Muhlenberg's experiences of some Indian atrocities led him to adopt a more negative and prejudiced attitude toward them. While evidences of paternalism and outright racism can be found among his comments, Muhlenberg, like Justus Falckner before him,[36] was relatively enlightened in his attitudes and actions toward the most oppressed and abused racial groups in this country.

Until nearly the close of the Revolutionary War, Muhlenberg remained doggedly neutral, condemned first by one side and then the other as a traitor. He was, as he put it, enclosed "between two fires." He was convinced that there was "no Christian principle at stake, nothing humane about the war at all," and so he tended to view it as a punishment sent by God upon both England and America.[37] From this perspective his comments to the effect that a pastor's duty is to preach Christ and to stay out of politics must be viewed, at least in part, as a religious rationale for his anguished neutrality.[38] The real reasons for Muhlenberg's oft-quoted statements about keeping politics out of the church appear to have stemmed more from a practical strategy than from theological conviction. They can be understood as resulting from the exceptional problems that the war presented in the midst of efforts to establish a new church, rather than as a demonstration of any strict confessionalism.

Muhlenberg was consumed with the gargantuan assignment of planting and organizing the Lutheran church in a "strange land." He could not

---

[35]Ibid. 2:439, as one example.

[36]Falckner appears to have been especially active in his ministry to both blacks and native Americans. See Sachse, *German Pietists of Provincial Pennsylvania:* and idem, *Justus Falckner: Mystic and Scholar* (Philadelphia: Printed for the author by New Era Printing, 1903). Some orthodox Lutheran pastors also demonstrated an enlightened spirit in this regard.

[37]Henry M. Muhlenberg, *The Notebook of a Colonial Clergyman,* trans. Theodore G. Tappert and John W. Doberstein (Philadelphia: Muhlenberg Press, 1959) 189.

[38]Ibid., 31.

permit the raging political crisis to deter him from that task. As he wrote to the Halle fathers, "The duties here are so extensive . . . that preachers have no time and strength left to engage in political affairs."[39] Closely related to this comment was his perception that to have taken sides on such a volatile political question might have divided the church he was serving as midwife and left it stillborn. Muhlenberg's *Journals* bear abundant testimony to his keen interest in the political scene,[40] as do the careers of his three sons. Frederick Muhlenberg was elected speaker of the First Congress of the United States, and either he or his brother Peter remained in Congress almost continuously from 1789 to 1801. No Lutheran family in America made a more direct or distinguished contribution to the political life of this country, and all of Muhlenberg's sons, like himself, were educated at Halle University.

It was in connection with the political events of his day that Muhlenberg gave the clearest evidence that his Pietism encompassed millennial convictions. He read and revered Johann Bengel on this subject[41] and in later years especially commented frequently in his *Journals* on attempts to decipher current events in the light of the coming millennium.[42] Any doubt that Muhlenberg's theological disposition remained under the influence of Lutheran Pietism is further dispelled by his firm and forceful, albeit respectful, opposition to the Lutheran orthodox leadership in the provinces of New Jersey and New York. The success of these efforts undoubtedly was due not only to the superior quality of Muhlenberg's personal leadership abilities but also to the prevalent strain of Lutheran Pietism in New York State.

PIETISM IN NEW YORK STATE

The history of Lutheranism in the Empire State is both interesting and significant. Lutherans from Holland had arrived as early as 1623 in what was then called New Netherlands, long before the rise of Pietism in Germany. By 1649, these orthodox Lutherans had organized their own congregation. Not until the beginning of the eighteenth century did large numbers of Lutherans, mainly of Pietist leanings, come to New York. In

---

[39]Muhlenberg, *Journals* 3:126.

[40]Muhlenberg, *Notebook of a Colonial Clergyman*, 111, 164.

[41]Muhlenberg, *Journals* 3:551.

[42]See, for instance, ibid. 2:706, 723, 754; 3:320, 406, 410, 487, 514, 633, 722, 749.

the summer of 1710, the largest single group of Germans ever to immigrate to North America arrived in New York City. They had come from their homeland by way of London, where they had sought sanctuary from the ravages of famine and war under England's Protestant Queen Anne. Since the British government was hard pressed to provide the necessary finances to care for such large numbers of refugees, arrangements were made to send them to the colonies in North America. Of the 3,000 who left England for New York, only about 2,500 survived the terrible sea voyage. Several hundred others were sent to the Carolinas, one group landing at the present site of New Bern, North Carolina, and the other on the Congree River in South Carolina. [43]

Since the majority of these persons had come from an area in southwestern Germany called the Palatinate, the whole group was referred to as Palatines, although many came from the surrounding districts of Hesse-Darmstadt, Franconia, Alsace, Baden, and Württemberg. [44] Nearly all of the emigrants were Protestants, about equally divided between Lutheran and Reformed. The Palatinate had been the birthplace of Philip Melanchthon, and the influence of his more irenic approach to Lutheran theology, as opposed to a rigid orthodoxy, prevailed throughout this entire area. [45] Spener's influence had been dominant in Württemberg, where he had made an extended visit early in his career, and it was also later directly influenced by Francke. [46] Lutheran church reform under Pietist leadership was at the peak of its influence at the time of the major exodus of 1709-1710. Among the Lutherans in this so-called Palatine immigration, it is most probable that the majority, while vigorously upholding their identity from Reformed churches on confessional grounds, [47] adhered to some variation of the churchly Pietism of the Spener-Francke school. [48]

---

[43]Jacob L. Morgan, Bachman S. Brown, Jr., and John Hall, eds., *History of the Lutheran Church in North Carolina* (United Evangelical Lutheran Synod of North Carolina, 1953) 14.

[44]Walter Allen Knittle, *Early Eighteenth Century Palatine Emigration* (Philadelphia: Darrance, 1937) 1-3. See also Don Yoder, ed., *Rhineland Emigrants* (Baltimore: Genealogical Publishing, 1985) 8.

[45]Lars P. Qualben, *The Lutheran Church in Colonial America* (New York: Thomas Nelson & Sons, 1940) 168-69.

[46]Aland, *History of Christianity* 2:245, 257.

[47]Claus-Peter Clasen, *The Palatinate in European History, 1559-1660* (Oxford: Basil Blackwell, 1963) 9-11, 19.

[48]Wentz, *Basic History of Lutheranism in America*, 28.

By 1725, most of the original Palatine emigrants had settled in an area of thirty square miles, comprising two large tracts of land in upper New York State. This picturesque country, bounded by the mighty Mohawk River and its slender sister, the Schoharie, lay northwest of Albany, in what is now Montgomery and Schoharie counties. Shortly thereafter, about 300 of these original settlers made their way down the Susquehanna River to Tupelhocken in Pennsylvania. Their leader was the illustrious Indian scout, Conrad Weiser, whose daughter Anna later became the wife of Henry Muhlenberg. The Palatines in New York and Pennsylvania were joined by other emigrants from the same districts of Germany at various times until after the Revolutionary War.[49] The original group of Palatine emigrants who landed in North Carolina in 1710 were nearly exterminated in conflicts with the native Indians, but some survived, and later Palatine emigrants from Pennsylvania made their way into Virginia and North Carolina, adding to the strong Pietist element that continued to dominate Southern Lutheranism.[50]

After the death of Justus Falckner in 1723, New York Lutherans were under the leadership of a staunch defender of orthodoxy, the Reverend William C. Berkenmeyer. A graduate of Hamburg University, Berkenmeyer arrived in New York in 1725 and soon became the recognized overseer of all Lutheran clergy and parishes in New York and New Jersey. In 1743, he was responsible for importing another orthodox graduate of Hamburg, the Reverend Peter Sommers, who established the first congregation among the Palatines of the Schoharie area. Sommers's long ministry there was well received, apparently due not only to his deep pastoral con-

---

[49]All factual material for this account of the German Palatine emigrants, unless otherwise noted, is found in the following sources: Knittle, *Early Eighteenth Century Palatine Emigration;* Sanford H. Cobb, "The Palatine or German Immigration to New York and Pennsylvania" (paper read before the Wyoming Historical and Geographical Society, printed for the society, Wilkes-Barre PA, 1897); idem, *The Story of the Palatines: An Episode in Colonial History* (New York, London: B. Putnam's Sons, Knickerbocker Press, 1897); Felix James Schrag, "Pietism in Colonial America" (Ph.D. diss., University of Chicago, 1948); P. B. Mattice, ed., *The Palatines of New York State: A Complete Compilation of the History of the Palatines Who First Came to New York State in 1708–1722* (Johnstown NY: Palatine Society of the United Evangelical Lutheran Church of New York and New England, 1953); Frederick S. Weiser, ed., *Johan Friederich Weisers Buch Containing the Autobiography of John Conrad Weiser, 1696–1760* (Hanover PA: John Conrad Weiser Family Association, 1976).

[50]Wentz, *Basic History of Lutheranism in America,* 19-20; Ernest L. Hazelius, *History of the American Lutheran Church* (Zanesville OH: Edwin C. Church, 1846).

cern but also to his unusual flexibility in dealing with doctrinal differences. Berkenmeyer was more typically rigid in his orthodoxy.[51] He was sharply critical of the Reverend John C. Hartwick, the Halle graduate and colleague of Muhlenberg who had ministered to the Palatine emigrants and later bequeathed the land for the first Lutheran seminary in this country. Hartwick was accused of "Moravian leanings."[52] Soon a whole series of controversies erupted within the parishes under Berkenmeyer's jurisdiction. In three of the most critical of these disputes, beginning in 1745, the congregations turned to Henry Muhlenberg to serve as an arbitrator.[53] While never directly challenging Berkenmeyer's authority, Muhlenberg handled these situations with such patience, skill, and tact that in each instance he replaced Berkenmeyer as the acknowledged leader.

A good part of Muhlenberg's success in this area of administrative endeavor stemmed from his pietistic stress on the spiritual priesthood of all believers. It revealed itself in his encouragement of more lay involvement. Throughout his life Muhlenberg was in demand as an arbitrator in parish disputes because of his willingness to allow the laity to present their grievances and to refrain from premature and arbitrary judgments. The flexibility of Pietism to adjust itself more easily than orthodoxy to this American tendency toward volunteerism and to other aspects of North American culture was not simply the result of a capitulation to the American environment, as many historians have contended. Rather, Pietism was essentially more concerned about its Christian mission and witness to all people than it was to preserve traditional doctrines or forms of procedure.[54] Equally important is the fact that Muhlenberg emphasized precisely those elements in his Lutheran Pietism that corresponded most closely to the American milieu—lay participation and representation in the decision-making process, constitutionality, and democratic procedure. This commitment to an American church, rising from the very heart of his Hallean heritage, helped to assure the victory of Muhlenberg's Pietism over the orthodoxy of Ber-

---

[51]Berkenmeyer, Wilhelm Christoph, *The Albany Protocol: Wilhelm Christoph Berkenmeyer's Chronicle of Lutheran Affairs in New York Colony, 1731–1750*, ed. John P. Dern (Cornwallville NY: Hope Farm Press, 1971) xxii.

[52]Ibid., xlvii.

[53]Muhlenberg, *Journals* 1:114.

[54]J. J. Mol, *The Breaking of Traditions: Theological Convictions in Colonial America* (Berkeley CA: Glendessary Press, 1968) 43, 55, 63-64.

kenmeyer.[55] By the time of Berkenmeyer's death in 1751, that victory was already assured. With few exceptions, the clergy who took pastorates in the Empire State thereafter were Halle-trained colleagues of Muhlenberg. Pietism, with its revivalistic, ecumenical, and missionary spirit, was clearly the most dominant and widespread expression of Lutheranism in North America.

MUHLENBERG'S PIETIST SUCCESSORS

By the time the War for Independence had ground to a close, Henry Muhlenberg's health, sapped of strength by his Herculean efforts to plant the Lutheran church in a chaotic new land, was in rapid decline. His last years were spent in semiretirement and shrouded in a cloud of increasing melancholia. When he died on 7 October 1787, a new era was dawning in North American history. Less than a month before his demise, a proposed constitution for the United States of America had been approved in convention, and the Continental Congress had issued a call for its ratification by the individual states. By this time, Muhlenberg's earliest colleagues were either dead or nearing the end of their active careers. But younger men had continued to arrive from Germany over the years to assist the patriarch in his efforts. The pre-Revolutionary era had witnessed the immigration of thousands of German Lutherans to colonial America. The greater part of them came from districts in southwestern Germany, where the Pietism of Spener and Bengel had made heavy inroads. The need for clergy to minister to the increasing numbers of these newcomers was urgent. Muhlenberg had repeatedly implored the fathers at Halle to send help, and the plea was not ignored.

About a quarter of a century after he launched his ministry in America, a new group of clergy began to arrive. Christopher Schultze came in 1765. Justus H. C. Helmuth and John F. Schmidt traveled together to Philadelphia in 1769. In 1770, John C. Kunze arrived in company with Muhlenberg's three sons, who had completed several years of study at their father's alma mater. All of these men had been ordained and had either studied, taught or both at Halle University and Orphan Home. They formed a close-knit circle. Helmuth and Schmidt had been inseparable friends from youth. Both Schultze and Kunze married Muhlenberg's daughters. There were other marriages within this family group. Most important for the future

---

[55]Harry Julius Kreider, *Lutheranism in Colonial New York* (Ann Arbor MI: Edwards Brothers, 1942; reprint, New York: Arno Press, 1972) 81-136; Nelson, "Critical Study," 149.

course of Lutheranism in this country was the unanimous theological accord with the basic principles of the Arndt-Spener-Francke school of Pietism. They were all endowed with a practical piety, evangelical in their preaching, and convinced of the importance of conversion, prayer meetings, Bible study, Sabbath schools, and catechetical instruction. Their piety was matched by scholarly abilities. Their intellectual capacities, particularly in linguistics, theology, and the natural sciences, were acknowledged and undisputed. They were missionary minded, imbued with the spirit of ecumenism and religious tolerance, concerned more with the caliber of the Christian life than with purity of doctrine in points they considered nonessential. Some were active crusaders for temperance, and all were involved in various forms of social and community reform.

Of the clergy who labored closely with Muhlenberg during the last ten or fifteen years of his ministry, Helmuth, Schmidt, and Kunze more than any others assumed the mantle of Lutheran leadership following the patriarch's death. These men in particular were destined to consolidate and extend the traditions of Lutheran Pietism at the beginning of the second half of its first century of existence in North America. During the early postwar years they were also influential in adapting this dominant Lutheran tradition to the new conditions of life in a constitutional democracy.

Justus H. C. Helmuth (1745–1825) and John F. Schmidt (1746–1812) became close friends during their teenage years at the Orphan Home at Halle, where they later served as teachers. Both were astute linguists and scholars, knowledgeable in a wide range of subjects. Helmuth served a parish in Lancaster, Pennsylvania, for ten years, and then spent the remainder of his life in a Philadelphia church. He believed in a revivalistic approach to preaching and conducted prayer meetings regularly, where the Scriptures along with Arndt's *True Christianity* were read and discussed. In his first parish these meetings met with strenuous opposition, and attempts were made on occasion to break them up forceably. By 1804, he had established a flourishing Sabbath school with over 200 pupils and 40 teachers. He taught German and Oriental languages for nearly twenty years at the University of Pennsylvania.

After serving a parish in Germantown, John Schmidt left it in 1785 to become Helmuth's colleague in Philadelphia. That same year they established a private Lutheran seminary, where two generations of native Lutheran ministers received much of their theological training. Helmuth's long life enabled him to extend his teaching to the third generation. It is said that Schmidt and Helmuth were in perfect agreement on everything, including a firm resistance to the use of English language in worship, a conviction that ran counter to most other Pietist leaders, including Muhlenberg.

In other respects, however, Helmuth and Schmidt faithfully communicated the traditions established by the patriarch. Their influence was extremely significant, primarily due to their role as teachers of the first native-born Lutheran clergy.

John C. Kunze (1744–1807) was a man of peerless learning. He had taught at the University of Halle before coming to North America and was a renowned Hebrew scholar. From 1784 until his death he served a congregation in New York City and taught Oriental languages at Columbia University. It is said that he possessed the largest private library of any clergyman in this country. He typified the Pietist synthesis of spirituality and intellectual knowledge. He was thoroughly ecumenical in outlook, fostering close relationships in particular with the Episcopal and Reformed communions and indicating that, in his opinion, "the time was over . . . when Protestant parties could exclude each other for the sake of unessential deviations."[56] Kunze was also a philanthropist who devoted himself to the relief of the poor and the afflicted. As a reformer, he was not afraid to voice convictions that ran counter to majority opinion, taking his fellow Germans to task for their desecration of the Sabbath. Unlike Helmuth and Schmidt, he sought with all of his energies to introduce the use of the English language into public worship. But the forces against him were too strong, and in his own parish he was largely unsuccessful. He persisted, however, and was the primary mover in the establishment of the New York Ministerium, which became the first Lutheran group to use the English language in its official proceedings. From its official organization in 1796 until his death, Kunze served as president of this second Lutheran synod established in North America.

His desire to Americanize Lutheran Pietism by training ministers who could use both English and German led Kunze to make several attempts to organize a Lutheran seminary. While he never saw this goal reach fruition, he did become a professor of theology for the Hartwick Foundation, made possible by a grant from the estate of Reverend John C. Hartwick. This bequest finally led to the establishment of Hartwick Lutheran Seminary following Kunze's death. Both as a teacher of clergy and as synodical president, Kunze exerted considerable influence upon the future course of Lutheranism in North America. During his years of leadership the New York Ministerium held consistently to a Pietistic interpretation of the Lutheran

[56]John C. Kunze, *History of American Lutheranism* (New York, 1801) in Microfilm Corpus of American Lutheranism (hereafter cited as MCAL), reel 1, p. 28, Archives of Jesuit-Krauss Memorial Library, Lutheran School of Theology, Chicago.

teachings, shaping its organization for the most part after the pattern Muhlenberg had established with the Pennsylvania Ministerium.

After 1792, neither group made any specific reference whatever to the Lutheran confessions in their constitutions, nor was any mandatory subscription to the symbolic books required of those who were licensed or ordained. Yet there is no evidence of any antagonism directed toward the confessional standards, and at least on certain occasions during this period in the New York Synod, candidates for ordination did pledge themselves to carry out their office "in agreement with the Word of God and the symbolical books of our Church."[57] Kunze, like his famous father-in-law, had a strong regard for the distinctive doctrines of the Lutheran church. German Pietism had never been anticonfessional. However, it had continued to assert with the original Reformers that the authority of the confessions was derived solely from their agreement with Scripture and that the extent of this agreement did not necessarily pertain alike to every part of the symbolic books. Furthermore, the tendency within German Pietism to test continually the conformity of Scripture and confession in the light of new knowledge and exegetical studies found an encouragement in the new democracy that had been absent in the Lutheran state churches of Germany and Scandinavia. It would appear that American Lutheran Pietists did not actually change their position toward the confessions in the post-Muhlenberg era, but rather that conditions had changed the manner of their usage. Instead of feeling a need to utilize the confessions for the practical purpose of establishing an identity in the midst of a scattered and chaotic constituency, this basic allegiance was now more often simply assumed or taken for granted.[58] By the time John Kunze died in 1807, Pietist traditions were firmly entrenched within the New York Ministerium.

The man who succeeded John Kunze as president of the New York Ministerium, Frederick H. Quitman (1760–1832), had attended Halle University nearly two decades after Kunze. He was an able scholar in the fields of theology, language, and the sciences. He emigrated to the United States in 1795 and for a few years served parishes in Schoharie and vicinity, after which he took charge of churches in the Rhinebeck area further to the south. One of his sons had a distinguished career as a general in the Mexican and Civil wars, and two of his stepsons, Philip and Frederick Mayer, were influential Lutheran pastors and teachers of other clergy.

---

[57]Harry J. Kreider, *History of the United Lutheran Synod of New York and New England*, vol. 1, *1786-1860* (Philadelphia: Muhlenberg Press, 1954) 14-24.

[58]Nelson, *Lutherans in North America*, rev. ed., 93.

Quitman has often been accused of fostering the spread of a rationalism or Socinianism that undermined basic Lutheran teachings.[59] It is true that, by the time Quitman attended Halle University, a number of its teachers had been influenced by the so-called biblical supernaturalism. This theology, which is evident in Quitman's writings, actually attempted to refute rationalism's basic critique of Christianity by asserting that, while matters of faith and revelation went beyond human reason, they were not thereby antithetical to it. It maintained that there could be no possible chasm between reason and revelation, since God was the creator of both.

In reality Quitman was a Pietist who was determined to prove that the basic tenets of Christianity were compatible with human reason.[60] This interest, coupled with a less personal evangelical fervor and revivalistic zeal than had characterized the earlier German Pietist tradition, undoubtedly led to more of an emphasis of the mind over the heart. The fact that Quitman was a prolific author as well as a capable and charismatic leader added to the impact of his views upon the New York Ministerium. However, the deeply spiritual and ethical elements of classical Pietism continued to remain vigorous in parts of the synod, especially in the Schoharie-Mohawk valleys, where its heritage was strongest.

It was in this area that Ernest Hazelius (1777–1853) was called in 1815 as the first full-time professor of Hartwick Seminary, located near Cooperstown, New York. Hazelius was descended from a long and illustrious line of Lutheran ministers of German and Swedish ancestry. He was reared in the Moravian faith and schooled in their seminary in Sweden. After coming to the United States in 1800, he taught for a time in the Moravian seminary in Nazareth, Pennsylvania, before deciding to return to the Lutheran faith of his forefathers. He was ordained by the New York Ministerium in 1809 and served parishes in New Jersey before assuming the professorship at Hartwick. Hazelius was the author of a number of important historical and theological works, in all points adhering closely to the Spener-Francke Pietist traditions. He was a moderate in both his views of revivalism and confessionalism. He opposed an unrestrained emotionalism, as well as an uncritical symbolism. His motto was that which classical

---

[59]See Paul W. Spaude, *The Lutheran Church under American Influence* (Burlington IA: Lutheran Literary Board, 1943) 364-67; also Krieder, *History of the United Lutheran Synod*, 41-47.

[60]Raymond H. Bost, "The Rev. John Bachman and the Development of Southern Lutheranism" (Ph.D. diss., Yale University, 1963) 18-60; Nelson, *Lutheranism in North America*, 106.

Pietism had voiced over the years: In essentials, unity; in nonessentials, liberty; in all things, charity. Hazelius's colleague at Hartwick, George B. Miller, also came from a Moravian background and had adopted similar views. Because this first Lutheran seminary in North America trained most of the ministerial candidates from the New York Ministerium, these two men were more responsible than any others for the continued vigor of classical Lutheran Pietism in that area.

By the first decades of the nineteenth century, however, deism—the fast-growing religion of reason and the faith of America's founding fathers—had managed to gain a toehold within Lutheranism, especially in the New York City area and in some parts of New Jersey and Pennsylvania. This deistic tendency, or, as it was usually called, Socinianism, became recognized as the primary foe of American Lutheran Pietists. Eventually, it would lead them back to a more overt confessional allegiance characteristic of Henry Muhlenberg.

POSTREVOLUTIONARY PIETISM IN THE SOUTH

Lutherans were not nearly as numerous in the South as in the Pennsylvania and New York areas and, as a result, were not as quick to receive the pastoral leadership that they needed. Except for the original settlement in Ebenezer, Georgia, which had remained small and isolated, most Southern Lutherans were located in the Carolinas and Virginia. The huge majority had come from the general area of the Palatinate in Germany, either directly or by way of Pennsylvania, and were therefore predominantly of Pietist stock. Muhlenberg had been far too busy to extend his journeys in that direction, or even to send any of his associates to labor there. For years these Lutherans were dependent upon the occasional visits of traveling ministers. Finally, in 1773, after laypersons from Carolina had traveled all the way to Germany in order to secure a pastor, the Reverend Adolph Mussmann and a schoolteacher, John Arends (who was later ordained), were sent from Halle through the consistory of Hanover.[61] These men labored faithfully and organized several parishes, but the real development of Lutheranism in the South did not take place until after the War for Independence. In 1786, Reverend Christian E. Bernhardt came to North Carolina from Württemberg, and two years later, the Reverend Carl A. G. Storch from the University of Helmstadt.[62]

---

[61]Hazelius, *History of the American Lutheran Church*, 117; Morgan, Brown, and Hall, *Lutheran Church in North Carolina*, 21.

[62]Morgan, Brown, and Hall, *Lutheran Church in North Carolina*, 23-25.

Carl Storch (1764–1831), more than any other individual, influenced the direction of Southern Lutheranism in the postrevolutionary period. Like Kunze, he personified the happy union of Pietist and scholar. He was a superior linguist, familiar with Greek, Hebrew, and Latin, and able to speak five or six languages fluently. His solid intellectual acumen was combined with an evangelical zeal that sought involvement in every benevolent endeavor of interest to humanity. Storch established his home parish at Salisbury, North Carolina, but he engaged in missionary work throughout the state and into Tennessee, Virginia, and South Carolina. His ministry covered a period of over forty years. He favored a revivalistic approach but was opposed to any form of fanaticism. The North Carolina Synod, which he helped to organize in 1803, sponsored three-day revivals with Moravian and Reformed churches. Like all of his fellow Pietists, Storch emphasized the individual's commitment to Christ over denominational distinction or confessional details. Thus, when Gottlieb Shober (1756–1838), a native-born fifty-four-year-old Moravian layman from Salem, North Carolina, informed Storch that he felt called to preach the gospel and wanted to be a Lutheran minister, he was not turned away.

Shober was well known and respected in the area. He had been a teacher, clerk, lawyer, businessman, postmaster, and elected representative in the state legislature. After being catechized by Storch in 1810, Shober accompanied him on a preaching mission to South Carolina and in the fall of that year was ordained by the North Carolina Synod. Establishing his headquarters at a parish in his hometown of Salem, Shober became a recognized leader of American Lutheran Pietism in the Southern states. He was an ardent preacher and a devoted friend of Sunday schools, Bible, tract, missionary, and education societies, and other benevolent activities. Above all he was a man of great practical wisdom and experience.

Following Shober's entry into the Lutheran church, American Lutheran Pietism experienced its first concerted challenge from orthodox confessionalism since the time of William Berkenmeyer in New York. The opposition arose in the person of the Reverend Paul Henkel (1754–1825). Henkel was a native North Carolinian whose great-grandfather Gerhard had emigrated from Germany and was one of the earliest Lutheran ministers in the New World. Paul Henkel adopted his strict confessionalist position late in life. In his early twenties he had a conversion experience. Afterward he received religious instruction from a Lutheran minister in Maryland and in 1792 was ordained by the Ministerium of Pennsylvania with the Reverend John F. Schmidt, Muhlenberg's Pietist colleague, officiating. Henkel's primary parish was in New Market, Virginia, but he made a number of missionary tours through frontier country as far west as Ohio and Indiana. His earlier ministry presents a pointedly Piestist profile. He was on friendly terms with Moravian clergy, helped form the North Carolina Synod with Storch as a colleague, was a revivalist missionary, and favored some of the Melanchthonian alterations to the original Augsburg Confession.

By the time of Shober's ordination, however, Henkel had begun to publish works on baptism and the Lord's Supper that professed a conservative theology, and in later publications his orthodoxy became even more advanced. His sons, Philip and David, carried his confessionalism to the point where fellowship with the dominant Pietist position was no longer possible. Shober and the Henkels became bitter doctrinal antagonists. The end result was the formation of the Tennessee Synod in July of 1820. It covered roughly the same territory as the North Carolina Synod and constituted the first official body of Lutherans in North America to take a strict conservative stance in opposition to the prevailing Pietism. Since Paul Henkel had also played a prominent role in the development of the Ohio Synod, which was organized in 1818, his conservatism was evident there too, but in a more limited degree.

The classic clash of Lutheran orthodoxy and Pietism in North America (or "Old Lutheranism" versus "American Lutheranism") thus first appeared full-blown in the South by the end of the first decade of the nineteenth century and was initiated by a native-born former Pietist pastor. In the North, following the miniclash of Berkenmeyer and Muhlenberg, the struggle was much slower to take definite shape. The issues were not clearly joined for nearly a quarter of a century. Even then, confessionalism in the North never assumed the ultraconservatism of the Tennessee Synod. When finally launched, however, its challenge, while more moderate, was far more pervasive and successful.

AMERICAN-EDUCATED PIETIST LEADERS

In the Northern states there appeared little concerted conservative resistance to classical Lutheran Pietism until thirty years or more after the turn of the century. As noted earlier, Muhlenberg's three sons were all educated at Halle University. The elder two left the ministry to pursue political careers, but the youngest, Henry Ernest (1753–1815), carried on a long ministry at Lancaster, Pennsylvania, in which the Pietist theology of his father was refined and extended. It expressed itself in a benevolent concern for the needy and in a willingness to labor together with any and all who were sound on those points generally regarded by Christians as of fundamental importance. Henry E. Muhlenberg was a diligent scholar and pursued the study of botany until he became the foremost authority on this subject in the entire country.

The first native-born pastor of the Muhlenberg era to exert an extensive influence over the shape of early nineteenth-century Lutheranism was Jacob Goering (1755–1807). Born on a farm in York County, Pennsylvania, he studied theology under Justus Helmuth and later married the daughter of Reverend John N. Kurtz. Ordained by the Pennsylvania Ministerium in 1774, he served parishes in York and vicinity for over twenty-five years. He exhibited all the classic marks of the Spenerian Pietism, cultivating close relationships with Reformed and Moravian clergy, preaching fervent, evangelical, and practical sermons, and initiating a number of extensive revivals, or "awakenings." He took an active part in community and political affairs, the latter involvement resulting in much controversy. His significance for the coming generation of clergy was enhanced by the fact that he was a man of rare intellectual endowment. Besides knowing Hebrew, Greek, and Latin, he was familiar with Syriac and Chaldean and was a thorough student of historical theology as well as the natural sciences.

Many young ministerial candidates sought out Goering for private instruction. Frederick D. Schaeffer (1760–1836), a young German who had emigrated with his uncle to York County at the age of sixteen, was one of the first to be taken under Goering's tutorship. Ordained in 1788, Schaeffer later succeeded Helmuth and Schmidt in their prestigious Philadelphia parishes, where he became involved in a bitter and unsuccessful attempt to allow the English language to be used in worship. Like Goering, he was a linguist and competent scholar, as well as a man of ardent piety and prayer. His partialities leaned entirely in the direction of the Arndt and Spener school of Pietism. Schaeffer had four sons, all of whom took up the ministry and followed in his theological footsteps. Two in particular, David F. in Maryland and F. Christian in New York City, became influential leaders in their own right.

Over the years, nearly two dozen individuals, a number of whom became the foremost leaders of early nineteenth-century American Lutheran Pietism, received their theological education and inspiration not only from Justus Helmuth but also from Jacob Goering. At least three of the individuals whom one or both of them instructed became the primary movers in the first effort to unite all the various Lutheran groups in this country, namely, J. George Lochman (1773–1826), Christian F. Endress (1775–1827), and John George Schmucker (1771–1854).

George Lochman and Christian Endress maintained a close association throughout their life. They were of a similar age, pursued their theological studies together under Helmuth at the University of Pennsylvania, entered the ministry at the same time, and died within a year of each other. Lochman served parishes in Lebanon and Harrisburg, Pennsylvania, and Endress at Easton and Lancaster, Pennsylvania, where he succeeded Henry E. Muhlenberg. They were capable scholars, and Lochman carried on the tradition of a private theological teacher, helping to prepare some thirty persons for the Lutheran ministry. Both he and Endress were steeped in the Pietist heritage, which had been passed on to them from family as well as teachers. They were men of public spirit and active in all the great benevolent movements of their day, with a deep concern for the needy and unfortunate. Lochman's practice of admitting all classes, including the poor, to the Sabbath school he established was something entirely new in the community. Neither was adverse to the confessions of the church as a formulation of the fundamental teachings of Scripture. However, they rejected any spirit of sectarianism and believed that, in spite of differences, there was a common ground on which all who loved the Lord in sincerity and truth could meet and labor together for the advancement of God's kingdom.

John George Schmucker was born in the duchy of Hesse-Darmstadt, in the town of Michaelstadt near Heidelberg, in the part of Germany heavily influenced by classical Pietism. At the age of fourteen he came with his father, Christopher, and family to North America. The Schmuckers first settled in southeastern Pennsylvania and after two years moved to a farm near Woodstock, Virginia, in the beautiful Shenandoah Valley. In addition to the Bible the primary devotional books in their home were Luther's catechism and John Arndt's *True Christianity*. Three of Christopher Schmucker's sons entered the ministry of the Lutheran church, but it was John George who became one of the most outstanding leaders of American Lutheranism during the first quarter of the nineteenth century. His life contained all the characteristic marks of Lutheran Pietism. At the age of eighteen he underwent a conversion experience that propelled him to prepare for the gospel ministry. Paul Henkel was then a pastor in the vicinity, and the young Schmucker accompanied him on several of his missionary journeys to the western frontier. It was in the years before Henkel moved to a more conservative theological position, and apparently Schmucker's pietistic convictions remained unimpaired or were even stimulated through this association. In 1790, he began formal theological studies under Helmuth and Schmidt, with Lochman and Endress as fellow students. Licensed by the Synod of Pennsylvania in 1792, Schmucker served several small parishes in York County, Pennsylvania. Here he became a close friend and student of Jacob Goering. In 1794, Schmucker took a parish in Hagerstown, Maryland, where he served until 1809, at which time he succeeded Goering at York, Pennsylvania. There he remained for over a quarter of a century.

J. G. Schmucker was a powerful preacher, revivalist, and moral reformer. He was a great admirer of Spener and Francke and other writers of the Pietist school and sympathized with them in their conflicts with the formalism of their day. When the Orphan Home at Halle was nearly destroyed by the armies of Napoleon, he made generous contributions for its restoration. He was particularly noted for the strength of his convictions, his great moral courage, and his help to the poor, the afflicted, and the oppressed. He served as vice-president of the American Tract Society, worked actively in the Foreign Missionary Society, the Temperance Union, and other benevolent and reform societies of his day. He conducted prayer meetings in the face of great opposition, and when at the age of sixty he took up the cause of temperance, he was rewarded by his irate German parishioners with a 50 percent cut in salary.[63] A promoter of peace and unity among all Christians, he believed that the fundamental doctrines of the Bible were contained in the confessions.

In addition to all of his other activities, J. G. Schmucker was a prolific writer, publishing more literary works than any other Lutheran pastor of his day.[64] His major effort was a two-volume study of the Book of Revelation which indicated that he, like Spener, was a staunch postmillennialist, who looked to the future of the church on earth with hopeful anticipation.[65] In this study Schmucker followed a pattern of interpretation similar to that of the English biblicist, Joseph Mede.[66] He also cited his great indebtedness to John Bengel, the renowned eighteenth-century biblical scholar and Pietist leader in Württemburg, calling him "the most able expositor" of the Apocalypse.[67] He concluded that, according to his calculations of prophetic time, the millennium would begin between 1850 and

---

[63]Paul Anstadt, *Life and Times of Rev. Samuel S. Schmucker* . . . (York PA: P. Anstadt & Sons, 1896) 11-12, 18-23.

[64]Abdel Ross Wentz, *Pioneer in Christian Unity, Samuel Simon Schmucker* (Philadelphia: Fortress Press, 1967) 3.

[65]J. George Schmucker, *The Prophetic History of the Christian Religion Explained; or, A Brief Explanation of the Revelation of St. John* (Baltimore: Schaeffer & Maund, 1817), vol. 1.

[66]LeRoy Edwin Froom, *The Prophet Faith of Our Fathers: The Historical Development of Prophetic Interpretation*, vol. 4 of *New World Recovery and Consummation of Prophetic Interpretation* (Washington, D.C.: Review & Herald, 1954) 225.

[67]J. G. Schmucker, *Prophetic History*, 24.

1860.[68] Schmucker's millennial views were received with wide favor by his fellow Lutheran Pietists and in particular were endorsed by two influential teachers of the clergy, Justus Helmuth and George Lochman.[69]

ORGANIZATION OF THE GENERAL SYNOD

John George Schmucker was serving as president of the Pennsylvania Ministerium at that momentous period in American Lutheran history when the first attempt to unite all the Lutheran groups in North America took place. While it never realized its ultimate goal, the effort did bear abundant fruit. It resulted in the organization of the General Synod, a federation of Lutheran bodies that for fifty years played a formidable part in determining the shape of American Lutheranism and that continued to be one of its major judicatories for an entire century. J. G. Schmucker along with his fellow leaders and former schoolmates George Lochman and Christian Endress played major roles in its creation and first precarious years of existence. In 1818, the Pennsylvania Ministerium took the lead in calling for a plan to unite the various Lutheran synodical groups. Expressions of approval came from both New York and North Carolina. Gottlieb Shober, then secretary of the North Carolina Synod, came in person to the Pennsylvania convention in 1819, bringing with him a proposed plan for the new General Synod. During the following year Shober's plan was modified. In particular the powers of the proposed new synod were sharply curtailed. It was given no authority to regulate orders of worship or to prescribe religious literature for its constituent churches. Neither could it render any binding judgment in disputes between member synods. For the most part its powers were purely advisory in nature.[70] The proposed constitution made no reference whatever to the Augsburg Confession.

---

[68]Ibid., chart at beginning of book.

[69]When not otherwise indicated, material on all the Lutheran clergymen noted up to this point in chapter 2 is taken primarily from the following sources: Martin Luther Stoever, "Reminiscences of Lutheran Clergymen," a series of articles in the *Evangelical Review*, vol. 5 through 10, extending from April 1854 through April 1859; Sprague, *Annals of the American Pulpit*, various volumes; *Dictionary of American Biography*, vols. 8-11 (New York: Scribners & Sons, 1943); Charles Hay, *Memoirs of Rev. Jacob Goering, Rev. George Lochman, D.D., and Rev. Benjamin Kurtz, D.D., L.L.D.* (Philadelphia: Lutheran Publishing Society, 1887); and Morgan, Brown, and Hall, *Lutheran Church in North Carolina*.

[70]*Constitution of the Evangelical Lutheran Synod in the United States of North America, Together with the Proceedings of the Convention in Which It Was Formed* (Lancaster PA: John Bear, 1820) 8-9, MCAL, reel 6.

The creation of the General Synod and Gottlieb Shober's active involvement in the endeavor probably did more than anything else to precipitate the open revolt of the Henkels and the formation of the Tennessee Synod in July 1820. For many years its members, scattered throughout the states of the South and West, formed a hard-core conservative opposition to the Pietist stance of the General Synod. They repeatedly accused it of having deserted or perverted the Augsburg Confession.[71] Evidences of this conservative resistance surfaced early in the newly formed Ohio Synod, which Paul Henkel had helped organize in 1818. Its members first approved the plan for a general synod but later rescinded their action and as a consequence did not send delegates to the organizing meeting.

The constituting convention of the General Synod took place at Hagerstown, Maryland, on 22 October 1820. Representatives were present from the New York Ministerium, the Pennsylvania Ministerium, the North Carolina Synod, and the Maryland-Virginia Synod. The latter group had been in existence for only two weeks. The clerical delegates were Philip F. Mayer and F. Christian Schaeffer from New York; George Lochman, F. W. Geissenhainer, Christian Endress, J. G. Schmucker, and Henry A. Muhlenberg (a son of Henry E. and grandson of the patriarch) from Pennsylvania; Gottlieb Shober and Peter Schmucker (brother of J. G.) from North Carolina; and J. D. Kurtz (son of John N.) and David F. Schaeffer from Maryland-Virginia.[72] It is significant that, without exception, these men were firm upholders of the classical Lutheran Pietism that Henry Muhlenberg had transplanted in North America and were in close agreement on matters of theological conviction. Three of the four synods represented at the first meeting adopted the constitution, the number required for the General Synod to continue its existence. The New York Ministerium, after considerable debate, voted not to be become a member, and in fact did not join the synod for another sixteen years. In one respect its resistance was similar to that of the Henkelites. Its members were concerned that the General Synod might impose unwanted standards of church polity or liturgical ritual. Unlike the more conservative opponents in the Tennessee and Ohio synods, however, the New York Ministerium voiced no criticism of the General Synod's moderation in regard to confessional matters.

The primary motivation for the creation of the General Synod was simply to unite the various organized bodies of Lutherans into a more closely

[71]David Henkel, *Carolinian Herald of Liberty* (Salisbury NC: Krider & Ringham, 1821) 3-5, in MCAL, reel 6.

[72]Edmund Jacob Wolf, *The Lutherans in America: A Story of Struggle, Progress, Influence, and Marvelous Growth* (New York: J. A. Hill, 1890) 327.

knit and cooperative organization. Its founders believed that Lutherans in the United States had no fundamental doctrinal disagreements. With the organization of the rival Tennessee Synod and the refusal of the Ohio and New York synods to affiliate, this conviction was seen to be overly optimistic. But unity was not viewed as an end in itself. There was a growing awareness of the need to combat the creeping Socinianism, or deism, that was challenging some fundamental beliefs such as the deity of Christ and justification by faith alone, threatening to repudiate them with its rational approach to the Scriptures. It was agreed that the best way to overcome this menace was for a federation of synods to establish a new Lutheran seminary that would be available to a large number of prospective clerical candidates. There was no major dissatisfaction with Hartwick Seminary, but its location in upper New York State posed the practical problem of accessibility for students in Pennsylvania and further south.

Two other important and intertwined factors led to the formation of the General Synod: the desire to coordinate Lutheran efforts for needed benevolent and moral reforms and an interest in cooperating more effectively with all other Protestant denominations in these endeavors. These twin tendencies of activism and ecumenism could be traced directly to the dominating Lutheran Pietist heritage of its founders. The constituting convention of the new synod specifically empowered it to set up plans not only for a new seminary but for other missionary institutions as well and for the aid of poor ministers along with the widows and orphans of ministers.[73] Committees were immediately appointed to begin the cooperative work necessary to effect these goals. At the time of the General Synod's organization, a number of important interdenominational benevolent associations were already in existence, including the Home and Foreign Missions Society, the American Bible Society, the American Education Society, and the African Colonization Society.[74] The founding fathers of the General Synod wanted it to engage in cooperative endeavors on these projects with other denominations.

Lutheran Pietists had never, either in this country or in Germany, favored organic union with other Protestant groups, and in this sense they always retained confessional convictions. This view was encapsulated in the organizing documents of the General Synod. There was pointed opposition to any union of Lutheran and Reformed churches. But there was

---

[73]*Constitution of the Evangelical Lutheran Synod*, 9, MCAL, reel 6.

[74]William G. McLoughlin, *Revivals, Awakenings, and Reform* (Chicago: University of Chicago Press, 1978) 112.

a wholehearted desire to establish a coordinated, organized, and official cooperative effort with the Reformed and all other denominations to do the Lord's work, and in this way hopefully to hasten the coming millennium. The missionary effort to bring the gospel to the whole world, combined with an all-out attack on the religious and moral evils that curtailed the effectiveness of that gospel, was seen as the overwhelming and urgent task of the church. To waste energy arguing over unessential points of doctrine was therefore viewed as a particularly heinous sin. The founders of the General Synod were thoroughly convinced that unity among Lutherans and cooperation among all Protestants were fundamental to Christian faithfulness.

SAMUEL SIMON SCHMUCKER

A young Lutheran minister who was present at all the organizing sessions of the General Synod, although not as a voting delegate, was destined to take the leading role in shaping its polity, organization, and confessional position for nearly forty years. His name was Samuel Simon Schmucker (1799–1873), the son of John George Schmucker. Samuel had recently been licensed to preach and was serving his first parish but had not yet been ordained. Working behind the scenes in close conjunction with his father, he played an important part in the formation of the General Synod. For the next fifty years he never missed one of its meetings and served as its president from 1828 until 1845.[75] During the entire antebellum period Samuel S. Schmucker stood without a rival as the most capable and qualified leader of the majority of Lutherans in the United States. The school of thought that he headed, while traditionally referred to as American Lutheranism, is more accurately described as American Lutheran Pietism. Born in 1799, just a dozen years after the death of Henry Muhlenberg, Samuel Schmucker attempted to cultivate, extend, and Americanize more fully the Spener-Francke brand of Pietism that the patriarch had transplanted in North America. In this effort he was for a time highly successful. Under his leadership, American Lutheran Pietism reached the pinnacle of its power and influence.

During his early years Samuel Schmucker was tutored by his illustrious father, and his entire life and thought retained the marks of that close association. The formative influence of his father's Lutheran Pietism was extended and reinforced. At the tender age of fifteen, Samuel traveled from

---

[75]Luke Schmucker, *The Schmucker Family and the Lutheran Church in America* (N.p., 1937) 37.

the family parsonage in York, Pennsylvania, to enroll at the University of Pennsylvania in Philadelphia. There he was tutored in theology by one of his father's old mentors, Justus Helmuth. It was not surprising that the seventy-year-old Helmuth took a special liking to the son of his former student, "taking him into his home, as well as his heart."[76] After two years of study Samuel returned to his home, where he taught for a year in the York County Academy. In the fall of 1817, he resigned his teaching work in order to accompany his brother George on a trip to the western frontier in Kentucky. It proved to be an eventful journey. For months the young schoolmaster had earnestly sought the sure signs of conversion, but without success.[77] During this pilgrimage he attended several frontier revival meetings and at last found the assurance he had been seeking. Upon his return home he made the firm decision to prepare himself for the gospel ministry.[78]

In August 1818, young Samuel Schmucker enrolled at the new Presbyterian seminary in Princeton, New Jersey. The fact that he chose Princeton Seminary indicated no lack of dedication to the Lutheran church, but it did imply an openness to other Protestant denominations. The location of Hartwick Seminary in central New York was a barrier to persons living as far away as Pennsylvania.[79] On the other hand, Princeton, while also a new school,[80] had already gained a solid reputation under its first professor, Archibald Alexander, and was much closer to Samuel's home in York. Between Alexander and Samuel Miller, the two professors at Princeton when Schmucker enrolled, the former exerted the greater influence, which was undoubtedly due to his closer affinity with Schmucker's own theological disposition.[81]

Archibald Alexander was a living embodiment of the close interrelationship that had always existed between English Puritanism and German Lutheran Pietism. As with August Francke and Cotton Mather, or with Henry Muhlenberg and Gilbert Tennent, so, with the student Samuel

---

[76]Wentz, *Pioneer in Christian Unity*, 8.

[77]Anstadt, *Life and Times of Samuel Schmucker*, 35.

[78]Ibid., 46. Samuel and his father were both the same age when they had a "conversion" experience.

[79]Wentz, *Pioneer in Christian Unity*, 15.

[80]Princeton Seminary had commenced operation in 1812.

[81]Wentz, *Pioneer in Christian Unity*, 17. Miller was a more precise scholar and more of a staunch Calvinist than Alexander (p. 19).

Schmucker and his teacher Archibald Alexander, the Pietist and the Puritan faced each other again and discovered in one another the reflection of their own basic theological convictions.

Alexander grew up in the same area in Virginia where Schmucker's father and grandfather had lived. As a youth he was greatly attracted to Baptist revivalist preaching and at the age of seventeen had a conversion experience that he always referred to as the most important event of his life.[82] He remained a friend of reverent revivals,[83] although in later life he strongly protested against the excesses of the so-called New Measures.[84] He endorsed, with his characteristic spirit of moderation, moral causes of the day, participating in a tract society, foreign mission society, Sunday school association, as well as the African Colonization Society.[85] His philosophy of theological education was to unite, in those who studied for the ministry, piety of heart with solid learning. He was convinced that a learned ministry without corresponding piety was a curse to the world and an offense to God.[86] But Alexander appeared never to have integrated the sharp dualism that existed in his mind between piety and learning, religious experience and reason. He emphasized both his Pietist heritage and his more formal orthodox rationalism, without ever synthesizing them into any coherent theological system.[87] He supported missionary endeavors, but his appeals to millennial hopes were not numerous.[88] His ecumenical views were centered in a vision of "invisible union." He believed that all who held the same fundamental beliefs were already members of the same church. On

---

[82]James W. Alexander, *The Life of Archibald Alexander, D.D.* (New York: Scribner's, 1854) 70-71.

[83]In the early years of teaching at Princeton, Alexander participated in revivals and conducted "Sunday conferences" with students which were aimed at stimulating their "awakening." See Lefferts A. Loetscher, *Facing the Enlightenment and Pietism: Archibald Alexander and the Founding of Princeton Theological Seminary* (Westport CT: Greenwood Press, 1983) 243-44.

[84]Alexander, *Life of Archibald Alexander*, 72.

[85]John Mackay, "Archibald Alexander," in *Sons of the Prophets*, ed. Robert T. Kerr (Princeton NJ: Princeton University Press, 1963) 11.

[86]Ibid., 14.

[87]Loetscher, *Facing the Enlightenment and Pietism*, 47, 170, 243, 253.

[88]Ibid., 206.

the visible level, though, he insisted that all churches who refused communion with others were guilty of schism. [89]

It appears that Samuel Schmucker took what he desired from the Pietistic aspects of Alexander's theology, imbibed also something of Alexander's scientific rationalism, and interpreted many of his teacher's ideas to fit in with his own more passionate devotion to moral reform, millennial hope, and ecumenical expectations. By the middle of the 1830s, Princeton Seminary had shifted from a moderate position to the more rigid orthodoxy of Old School Presbyterianism, and Alexander participated in the move, although with some reluctance. [90] In the meantime, Nathaniel Taylor's so-called New Haven Theology had made Andover Seminary the champion of the New School Presbyterians. By then Schmucker had transferred his allegiance from his alma mater to Andover, where he published his first work in 1826. [91] But Archibald Alexander remained Schmucker's ideal of a godly minister. [92]

Samuel Schmucker's other teacher at Princeton, Samuel Miller, came from a much more orthodox Presbyterian background. Tutored in theology by his minister father, Miller had filled the pulpit of the First Presbyterian Church in New York City for a number of years before coming to Princeton Seminary as its second professor in 1813, at the age of forty-four. In later years, Miller became one of the staunchest pillars of Old School Presbyterianism. But his early years at Princeton were characterized by a much more expansive, open, and liberal attitude. In 1795, he had preached a sermon berating the institution of slavery and insisting that all persons are born free and equal. By 1843, he had come to view this whole issue as lying outside the realm of religion. It was probably not until the 1830s that his thinking took a sharply restrictive turn, with its rigid resistance to change. [93] Miller also held a highly positive view of German Lutheran Pietism. He considered the Pietism of Spener as a reformation of Lutheranism that restored it to the shape originally given to it by Martin Luther. He

---

[89]Mackay, "Archibald Alexander," 20; and Loetscher, *Facing the Enlightenment and Pietism*, 209.

[90]Wentz, *Pioneer in Christian Unity*, 25.

[91]This book was Schmucker's translation with additions from the German of Professors Storr and Flatt's *Elementary Course of Biblical Theology* (Andover: Flagg & Gould, 1826).

[92]Wentz, *Pioneer in Christian Unity*, 17.

[93]Belden C. Lane, "Miller and the Eldership: A Knickerbocker Goes to Nassau," *Princeton Seminary Bulletin*, n.s., 6 (1985): 211-15.

even asserted that it was in the followers of Spener that the true church was to be found in Germany during the seventeenth century.[94]

It appears that both of Samuel Schmucker's professors at Princeton tended more to invigorate rather than revise the Lutheran Pietist theology that he had carried with him into this stronghold of Presbyterianism. Yet when he left Princeton Schmucker had changed. He had grown intellectually and spiritually, through close association not only with his teachers but also with fellow students like Charles Hodge, later to become the champion of Presbyterian conservatives, and his roommate Robert Baird, who became a world traveler for causes like Sabbath schools, temperance, and ecumenism.[95] Schmucker's conviction that reason always ratified the claims of revelation was heightened, his sympathy for moral causes confirmed, his devotion to personal piety and revivalism expanded, and his understanding of other Protestant denominations broadened and sharpened. The Presbyterian church had afforded Schmucker a positive and highly creditable educational experience, but in no discernible way had it diminished the dedication to his Lutheran heritage. He left Princeton as he arrived, a devotee of classical Lutheran Pietism.

ORGANIZATION OF SYNOD AND SEMINARY

At the time of his graduation from seminary, Samuel Schmucker's basic convictions and goals were already firmly formulated, and they never really changed. Utilizing the term made famous by Spener, he noted, as he left Princeton in 1820, that he had three *pia desideria:* an English translation of an eminent work of Lutheran dogmatics, a Lutheran theological seminary, and a Lutheran college.[96] For Schmucker, "pious desires" were not idle dreams or sentimental wishes, and within ten years all three had become realities. But before any of them came to fruition, the young clergyman found himself intimately involved, as we have already noted, in the organization of the General Synod.

Samuel Schmucker not only helped determine the shape of the General Synod, he almost single-handedly saved it from early extinction. The newborn synod received what appeared to be a mortal wound when, in

---

[94]James Lawton Haney, Jr., "The Religious Heritage and Education of Samuel Simon Schmucker: A Study in the Rise of 'American Lutheranism' " (Ph.D. diss., Yale University, 1968) 436-37.

[95]Henry H. Baird, *The Life of the Rev. Robert Baird, D.D.* (New York: A. D. F. Randolph, 1866) 32-35, 227-35.

[96]Anstadt, *Life and Times of Samuel Schmucker,* 112.

1823, after sending delegates to only one meeting, the Pennsylvania Ministerium withdrew its membership. The action was apparently taken out of fear that the new synod, with its plans to establish a seminary and unite with interdenominational Bible and tract societies, was too thoroughly "unionistic" and would exercise too much authority over the rights of its constituent congregations and districts. These rights were particularly cherished by immigrants who had fled from similar systems of religious control in their fatherland. In addition, many German Lutherans clung tenaciously to their native language and resisted vigorously the General Synod's use of English.[97] Since the Pennsylvania Ministerium contained over half of the General Synod's membership, it was concluded that the life of the infant federation was at an end, and its officers made no plans even to call another meeting. At this point Samuel Schmucker launched himself into feverish activity and, with a flurry of correspondence, secured a respectable attendance of delegates to attend a meeting of the synod in Frederick, Maryland, in October 1823. Delegates attended from the synods of North Carolina, Maryland and Virginia, Ohio, and from the West Pennsylvania Conference.[98] The survival of the General Synod was no longer in doubt. Before the outbreak of the Civil War, the Pennsylvania Ministerium itself had rejoined,[99] and nearly two-thirds of all the Lutherans in this country had affiliated with the synod whose existence owed so much to one man's prodigious efforts at a critical moment in its young history.

Another major contribution that Schmucker made to the early life of the General Synod lay in his authorship of a comprehensive document on church polity and discipline. Schmucker had begun work on it during his first year in the parish ministry. Several years later it was published by the General Synod and for nearly two generations gave valuable guidance to its various judicatories at all levels of their organization.[100] Schmucker's son

---

[97]Ibid., 149-50.

[98]Ibid., 126.

[99]This action occurred in 1853.

[100]Samuel S. Schmucker, "Formula for the Government and Discipline of the Evangelical Lutheran Church," in *Elements of a Popular Theology, with Occasional References to the Doctrines of the Reformation Avowed before the Diet of Augsburg in 1530*, 9th ed. (Philadelphia: Smith, English, 1860) 420-50. Unless otherwise noted, all quotations from *Elements of a Popular Theology* are from the 9th and last edition. Publishers for the other editions consulted are, for 1st ed., Andover: Gould & Newman, 1834; 2d ed., New York: Leavitt, Lord, 1834; 3d ed., Baltimore: Publication Rooms, 1842; 5th ed., Philadelphia: J. S. Miles, 1845; 6th ed., Philadelphia: E. W. Miller, 1848; 8th ed., Philadelphia: Miller & Burlock, 1857.

Beale later referred to this so-called Formula as the most "important, influential and enduring work" of his father's life.[101]

Samuel Schmucker's deep interest in maintaining a viable union of Lutheran synodical groups, and his consequent lifelong commitment to the General Synod, was related both to his determination to combat heresy and to his dream of larger Protestant union. Schmucker was concerned about the creeping rationalism that had infiltrated the church since the days of Muhlenberg and particularly during and following the War of 1812. On visiting New York City shortly after his sojourn at Princeton, he commented in his journal that the majority of Lutheran preachers were "rank socinians."[102] It is clear from his comments that he associated the term *Socinians* primarily with the denial of Christ's divinity, or the rejection of its fundamental importance. Intuitively, Schmucker understood that a weak and fragmented Lutheranism could never rid itself of this insidious worship of human reason and its consequent rejection of divine revelation. Only a united church could provide a strong college and seminary where its prospective ministers would be solidly grounded in the fundamental doctrines of the Bible. Such a church could demand that every applicant for the Lutheran ministry be examined in the presence of the whole synod on the subject of personal piety and be required to subscribe to the basic teachings of the Augsburg Confession.[103] As early as 1820, Schmucker records in his journal the opinion that "a confession should be adopted [by the synod] which ought to include only fundamental doctrines, and that would leave sufficient room for . . . liberty of thought. . . . This would enable us to exclude from the Church of Christ those pests of society, the socinians."[104]

Schmucker's early struggle to keep the General Synod alive and his ongoing dedication to its welfare were also directly related to another lifelong commitment—a broader Protestant union. Like his German Pietist forebears, Schmucker was an ecumenist at heart. He knew that, if the Lutheran church was to realize its potential contribution to the interdenominational societies of a missionary and moral nature, which were already beginning to characterize American Protestantism, it must first unite its own forces. He viewed the General Synod as a necessary step for Lutherans toward the greater goal of strengthening the evangelical piety of the whole church.

---

[101]Quoted in Wentz, *Pioneer in Christian Unity*, 81.

[102]Anstadt, *Life and Times of Samuel Schmucker*, 62.

[103]Ibid., 62, 72.

[104]Ibid., 71.

While Schmucker was engaged in efforts to save the General Synod, his thoughts were preoccupied with future tasks far beyond the confines of the small parishes he served in the backwoods of Virginia. This plethora of planning and perhaps even his hectic activity on behalf of the synod had been stimulated by a personal tragedy that for a time left him nearly immobilized with grief. In July 1823, his young wife, after having given birth to their first child a few months earlier, became ill and died. [105] As Schmucker began to emerge from the trauma of his bereavement, he immersed himself in activity as well as thoughts about the future. In addition to his pastoral duties and studies, he continued translating a volume of dogmatics by Storr and Flatt and made a little parish seminary out of his home, where he tutored and prepared students for the Lutheran ministry. [106] He thought for a time of founding an orphan's home and publishing house like that of Francke in Halle, but his mind kept gravitating back to one of his "pious desires," the establishment of a full-fledged Lutheran seminary. Still struggling to find a way out of his sorrow, he wrote in his diary at this time, "Sometimes I think it is the will of God that I should devote myself entirely to the education of youth, principally for the Gospel Ministry: then I desire to establish a Franckean Seminary."[107]

Within three years, Schmucker's thoughts had been translated into deeds. In 1825, he was the prime mover of a resolution that came from his

---

[105]Wentz, *Pioneer in Christian Unity*, 74. Schmucker's first marriage was to Elnora Geiger. Then in October 1825, he married Mary Catherine Steenbergen. This union lasted nearly twenty-three years, until her death in 1848. They had twelve children in addition to the son from his first marriage, of whom eight lived to maturity. In 1850, Schmucker married his third wife, Esther M. Wagner, who survived him. Three of his sons became Lutheran ministers. See pp. 332-42.

[106]Anstadt, *Life and Times of Samuel Schmucker*, 176. Six students were tutored over the years in this parish seminary.

[107]Ibid., 175-76. The reference to an orphanage like Francke's and to a "Franckean Seminary" are typical and reveal Schmucker's admiration for the German Pietist father. The same was true of his feelings for Spener, for whom he named one of his sons. Samuel Schmucker's references to Spener, Francke, and Arndt are numerous and, without exception, filled with respect and veneration. See, for example, "Portraiture of Lutheranism" and "Patriarchs of American Lutheranism" Schmucker, *American Lutheran Church*. Schmucker, like the Pietist fathers themselves, had the highest regard for Luther but expressed more openly than they ever did his dissatisfaction with the excessive veneration for Luther, which causes "all attempts to continue the work of the reformation he began to be denounced as treason to his cause" (p. 60).

own Maryland and Virginia Synod to the convention of the General Synod, calling for an immediate organization of a theological seminary under the official auspices of the General Synod. The resolution was adopted and the first board of directors elected, with Schmucker's father as chairman. The board of directors, by nearly unanimous choice, elected Samuel Schmucker as the first teacher in the proposed seminary, which they later decided to locate at Gettysburg, Pennsylvania. The newly appointed professor composed the proposed constitution for the seminary, which was adopted by the board with only a few minor changes. In September 1826, Schmucker subscribed to the oath of office that he himself had written. In it he affirmed a belief in the Augsburg Confession and Luther's *Small Catechism* as "summary and just exhibitions of the fundamental doctrines of the Word of God" and promised to "vindicate and inculcate these doctrines in opposition to all errorists."[108]

Exactly fifty years after the United States declared its independence, Lutherans thus established their second seminary in the United States, the oldest one still in operation today. Shortly after taking up his teaching duties, Schmucker realized that many of his students were ill-equipped to begin theological studies, and he began to plan for a preparatory school. Within a year's time, a small classical school was started and housed in the seminary building. Schmucker personally purchased a separate building for the school and addressed the Pennsylvania House of Representatives in regard to its purpose.[109] As a result, a charter was granted, and Gettysburg College, then called Pennsylvania College, was formally organized on 4 July 1832. All three of Schmucker's "pious desires" were fulfilled. He now devoted himself to teaching in the seminary he had helped to found and to leading the synod he had helped to save. During his nearly forty years of teaching, it has been estimated that his views influenced the pliable minds of more than 400 students, who for the most part served in Lutheran parishes and institutions throughout North America. It was largely through Schmucker's teaching at Gettysburg that the traditions of German Lutheran Pietism, adapted to the peculiar cultural and political environment of the United States of America, continued their pervasive influence within the life of the Lutheran church in this country for another generation.

---

[108]Wentz, *Pioneer in Christian Unity*, 128-32.

[109]Anstadt, *Life and Times of Samuel Schmucker*, 220.

C·H·A·P·T·E·R 3

Activism

As the respected leader of the General Synod and first professor of its newly established seminary, Samuel Schmucker was by 1830 the acknowledged spokesman for the majority of Lutherans in this country. From the beginning he had made it clear that, like his father, he stood squarely within the tradition of German Lutheran Pietism. In a synodical address delivered in 1824, he had invited his audience "with the aid of history . . . [to] contemplate our Church in the splendor of her morning glory . . . in the land . . . where Spener sowed the seed of truth,—where Arndt wrote and preached and lived his 'true Christianity', where Francke wrought his works of love."[1] Schmucker maintained that, under the influence of Spener and his colleagues, "the dead formality of the seventeenth century had been broken up," that a great and extensive reformation or revival of spiritual religion was thereby effected within German Lutheranism, restoring it to "the divine light and heat of grace" and "causing it to bud and blossom as the rose."[2] He read most of the works of Spener and Francke either from the original or secondary sources and made frequent references to them in his own compositions. He drew an undeviating line of descent from German Lutheran Pietism to the fathers of Lutheranism in colonial America to himself. He stated categor-

---

[1]S. S. Schmucker, "Intellectual and Moral Glories of the Christian Temple" (1824), MCAL, reel 6, p. 10.

[2]S. S. Schmucker, "Patriarchs of American Lutheranism," in *American Lutheran Church,* 94. See also idem, *The Church of the Redeemer* (Baltimore: T. Newton Kurz, 1867) 78.

ically that Muhlenberg, Helmuth, Brunholz, Handschuh, and Kunze along
with their other Hallean colleagues "belonged to the most zealous and
faithful preachers of the Pietistic school of Spener and Francke, and had
only modified their ministrations to suit the altered circumstances of our
country."[3]

Samuel Schmucker understood his own ministry and mission in exactly
this manner. But just as Muhlenberg and the other American Lutheran fathers had modified the primary postulates of Pietism to meet the "altered
circumstances of our country," so Schmucker aimed to apply its fundamental insights to the culturally changed conditions of a constitutional democracy.

From this perspective, then, what was the precise nature of the American Lutheran Pietism that Schmucker led during the crucial years from 1830
to 1860? How can it be most accurately defined? First, it traced its theological roots back to Martin Luther and to the classic doctrines of the Reformation. On these well-accepted Lutheran foundations it continued to
promote the strong strain of spirituality that had been a major characteristic of German Pietism. Like its predecessor, American Lutheran Pietism
directed this spiritual emphasis into practical forms of active expression
rather than intricate doctrinal definitions. It moved more in the direction
of ethics than of dogma, practical religion rather than doctrinal formulation, activism rather than theological analysis. In these differences lay the
heart of that which distinguished it from the more orthodox and conservative stance of the "Old Lutherans." The key theological factors that accounted for the activist approach of American Lutheran Pietism appear to
be precisely those that separated German Pietism from Lutheran orthodoxy a century earlier, namely, its revitalization and extension of the doctrine of sanctification and its hopeful and optimistic millennial eschatology.

SANCTIFICATION

American Pietism, in keeping with its German antecedents, held justification in close and inseparable conjunction with sanctification. Samuel
Schmucker insisted that true faith was always active and living, expressing
in tangible acts the new life in Christ. "Faith must bring forth good works,"

---

[3]S. S. Schmucker, "Patriarchs of American Lutheranism," in *American Lutheran
Church*, 98. Schmucker frequently asserted that Muhlenberg was a direct spiritual
descendant of Francke. See his *Inaugural Address, Delivered before the Directors of the
Theological Seminary of the General Synod of the Evangelical Lutheran Church* (Carlisle PA:
J. Tizzard & J. Crover, 1826) 27.

he wrote, "and . . . it is our duty to perform them, not in order to be justified, but because God commands it."[4] Even with this strong emphasis on sanctification, there was no corresponding disregard of the doctrine on which it has been contended that Lutheranism stands or falls. On the contrary, justification through grace by faith alone retained an unquestioned position of eminence. Schmucker described justification in explicitly orthodox terms, as "not a change in man, but a forensic or judicial act . . . the imputation of the Savior's righteousness to the sinner."[5] It was, in fact, a reticence to deviate from the principle of *sola fides* that led Schmucker and his Pietist colleagues to question orthodoxy's insistence on regeneration in the baptism of infants and the presence of Christ in the Supper, regardless of the presence or absence of faith in the communicant.

With undeviating consistency Pietism viewed salvation as absolutely dependent upon the atoning act of Christ as Redeemer and Savior. In this respect Pietism's interpretation of justification emphasized not only the concept of "faith alone" but even more the classical Reformation doctrine of "Christ alone." Here lay the heart and core of Pietist spirituality. And here again the intimate and indissoluble connection between justification and sanctification was taken for granted. Pietism was never content to allow the justification of the believer through faith in Christ to exist in isolation. To be justified meant to receive the goodness of God and simultaneously to be consumed with the compulsion to do good for others. It meant to be filled with the desire to witness and to serve. Schmucker thus described the grand object of the Christian ministry and Christianity itself as "to bring souls to Christ."[6] After describing Francke as the "great father of missionaries," Schmucker quoted the Halle professor as having written, " I regard it as the greatest happiness of my whole life, if God so highly honors me . . . as to make me the instrument of rousing a single soul from sleep to sin, and bringing it to Christ."[7]

American Lutheran Pietism did not in any way reject the importance of justification but insisted on its propinquity with sanctification. This theological emphasis motivated its adherents to continue in a tradition of

---

[4]S. S. Schmucker, *Elements of a Popular Theology,* 191.

[5]Ibid., 169-70, 202.

[6]S. S. Schmucker to his son Beale, 7 November 1849, S. S. Schmucker Papers, Lutheran Theological Seminary Archives, Abdel Ross Wentz Memorial Library, Gettysburg PA (hereafter cited as Schmucker Papers). See also S. S. Schmucker, *Inaugural Address,* 39.

[7]S. S. Schmucker, "Intellectual and Moral Glories," 27.

activism characterized by an accentuation on evangelism, conversion, revivals, missions, ecumenism, and moral reform. Pietism's practical commitment to these goals, generated by its accent on the nexus of faith with life, was given added impetus, widened horizons, and a more precise political focus by its millennial expectations.

MILLENNIALISM

During the latter part of the eighteenth century and the first half of the nineteenth century, most of American Protestantism was definitively influenced by some form of millennialism. It was expressed in widely diverse forms. In general, premillennialists looked for the world to grow worse and worse until Christ came suddenly to rule in power on earth for 1,000 years previous to the final judgment. Postmillennialists, on the other hand, generally envisioned a gradual improvement of conditions along with an increase of justice and peace on earth as a prelude to the coming kingdom. In the tradition of Philipp Spener, American Pietism stood for the most part within the latter group. They believed that lending themselves as instruments of God to the work of conversion and moral reformation would hasten the day when the kingdoms of this earth would become the kingdoms of the Lord. This brand of millennialism was similar in many respects to that espoused by numerous other Protestant evangelicals and by popular evangelists like Charles G. Finney. But Lutheran Pietists tended to trace their convictions regarding the coming kingdom back to Spener's "hope for better times" and to the interpretation of the Apocalypse expounded by the Württemburg Pietist leader and biblical scholar Johann Bengel. A notable product of the eschatology that permeated the Pietist interpretation of the millennial hope was an optimism about the future of the church and world. This assurance in turn provided strong motivation to human efforts and activist ethics.

During the first half of the nineteenth century, the eschatological stance of the more conservative branches of American Lutheranism tended to denigrate any faith in the hope of historical progress before the second coming of Christ. Some strict confessionalists echoed Luther's belief that the millennium lay in the past and that only the final dissolution of this world marked the future. They lumped all who believed in a future reign of Christ on earth under the category of chiliasts and argued that such persons were condemned as heretics by Article 17 of the Augsburg Confession.[8] There were, however, a few conservative Lutherans who did express

---

[8] Gustav Seyffarth, "Chiliasm, Critically Examined according to the Statements of the New and Old Testaments, with Reference to the Most Recent Theory of the Millennium," *Evangelical Review* 12 (January 1861): 341-43, 363.

millennial convictions and offered extensive arguments for the thesis that the Augsburg Confession opposed only one specific form of chiliasm.[9] However, the millennialism these writers explicated anticipated no expected increase in righteousness, justice, and peace to usher in Christ's reign on earth. By divine decree, all efforts at social and political reform were doomed to fail. Conditions would inevitably worsen until, at the darkest hour, Christ would appear to initiate his earthly kingdom. The chief exponent of this view, Joseph Seiss, a respected Lutheran theologian, wrote: "Some thought that the great Bible, Tract, Sunday School and missionary movements would soon win the nations to faith in Jesus . . . they see signs of promise in the movements of reform. . . . I have no confidence in such hopes. . . . I see more promise in the darkest features of the times than in all these pious dreams."[10]

This interpretation did not of necessity lead to a quietistic approach to ethics. It was often invoked to urge individual Christians to live a life of faith and piety, since Christ would come suddenly and unexpectedly in judgment.[11] But it was bereaved of any real hope for the renewal of the world, nor did it view this concern as having primary importance or any intimate relation to matters of salvation. In practice, this pessimistic view of the possibility of earthly improvement led to an ethic that was confined almost completely to the personal life of the individual believer.

American Lutheran Pietists, for the most part, rejected a premillennialism that anchored the motive for ethical behavior in the fear of Christ's sudden and unexpected coming in judgment. When the adventism of William Miller gained increasing popularity during the 1830s and early 1840s, a synod in New York State caustically characterized it as the phantom of "a deluded imagination." Miller's followers were described as living in a state of "marked restlessness" alternating between hope and fear that each day would be the last. In contrast, these Lutheran Pietists described themselves as "those who are contented to live and prepared to die, free from anxiety about the times and the seasons which the Father has put in his own hands."[12]

---

[9]Joseph A. Seiss, *The Last Times and the Great Consummation* (Baltimore: T. Newton Kurz, 1856; reprint, Philadelphia: Smith, English, 1867) 327-35. See also Francis W. Monseth, "Millennialism in American Lutheranism in the Light of Augsburg Confession, Article XVII" (Th.D. diss., Concordia Theological Seminary, 1986) 53-66.

[10]Ibid., 299-300.

[11]Seyffarth, "Chiliasm," 400.

[12]*Lutheran Herald*, n.s. 1 (30 October 1844): n.p.

Samuel Schmucker was an articulate advocate of the moderate type of postmillennialism that had characterized Lutheran Pietism from the time of Spener. His father was recognized as a leading authority on the subject. As a young man Schmucker was not only exposed to books and to frequent sermons on this topic[13] but had undoubtedly read carefully his father's two-volume study of the Revelation of St. John, in which a reliance upon Johann Bengel was frequently asserted.[14]

In his lectures to the seminary students at Gettysburg, Samuel Schmucker presented his own millennial views in great detail and compiled them in his textbook *Elements of a Popular Theology*. In keeping with Article 17 of the Augsburg Confession, Schmucker divorced himself from the concept held by the "ancient Jews and Chiliasts, as well as some Anabaptists of the 16th century, that the . . . Savior would . . . personally appear on earth and establish a theocracy not unlike that of the Old Testament."[15] But then in carefully chosen and precise wording, he portrayed his own understanding of the coming millennium. It would

> consist of an extraordinary and general diffusion of Christianity . . . among all the nations . . . by professing Christians, accompanied by extraordinary effusions of the Holy Spirit; facilitated by the improvement of science and the arts. This prevalence of Christian principle will . . . be the harbinger of peace and good will among men . . . [and] the triumph of the Gospel will everywhere be accompanied by its legitimate train of benevolent influences on the civil and social institutions of the world, and war itself, the prolific mother of all evil, will retire before the progress of the Prince of Peace.[16]

On the surface, Schmucker's millennialism appeared to hold much in common with the Enlightenment's emphasis upon an inevitable progress rooted in scientific achievement. But in one vital respect his apocalyptic view was directly opposed to this popular mentality. Schmucker's hope was based not upon faith in the power of human reason but on the utter reliability of God's promises. Like Jonathan Edwards, Schmucker applied the biblical concept of necessity to historical as well as personal salvation.[17]

---

[13]Wentz, *Pioneer in Christian Unity*, 244.

[14]J. G. Schmucker, *Prophetic History*, chart at beginning of book.

[15]S. S. Schmucker, *Elements of a Popular Theology*, 346.

[16]Ibid., 347.

[17]Ernest Lee Tuveson, *Redeemer Nation: The Idea of America's Millennial Role* (Chicago: University of Chicago Press, 1968) 51.

"That the Kingdom of the Messiah will be extended over the whole earth, "
Schmucker wrote, "is absolutely certain. " This certainty was not grounded
in the confidence that humanity would use their God-given intelligence to
solve problems and establish God's kingdom on earth. Rather, it was "because the sacred volume has expressly predicted the fact, . . . not only in
figurative language, but in literal terms. "[18] The true sign of the approaching millennium Schmucker saw in the conversion of the world through the
preaching of the gospel. He did not believe that every individual person
would accept the gospel but maintained that all nations and all people would
hear it proclaimed and therefore have the opportunity to receive its blessings. [19]

Since Schmucker looked upon Protestantism as the only true form of
Christianity, he envisioned the coming mass evangelization as encom-
passing not only pagans and Jews but Roman Catholics as well. According
to his interpretation of the books of Revelation and Daniel, the conversion
of the papists and of the papacy itself was a necessary prelude to the millennium. [20] Schmucker's enlightened and tolerant attitude toward Protestants did not extend to the Roman church. Like many others, he was caught
up in the anti-Catholic hysteria of his day. At times he appeared willing to
give credence to almost any slander against them, no matter how ludicrous
or extreme. He personally interviewed a young former nun, Maria Monk,
and accepted without question her scurrilous and sensational revelations of
scandal regarding the Roman church. [21] Schmucker's opposition to Ca-
tholicism approached the level of outright fear and led him to express alarm
over the reestablishment of the Inquisition and to portray the Jesuits as the

---

[18]S. S. Schmucker, *Elements of a Popular Theology*, 348.

[19]Ibid., 347.

[20]S. S. Schmucker, "The Papal Hierarchy, Viewed in Light of Prophecy and
History, Being a Discourse Delivered in the English Lutheran Church, Gettysburg, February 2, 1845, " in *Sermons and Papers against the Roman Catholic Church, 1833–
1852* (Gettysburg: H. C. Neinstadt, 1845).

[21]S. S. Schmucker to his wife, 10 June 1836, Schmucker Papers, 3100.0001.
See also John R. Bodo, *Protestant Clergy and Public Issues, 1812–1848* (Princeton NJ:
Princeton University Press, 1954); and S. S. Schmucker, "Discourse in Commem-
oration of the Glorious Reformation of the Sixteenth Century, with a Reference
to the Relation between the Principles of Popery and Our Republican Institu-
tions, " delivered before the Evangelical Lutheran Synod of West Philadelphia, in
A Commentary on Saint Paul's Epistle to the Galatians, by Martin Luther (Philadelphia:
Salmon S. Miles, 1840) 83-123.

Pope's spies operating in a conspiracy directed against the Protestant church.[22] This same fear led Schmucker to oppose Irish immigration because it was Catholic[23] and to express approval for some of the anti-Roman planks of the Nativist political party platform.

CONVERSION, MISSIONS, AND REVIVALS

The millennial hope of Lutheran Pietism contained positive ramifications that went far beyond its anti-Catholicism. Foremost among these implications was the basic conviction that the promised "better things" could not be realized until the gospel had been proclaimed to all people and that God had committed this divine work of proclamation into human hands. This same belief had propelled August Francke to become the "great father of missionaries" and had motivated the prodigious efforts of men like Muhlenberg to plant the gospel in new lands.

In this same spirit Samuel Schmucker in the early 1830s challenged the followers of Christ to "go to work," with full confidence that the task of bringing the gospel to the whole world was possible within a single generation.[24] In keeping with this emphasis on evangelism, Schmucker was an avid supporter and active participant in the Home and Foreign Missionary Society, along with the American Bible and Tract societies. This missionary motif also motivated Schmucker to continue the Americanization of Lutheranism that Muhlenberg had begun. In Schmucker's eyes, Americanization did not mean a desertion of the historic Lutheran doctrines or confessions or a capitulation to other forms of Protestantism. It meant, rather, a willingness to relate the Lutheran understanding of the Christian faith to the English-speaking citizens of a democratic republic.

This effort entailed, first of all, cutting the umbilical cord that still connected Lutheranism in America to the German language. In pressing for the use of English in its church life and worship, Pietists were primarily concerned about mission. They realized that a German-speaking church could never bring the message of the gospel to the growing numbers of unchurched youth who had been born in this country and spoke only English. The language struggle was long and bitter and costly. While there were major exceptions, for the most part it was a story of the struggle of

---

[22]S. S. Schmucker, "Papal Hierarchy."

[23]Frederick W. Wentz, introduction to *Fraternal Appeal to the American Churches, with a Plan for Catholic Union on Apostolic Principles*, by S. S. Schmucker (1838; reprint, Philadelphia: Fortress Press, 1965) 18.

[24]S. S. Schmucker, *Elements of a Popular Theology*, 212-13.

American Pietists against the determined efforts of strict confessionalists to retain a German church.

The activist nature of American Pietism and its priority on missions and conversion also led it to continue in the Spener-Francke tradition of prayer meetings and religious revivals, modifying them to meet the new conditions and accepted practices of the American scene. The entire Pietist movement within the Lutheran church in Germany was regarded by its American descendants as a revival of the true understanding of Christianity initiated by Luther. Schmucker thus could ask concerning John Arndt and his followers, "Who in glancing his eye over the history of our Church, does not dwell with wonder and gratitude and amazement on the extensive and glorious revivals far spread and radical, the fruits of which extended throughout the whole of that century?"[25]

American Lutheran Pietists looked favorably upon the revivalism that characterized so much of Protestantism in the United States because it was largely compatible with their own traditions. But the revivalism of all other denominations had to be tested by the example of the "fathers" before it was adopted. As a result, American Lutheran Pietism consistently took a moderate position with regard to the highly controversial New Measures, which had been popularized by the famous evangelist Charles G. Finney. Among these New Measures was the practice of holding "protracted meetings," lasting from a few days to several weeks, where a conscious attempt was made to stir up the emotions in order to produce conversion. In particular controversy raged over the "anxious bench" (or "mourner's bench"), where persons were asked to come forward in order to become the special objects of intensive prayer. Philip Schaff declared that one might "make a book on the 'anxious bench' controversy in the German Church in America."[26] Opposition of conservative Lutherans to the adoption of the New Measures was often heated.[27] It usually took the form of declaring them a capitulation to the ways of Methodists and other Protestant revivalists and an antithesis to historical Lutheranism. In 1838, one such writer blasted the editor of the *Lutheran Observer* for his alleged approval of these revivalistic measures. "Alter, for the Lutheran Church's sake, the name of your

---

[25]S. S. Schmucker, "Intellectual and Moral Glories," 21.

[26]Timothy Smith, *Revivalism and Social Reform* (Nashville: Abingdon Press, 1957) 31, 57.

[27]L. Schmucker, *Schmucker Family and the Lutheran Church*, 27.

paper; call it *New Measure, Fanatical, Methodistical, Anti-Lutheran Engine,* or *Advocate of Screaming, Falling, Clapping of Hands, of Hypocrisy and Lies.*"[28]

A variety of opinion existed even among Lutheran Pietists as to the extent to which the New Measures were validated by biblical directives. On the whole, they defended a moderate use of these measures, honed to the test of their own traditions. A Hartwick Seminary professor who was positive toward revivalism nevertheless warned, "The mere excitement of animal passions will leave us no better than they found us . . . . It brings genuine revivals into disrepute."[29] Typical of this position was an official resolution passed by the English Synod of Ohio during the midst of the New Measures controversy. "On revivals of religion [we] recommend opposition to all disorder and ultraism . . . whilst . . . we earnestly encourage our Churches to promote genuine revivals by faithful preaching of the word, by prayer, and such other means as accord with the holy religion of our Redeemer."[30]

In lectures to his students on this subject, Schmucker commented favorably on "calling out" before the congregation those who were convicted, but he opposed all unnecessary noise and confusion. Like Muhlenberg, he was concerned that prayer meetings and revivals be conducted decently and in order. Above all he felt that there should always be a follow-up on those who came under "conviction" by revivalistic preaching. Education should follow the experience of conversion. "The fathers," Schmucker said, referring as always by this phrase to his Pietist forerunners, "would not sanction the neglect of cathechization."[31] Ideally, confirmation was to follow conversion and not precede it, as was so often the case within Lutheranism. Schmucker was in complete accord with the criticism of another Pietist leader who complained, "How often are young people confirmed in the church who have no experimental knowledge of . . . faith in Christ. With such it is an empty form."[32]

---

[28]*Lutheran Observer* 5 (30 March 1838), quoted in Willard D. Allbeck, *A Century of Lutheranism in Ohio* (Yellow Springs OH: Antioch Press, 1966) 106.

[29]L. Sternberg, "Revivals," *Evangelical Quarterly Review* 15 (1864): 279.

[30]*Minutes of the English Synod of Ohio,* 1841, 13, quoted in Allbeck, *Century of Lutheranism in Ohio,* 91.

[31]S. S. Schmucker, "Notes on Lectures on Pastoral Theology, 1842" (delivered annually, 1842–1850), Schmucker Papers, 3450.000001.

[32]Nicholas Van Alstine, *Historical Review of the Franckean Evangelical Lutheran Synod of New York* (Philadelphia: Lutheran Publishing Society, 1893) 6.

While Pietists approved moderate revivalistic measures adjusted to the American milieu, they adamantly refused to admit that this adaptation was un-Lutheran. Schmucker consistently defended his position by Lutheran standards and insisted that revivalists were true Lutherans.[33] He referred to Luther as a man of "fervent piety" who not only believed in conversion but also "professed to have experienced it, and to know the exact time when this gracious change occurred." In similar fashion he described Spener as a "new measure" man.[34] As with Spener and Francke, American Lutheran Pietism was convinced that a converted ministry was an absolute necessity for a true renewal and reform of the church. A radical change of heart, resulting from the awareness of one's lost condition apart from faith in Christ's saving act, was most often referred to in the biblical phrase "born again" or simply called conversion. Not only were the clergy required to give some tangible evidence of this change of heart, but also in most cases a demonstration of conversion was considered as the doorway to adult membership in the church. In his model constitution for congregations Samuel Schmucker had advocated that, before admitting a person into membership, "The church council in all cases . . . require evidence of those changes and acts which constitute genuine conversion."[35] With few exceptions the English-speaking congregations connected with the General Synod accepted this suggestion and put it into practice, particularly throughout the third and fourth decades of the nineteenth century.

During this period the South Carolina Synod reported that two-thirds of its pastors participated in revivals. When the editor of the *Lutheran Observer* asserted that the synod's seminary in Lexington, South Carolina, was somewhat cool toward the New Measures, he received a swift reply from a seminary spokesman, "Four-fifths of the Board are advocates of *New Measures* . . . still further. . . . *All the students* who have been educated at Lexington, with not more than two or three exceptions, are New Measure Men . . . and have no scruples in using the 'anxious seat.' "[36] With rare exception, Lutheran leaders throughout the South, as well as its seminary teachers, were firm believers in "heart religion." They advocated revivals and participated in them. However, like Schmucker, they never viewed the conversion experience as a substitute for catechetical instruction. Further-

---

[33]Smith, *Revivalism and Social Reform*, 58.

[34]Ibid., 224; see also S. S. Schmucker, "That Eminent Man of God: Dr. Martin Luther" (handwritten lecture), Schmucker Papers, 3420.5001.

[35]S. S. Schmucker, *Church of the Redeemer*, 206-207.

[36]*Lutheran Observer* 10 (21 July 1843).

more, they frowned upon revivals that elicited excessive emotional displays and insisted that decorum and order always be maintained.[37]
Revivalism predominated likewise in the North Carolina and Virginia synods. Throughout the entire South, only the archconservative Tennessee
group, led by Paul Henkel, stood opposed to the practice. The Maryland
and West Pennsylvania synods, the latter of which Schmucker was a member, rejoiced over countless revivals held in their congregations, as was true
also in the English Synod of Ohio. Revivalism was widespread in Lutheran
congregations throughout the United States and Canada, but nowhere did
it reach such a feverish peak as in upstate New York, where it led at least
indirectly to the birth of two new synods.[38]

SCHISM IN NEW YORK STATE

In the New York Ministerium, reports of revivals were scarce,[39] an apparent result of the rationalistic tendencies introduced during the 1820s by
its president, Frederick Quitman. A negative attitude toward revivalism
continued to dominate the churches connected with the ministerium
throughout the 1830s and 1840s. But the Pietist spirit of revivalism was
strong among New York Lutherans, and opposition soon arose within the
synod. Those who composed the heart of this rebel nucleus resided in the
areas of upper New York State settled by the Palatine Pietist pioneers. They
favored a greater emphasis on revivals, prayer meetings, and involvement
with moral reform. In addition, some of them wanted to adopt the moderate confessional posture of the General Synod, which the ministerium
had rejected.[40] The man who emerged as the leader of the opposition group
was George A. Lintner, pastor of the largest congregation, located in
Schoharie. He was also among those who pressed for a more definite
confessional position. While Lintner approved of revivals and moral reform, he did not share fully the fervent Pietist concern for holiness of life
expressed in a converted clergy and lay membership. As early as 1823, he
had pressed the ministerium to unite with the General Synod. In 1826, a
resolution to this effect evoked a lengthy discussion, but in the end, action
was indefinitely postponed. Later that year Lintner helped to form the
Western Conference of the ministerium, for the purpose of creating greater

---

[37]Bost, "Rev. John Bachman," 347-53.

[38]Nelson, Lutherans in North America, 136.

[39]Krieder, History of the United Lutheran Synod, 181.

[40]Ibid., 106.

fellowship among the dissenters.[41] At this time Ernest Hazelius of Hart-wick Seminary preferred not to consider the issue further in order to prevent a division.[42] Three years later, however, Hazelius himself was calling for immediate union with the General Synod.

By this time the advocates of union had lost patience, and in 1830 they separated from the ministerium and formed the Hartwick Synod. The sanction of the parent body was never sought. The organizing convention was held at George Lintner's parish in Schoharie on 26 October 1830, and he was elected the first president. Ten pastors and fifteen parishes were represented, nearly half of the total of congregations in the ministerium.[43] One of the main reasons given by the Hartwick founders for the schism was the ministerium's alleged socinianism.[44] At its first regular convention in 1831, the Hartwick Synod, after hearing a letter of encouragement and invitation from Samuel Schmucker, voted to unite with the General Synod and to adopt its "Formula" for government and discipline.[45]

From the beginning, the Hartwick Synod expressed its strong approval of revivals and encouragement of greater emphasis on missionary endeavors at home and abroad,[46] as well as the cause of moral reform.[47] During the first year of its existence, it reported that "upwards of 1,000 souls" had been converted.[48] These priorities would appear to have met the major objections raised by those who had been dissatisfied with the ministerium. A significant portion of the original objectors, however, were unappeased. While there is little or no indication of differences recorded in the official minutes of the Hartwick Synod, later actions and testimony indicate that serious disagreements among members of the newly formed group surfaced

---

[41]Ibid., 71.

[42]Ernest Lewis Hazelius to S. S. Schmucker, 26 October 1826, Schmucker Papers, 3226.1026.

[43]Kreider, *History of the United Lutheran Synod*, 67-69.

[44]*Lutheran Herald* 1 (16 October 1839): 158.

[45]*Minutes of the Hartwick Synod and Ministerium of the Evangelical Lutheran Church in the State of New York*, 1st Session, September 1831, 9-10, Metropolitan-New York Synod Archives, Hormann Library, Wagner College, Staten Island NY.

[46]Ibid., 19-21.

[47]P. A. Strobel, *Memorial Volume to Commemorate the Semi-Centennial Anniversary of the Hartwick Lutheran Synod of the State of New York. . . .* (Philadelphia: Lutheran Publication Society, 1881) 42; Kreider, *History of the United Lutheran Synod*, 91.

[48]*Minutes of the Hartwick Synod*, 1832, 21.

early in its young life. On matters of general principles there was much unanimity, but in regard to the desired degree of commitment to those principles and the strategy by which they were to be carried out, dissension accelerated. The major points of controversy appear to have centered on the educational and moral requirements for the ministry and the degree of commitment to movements of moral reform.

In regard to home-missionary activity, all agreed that more ministers should be recruited and trained as quickly as possible to fill vacant congregations and organize new ones. But one group felt that this goal should not be accomplished at the cost of watering down the stringent theological training traditionally required for Lutheran clergy, while the other felt just as strongly that a crisis situation called for innovative measures. The latter group believed that the pressing need for ministers demanded that ways be devised to enable older men who had undergone conversion but who were without the advantages of a college education to prepare themselves for ordination. In these cases, they wanted strict intellectual requirements to be moderated in lieu of piety and religious experience.[49] Also, they pressed for the licensing of lay preachers who had little formal theological education, provided that they confined themselves to the tasks of teaching and preaching. The two groups agreed that the requirement of a "radical change of life," or conversion, both in regards to the ministry and the membership of the church, was in keeping with the teachings of Scripture. But there was sharp disagreement over setting up specific moral requirements as a test for admission to the ministry and membership of the church.

Finally, opinions differed about the desired degree of commitment to various moral reforms. These conflicting convictions surfaced during the convention of the Hartwick Synod in 1836 and resulted in yet another schism. In May 1837, just seven years after the first break with the ministerium, a dissendent group of laymen and clergy, most of whom were direct descendants of the eighteenth-century German Pietist immigrants from the Palatine, organized the Franckean Evangelic Synod, naming it in honor of their acknowledged hero, August H. Francke. No Lutheran synod in the United States was ever more thoroughly committed to a converted membership, missionary activity, moral reform, and revivalism. While the center of their activity remained in Schoharie and Montgomery counties in upstate New York, the Franckeans sent missionaries as far west as Wisconsin and Illinois, and north into Canada. Within five years these mission-minded Lutherans received nearly 2,500 adult members into their par-

---

[49]N. Van Alstine, *Historical Review*, 4-6.

ishes, largely by baptism and confirmation.[50] In just over a decade they more than doubled their membership,[51] a remarkable accomplishment, particularly in view of the stringent requirements they demanded in regard to personal piety. "Four-day meetings" were conducted regularly throughout their congregations, and most of the New Measures were utilized, including the "anxious seat."[52] Some of the Franckean leaders, the Reverend Philip Wieting in particular, were recognized as among the most powerful revivalist preachers in their area.[53]

The Franckeans devoted at least one session of each synodical convention to "experimental" religion. It was a period of time given over to "fervent prayers" and "speaking upon points of Christian experience."[54] Experimental religion was not only aimed at the unconverted but directed toward a renewal of the spiritual life of those already "born again." The concern was to foster a personal commitment to Christ. Like their Pietist colleagues throughout the country, the Franckeans were also acutely aware of the dangers of excessive emotionalism. One of their most respected leaders, the Reverend Nicholas Van Alstine, himself a noted revivalist, gave clear expression to this critical concern. "I am sick to heart of mere ranting . . . men should be taught to act from . . . principle, and not from blind impulses and emotions. One of the former is worth a score and a half of the later."[55] Still, the Franckeans defended all genuine revivalism, convinced that its authorization was found in the Bible and their own Lutheran heritage. When accused by the Tennessee Synod of being "present day enthusiasts" and denounced for utilizing New Measures, they replied, "What are the old measures? The old measures are revivals of religion, as in the days of the apostles, and of Luther, Arndt, Spener, and Francke, prayer meetings, family worship . . . evidence of a change of heart."[56]

---

[50]*Journal of the Franckean Synod* (hereafter cited as *JFS*), 1844, 7, Lutheran Theological Seminary Archives.

[51]N. Van Alstine, *Historical Review*, 10; Robert Fortenbaugh, "American Lutheran Synods and Slavery, 1830-1860," *Journal of Religion* 13 (1933): 86.

[52]H. L. Dox, *Memoir of Rev. Philip Wieting, a Pastor Forty Years in the Same Field* (Philadelphia: Lutheran Publication Society, 1870) 154, 164.

[53]Ibid., 152.

[54]*JFS*, 1840, 28; 1857, 19.

[55]Nicholas Van Alstine to Philip Wieting, Franckean Evangelic Lutheran Synod, Collected Papers and Correspondence, Metropolitan-Upper New York Synod Archives (hereafter cited as Franckean Papers).

[56]Editorial, *Lutheran Herald* 4 (15 March 1842): 45.

Revivalism, along with its insistence on an experience of personal commitment or conversion, was an integral aspect of the activist theology of Lutheran Pietism. As such it was not confined, as it has often been implied, to a minor radical wing of American Lutheranism. After 1830, it was one of the critical issues that separated Lutheran Pietism from orthodoxy. From New York to Georgia and as far west as Ohio, wherever Pietism prevailed, revivalism and conversion were normative aspects of American Lutheranism for the first century and a half of its existence. It is also important to remember that nineteenth-century revival measures, far from associating themselves with a conservative approach, as is often the case in our own day, went hand in hand with progressive theology, ecumenism, and a commitment to moral and humanitarian causes. [57]

ECUMENISM

The missionary enthusiasm and emphasis on revivalism and conversion of American Lutheran Pietism was directly related to its concern for the unity of Protestant churches throughout the world. Spener and Francke had promoted the ecumenical posture of German Lutheran Pietism, which had been initiated by John Arndt and George Calixtus. They had placed priority on the incorporation of the believer into the life of Christ, with its tangible expression of Christian love, rather than on denominational distinctions. Spener had written, "Christians are all one in the community of Spiritual blessings. No one has a better God, or better Christ, or Spirit, or faith than the other."[58]

In close accord with Spener, American Lutheran Pietism's understanding of church union did not entail an institutional, organic unity that involved the surrender of denominational uniqueness or congregational authority. Neither did it foresee the necessity for any complete doctrinal agreement as a prerequisite for meaningful cooperative endeavor. Rather, Pietists were convinced that Lutheran believers shared the same great fundamental truths of the Bible with all other evangelical Christians. This platform was believed to be wide enough to enable all denominations to labor harmoniously, and in full Christian fellowship, for the common goals of the gospel. This practical ecumenism was understood as a basic ingredient of genuine Christianity. Union with Christ in holiness of life automatically created communion with all other believers. This union was

---

[57]Smith, *Revivalism and Social Reform*, 60.

[58]Quoted by S. S. Schmucker, *Fraternal Appeal*, 78.

believed to be best promoted by simply manifesting the spirit of Christ in relations with all other ecclesiastical bodies.

The Pietist commitment to ecumenism was never conceived as an end in itself. It was a means for the accomplishment of the divinely ordained missionary goal and millennial promise. The chief concern of American Lutheran Pietist theology was always the salvation of souls, the redemption of the human race. All else was secondary. Sectarianism was considered an evil because it frustrated the ultimate missionary task that God had bestowed upon the church. Writing about a revival in which he had participated, a member of a Franckean Synod congregation noted that Baptists, Presbyterians, Methodists, and Lutherans were all present. Yet, he said, "I would have supposed there were no such names in existence. They appeared to have been all one in Christ Jesus, and their prayer was, 'Lord revive your work.' "[59] Lutheran Pietists believed that Christians were obligated to renounce all internal feuding as a sinful waste of energy. All energies needed to be directed against the wiles of the devil.

No one expressed this ecumenical concern more clearly and convincingly, nor with such enduring dedication, than did Samuel Schmucker. He believed that the success of the missionary task required primarily the willingness of churches to work together, offering their "united sacrifice on one common altar."[60] He was convinced that Christians who "believed in the same gospel and are traveling to the same heaven . . . acknowledge each other as brethren and . . . forget minor differences . . . are needed for the dawn of the millennium."[61] This goal could never be accomplished if the church "splits up and fritters away . . . her aggressive powers . . . wasting by want of concert, . . . and internal contention, these resources which ought to have been expended in converting the heathen."[62]

Schmucker viewed cooperative efforts so vital to the mission of the church that he described "dis-union" as the antichrist.[63] However, it was never his desire to eliminate denominations with their distinctive doctrines.[64] He did not envision an organic union or merger but desired a co-

---

[59]*Lutheran Herald* 1 (1 June 1839): 85.

[60]S. S. Schmucker, *Elements of a Popular Theology*, 35, 354.

[61]S. S. Schmucker, "A Plea for the Sabbath School System," delivered 2 February 1830 at the anniversary of the Gettysburg Sunday School, in *Sunday School Addresses and Reports, 1829–1834* (Gettysburg: Theological Seminary Press, 1830) 31.

[62]S. S. Schmucker, *Church of the Redeemer*, 246.

[63]Ibid., 247.

[64]Ibid., 249.

operative federation of sovereign units. In his book *Fraternal Appeal*, first published in 1838, Schmucker set down as the first feature of his plan for the restoration of Catholic union on apostolic principles that "the several Christian denominations should each retain their own present . . . organization, government, discipline, and mode of worship."[65] He based this proposed federation of churches on the concepts of union that he claimed had existed in the apostolic age. He called for a convention of the united churches in a council or synod, mutual acknowledgment of each other's acts of discipline, and sacramental and ministerial intercommunion.[66] This latter point meant that, both in regard to lay members and ministers, a certificate of good standing in one denomination would be accepted by all other member churches.[67]

The union that Schmucker contemplated placed priority on mutual love and cooperation rather than on a unified doctrine. Still, in order to "keep heretics out of the church," the adoption of an apostolic, Protestant confession was proposed.[68] This confession of faith contained the Apostle's Creed and twelve other fundamental doctrinal articles, drawn verbatim from the officially adopted creedal statements of various Protestant denominations.[69] This rather curious approach to doctrinal consensus testifies to Schmucker's concern for a confessional unity that would encompass the fundamental doctrines of Christianity. The last feature of Schmucker's plan, however, made it clear that the real purpose of his proposed union was not doctrinal agreement but the fuller proclamation of the gospel throughout the world. "Missionaries going into foreign lands ought to . . . profess no other creed than the Bible and the Apostolic Protestant Confession, and connect it with whatever form of Church government and worship they prefer. For the sake of [the] bleeding savior . . . sectarian divisions ought not to be transplanted into foreign lands."[70]

After his plan was approved by the General Synod in 1839, Schmucker organized an interdenominational group called the American Society for the Promotion of Christian Unity.[71] His *Fraternal Appeal* received wide-

---

[65]S. S. Schmucker, *Fraternal Appeal*, 36, 140.

[66]S. S. Schmucker, *Church of the Redeemer*, 244-45.

[67]S. S. Schmucker, *Fraternal Appeal*, 166.

[68]Ibid., 156.

[69]Ibid., 176-83.

[70]Ibid., 172.

[71]Wentz, *Pioneer in Christian Unity*, 280.

spread endorsement by Lutheran and other Protestant leaders both in this country and abroad. At the organizational meeting of the World Evangelical Alliance, which he attended at London in August 1846, Schmucker was officially recognized as a leading advocate of Christian unity.[72] The alliance developed branch organizations throughout the world, utilizing a modified form of Schmucker's plan. Due primarily to divisions arising over whether or not slaveholders could be members of the organization, its influence fell far short of what Schmucker had hoped it might be.[73] The times were not propitious for the promotion of Christian union and would not be for years to come. But Schmucker promoted this cause for the remainder of his life. His immense contributions to ecumenical thought and practice have been recognized by a number of contemporary historians.[74] He has been hailed as a pioneer architect of the modern concept of church federations, and of the World Council of Churches in particular.[75]

Lutherans who, like Schmucker, labored for denominational rapprochement during this period faced a determined and growing opposition. The Pietist passion for Christian unity flew directly in the face of the antebellum tendency to renew and emphasize denominational loyalty. This direction was evident not only among the Old Lutherans, but in other mainline conservative Protestant groups as well. The emphasis was placed on what constituted the denomination's own particular identity, what made it different from all the others and superior to them as well. Efforts in the direction of Christian fellowship and cooperative effort were condemned as "unionistic." *Unionism* became an epithet as much despised then as its synonym *ecumenism* is admired today. The Lutheran Pietist search for harmony based on mutual assent to fundamental biblical principles was characterized as an indifference to doctrinal veracity.

Charles Hodge, for example, a noted Presbyterian theologian who had been a fellow student at Princeton Seminary with Schmucker, wrote to him after reading his *Fraternal Appeal* and admonished the Gettysburg professor for having fallen in with "the faults of the age . . . an indifference to the truth, and disregard for authority in Church and State." Hodge went on,

---

[72]Ibid., 286.

[73]S. S. Schmucker, *Church of the Redeemer*, 254.

[74]Chief among them, A. R. Wentz (*Pioneer in Christian Unity*). See also Ruth Rouse and Stephan Charles Neill, eds., *A History of the Ecumenical Movement, 1517–1948* (Philadelphia: Westminster Press, 1961).

[75]Frederick K. Wentz, introduction to S. S. Schmucker, *Fraternal Appeal*, 31-32.

"The liberals of our day, are . . . liberal because they are indifferent."[76] The charge of "indifference to the truth" carries a false ring when directed at Schmucker, and American Lutheran Pietists in general. The motivation for their ecumenical activity, like that of revivalism and missions, was firmly rooted in biblical and theological convictions. Among the most powerful of these motivating beliefs was an eschatological hope, anchored in the faith that the promised millennium was about to dawn and that Lutheran Christians were commissioned to work together with all fellow believers in preparing the way for its arrival.

MORAL REFORM

The optimistic hope that American Lutheran Pietism maintained in the coming millennium constituted an additional impulse toward active involvement with the movements for social and moral reform. Since faith had to express itself in being useful and in doing good, and since the imminent coming of Christ meant that the world must be made fit for his return, the essential spirit of Lutheran Pietism was that of the reformer. It was a spirit keenly in tune with the temper of the times and with American evangelicalism in general. The ethical activism of Lutheran Pietism was without question strongly stimulated by close contacts with the major movers of what has been called the "most powerful reform era in American history."[77] But the spiritual sources of this identification came more from within than from without.

Orthodox and conservative Lutherans did not agree that moral reform was an integral part of Christian mission. In essence they condemned it as misdirected and unscriptural. One of its leaders exclaimed, "The loud cry for reform, change and something new only proves that *Society is sick* and nearing its dissolution. . . . Alas, Alas for the projects and dreamy hopes of modern reformers."[78]

But Pietists were convinced, on the basis of their own traditional Lutheran theology, that all moral evils would indeed be largely eradicated before the coming of the promised reign of Christ on earth. Furthermore, they believed that Christians were called to express their faith by lending themselves as instruments in this divine operation. This conviction more than anything else accounted for their close association with a whole myriad of moral reforms and their affinity with other Christians who were sim-

---

[76]Charles Hodge to S. S. Schmucker, 22 February 1839, Schmucker Papers.

[77]McLoughlin, *Revivals, Awakenings, and Reform*, 130.

[78]Seiss, *Last Times*, 298.

ilarly inclined. Among the most important of these reform movements were Sabbath observance, temperance, and peace.

SABBATH OBSERVANCE

The "sanctification of the Christian Sabbath" as a day of worship and rest had always occupied an important place among the priorities of Lutheran Pietism. It was considered as indispensable to both the life of the individual Christian and the church as a whole. It is not surprising, then, that as the movement to improve Sabbath observance gained momentum throughout the United States, Lutheran Pietists became actively engaged in its behalf. Samuel Schmucker believed that the clear command of the Almighty to "keep the Sabbath Day holy" had been slighted and even misconstrued in the Augsburg Confession. He traced this error to its placement in the category of "adiaphoria," which implied that it was only a human institution, leaving believers free either to observe it or not. The Franckean Synod agreed with Schmucker and commented that this was probably the reason "so many Augsburg Confession men disregard the Sabbath and desecrate the holy day."[79]

During the 1830s and 1840s, numerous moral reforms became agents of social and civic change, stimulating the rise of third-party movements in the political sphere. Sabbath observance too took on strong political ramifications, and those vying for public office found it incumbent to take a stand on the issue. When efforts were made through legislative channels to close post offices, stop the delivery of mail, and halt all public transportation on Sunday, many Lutheran Pietists, including Samuel Schmucker, gave these political aspects of the Sabbath controversy their full support.[80] The Franckean Synod openly attacked politicians whom they suspected of "Sabbath breaking." They complained that "the seeds of this abomination," which was growing throughout the land, were being sown within the legislative halls of the United States Congress.[81]

Closely connected with the emphasis on Sabbath observance was the movement to organize Sabbath schools. No institution of the General Synod so fully embodied in a practical way the vision of its Pietist founders. The Sunday School Union was organized in 1829, and subsequently its meetings were held in conjunction with the General Synod conventions. Sabbath (or Sunday) schools were established either independently

---

[79]*Lutheran Herald* 1 (16 November 1839): 175.

[80]S. S. Schmucker, *Elements of a Popular Theology*, 127.

[81]*Lutheran Herald* 1 (16 June 1839): 91.

or by congregations throughout the General Synod. Designed primarily for the religious and moral instruction of young people, they were often operated jointly by Lutherans and Reformed. They became a training ground for lay leadership. Classes were invariably taught by the laity rather than clergy.[82] In the Southern synods active laymen established flourishing Sunday schools, often in conjunction with Methodists and Baptists, which later became the nucleus of established congregations.[83]

Samuel Schmucker was recognized nationally as a leading advocate of the Sunday school. He believed that the universal observance of the Christian Sabbath, coupled with a strong Sunday school system, could instill respect for morality among the masses, diminish juvenile delinquency and crime, and contribute to the establishment of justice and peace throughout the world.[84] In this light he expressed the hope that Sabbath schools would help "train up a generation of Christians for millennial plans and millennial actions."[85]

TEMPERANCE

Temperance was a major and enduring reform to which Protestant evangelicals of almost every persuasion turned their attention during the first decades of the nineteenth century. Here again the earliest practices of Lutheran Pietism pointed its adherents to active participation in the movement. Samuel Schmucker became a member of the American Temperance Society shortly after its formation in 1826 and was one of the earliest organizers of temperance societies in this country.

Following the explicit example of the Halle fathers and the patriarch Henry Muhlenberg, nineteenth-century American Pietists understood that intemperance was a social as well as an individual problem. They considered it a major cause of family disintegration, moral degeneration, and religious distraction. While Schmucker himself was a total abstainer from intoxicating beverages,[86] his battle against the sale of alcohol was never waged simply on the basis of personal practice. His deeper concern was

---

[82]Crista R. Klein, "General Synod Shaped by America," *Lutheran Standard*, 6 February 1987, 13.

[83]Hugh George Anderson, *Lutheranism in the Southeastern States, 1860–1888* (The Hague: Mouton Press, 1969) 129.

[84]S. S. Schmucker, "Plea for the Sabbath School System," 16, 32.

[85]Ibid., 17.

[86]Anstadt, *Life and Times of Samuel Schmucker*, 291.

for the salvation of the entire social fabric of the nation, and he realized then what a more recent historian has since confirmed, that "the basic moral problem of the average community grew directly or indirectly out of the abundant supply of intoxicating liquor."[87]

Like his father, Samuel Schmucker also experienced intense opposition from fellow Lutherans in regard to his stand on temperance. Germans liked their beer and often brewed it in their homes. They sometimes appealed to Luther as an authority not only for the unaltered Augsburg Confession but for the uninhibited consumption of alcohol. Schmucker at times found himself standing alone in defending his temperance convictions.[88] However, he reacted in typical fashion by simply redoubling his efforts.

By the 1840s, many reformers had begun to turn from moral suasion to electoral means and legislative acts in their efforts to transform society. The temperance movement provides perhaps the best example of this shift in emphasis from the personal to the political.[89] Previously temperance had been primarily a matter for the individual conscience. Now its advocates also turned their attention to cutting off the supply of the "poisonous waters" at their source. The attack on alcohol was extended to include its manufacturers and distributors. Involvement in this type of direct political action presented few theological problems for the Lutheran Pietist constituency. Many regional synodical bodies throughout the entire General Synod set up their own temperance societies, which in turn organized groups in local congregations and communities. Nearly all English-language Lutheran newspapers supported these societies.[90] During the 1830s, both the Maryland and Hartwick synods passed resolutions calling for legislative action curtailing the production and sale of liquor,[91] and other groups followed their example. No moral question elicited the volume of synodical actions on the part of Lutheran synods in the South than did temperance. The campaign continued through the post-Civil war period,

---

[87]W. W. Sweet, "The Churches as Moral Courts of the Frontier," *Church History* 2 (1933): 21.

[88]S. S. Schmucker to his wife, 20 July 1838, Schmucker Papers.

[89]Lori D. Ginzberg, " 'Moral Suasion Is Moral Balderdash': Women, Politics, and Social Activism in the 1850s," *Journal of American History* 73 (December 1986): 603.

[90]Nelson, *Lutherans In North America,* 141.

[91]"Minutes, Maryland Synod, 1830," in the *Lutheran Intelligencer,* December 1830, 294, MCAL, reel 6; and *Lutheran Observer* 1 (12 September 1834): 11.

when all but two of the Southern groups made statements against the sale and use of alcoholic beverages.[92]

The Constitution of the Franckean Synod required that all ministers and elected lay delegates pledge themselves to total abstinence from all intoxicating liquors. In addition, anyone engaged in the "manufacture or traffic of intoxicating liquors as a beverage" was ineligible for election as a synod delegate and was designated as unworthy of being recognized "as a Christian by any evangelic Church."[93] Abstinence was strongly and "affectionately" recommended to all members of the synod.[94] In their first session in 1838, the Franckeans identified temperance with "the cause of Christ" and indicted the use of liquor as "an alarming evil, wasting the intellect, deadening the moral sensibilities, and destroying the present and eternal interests of man."[95] Political action was also taken. In the 1838 session a call was made for the repeal of the "license law" then operating in New York, and petitions were presented for a temperance bill to be introduced in the state legislature. Anticipating the objection of their more conservative colleagues that political matters did not warrant ecclesiastical action, the Franckeans asked, "When was there a time when Christians refused to do what was right, and to come up to the high and holy standard of the Gospel?"[96]

Although moral persuasion was never neglected, the Franckeans eventually turned more and more to legislative channels in pursuance of their temperance goals. In 1849, one of their leaders issued a blanket condemnation of all who claimed the sanction of civil laws for their "traffic in the waters of death." These laws were branded as immoral. They were "not a law but a lie."[97] By the middle of the century these activist New York Lutherans were ready to "buckle on the armor and plunge into the hottest battle" in the effort to establish prohibition by law. "Such a law," it was argued,

---

[92]Anderson, *Lutheranism in the Southeastern States,* 147.

[93]*Constitution and Standing Ordinances of the Franckean Evangelic Lutheran Synod* (1839), Standing Resolutions, 52-53; Art. 7, p. 9; Art. 8, p. 11; Lutheran Theological Seminary Archives. The clause "as a beverage" was intended to allow for the use of liquor for medicinal purposes, communion, etc.

[94]*JFS,* 1838, 18.

[95]Ibid.

[96]Ibid., 30.

[97]Sefferenas Ottman, "An Acceptable Fast unto the Lord," delivered on the occasion of a National Fast (3 August 1849), *Pohlman Collection,* vol. 206, New York State Library, Manuscripts and Special Collections, Albany.

was "right, constitutional and feasible."[98] At his seminary post in Pennsylvania, Samuel Schmucker agreed. He too was an advocate of prohibition, campaigning for the enactment of legislation that would outlaw the sale of alcoholic beverages. He warned that, "as long as liquor is publicly sold there will always be . . . [those] unprincipled enough to buy it."[99]

PEACE

American Lutheran Pietists frequently exercised a prophetic role toward government by issuing warnings about the evils of war and by taking an active role in the peace movements of its era. In a day when the philosophy of manifest destiny fanned the flames of the war spirit within a young and expanding nation, Samuel Schmucker and the Franckean Synod along with other Lutheran Pietists expressed fervent antiwar convictions that approached pacifist dimensions.

In 1839, when a dispute with England over the northern border of the United States threatened to erupt in armed conflict, Schmucker preached a sermon in which he pleaded with his hearers to "avoid all language and conduct that might produce this evil" and to do all in their power "to induce our rulers to avoid war."[100] Some seven years later Schmucker became the only Lutheran leader of note to oppose publicly the controversial war with Mexico.[101] In language that must have deeply offended many of his fellow citizens and fellow Lutherans, he accused the United States government of having invaded Mexico and condemned aggressive wars as "possessing all the essential features of robbery and murder by the individual, whilst their enormity is aggravated by the stupendous scale of their execution."[102] He predicted that, if the United States continued to foster the spirit of conquest, it would spell the end of its true national glory, and he called for "other remedies far better than war"—negotiation, arbitra-

---

[98]*JFS*, 1852, 21.

[99]Anstadt, *Life and Times of Samuel Schmucker*, 291.

[100]S. S. Schmucker, Sermon manuscript no. 84, Samuel Simon Schmucker, Collected Sermons and Addresses, Gettysburg College Archives, Musselmann Library, Gettysburg PA.

[101]Bodo, *Protestant Clergy and Public Issues*, 220.

[102]S. S. Schmucker, *The Christian Pulpit, the Rightful Guardian of Morals, in Political No Less Than in Private Life: A Discourse Delivered at Gettysburg, November 26, the Day Appointed by the Governor for Public Humiliation, Thanksgiving, and Prayer* (Gettysburg: H. C. Neinstedt, 1846) 31, 20.

tion, and mediation.[103] Of all the moral reforms that Schmucker supported, the crusade for peace appeared to arouse the deepest passion. He did not often write with obvious emotion, but when it came to this subject he seemed hardly able to find words strong enough to convey his revulsion. "What a horrible thing war is," he wrote to his wife, "what entire and perfect reversion of the Saviour's law of love to all mankind."[104] In another place he described war as "that prolific mother of all evils which stops the progress of piety" and added that it could be banished only by the coming of the millennium and the progress of the Prince of Peace.[105]

Opposition to war was such a vital concern to members of the Franckean Synod that it was included as a standing resolution in their constitution. The article condemned armed conflict as "morally wrong; contrary to the spirit of the Gospel; . . . a hindrance to the progress of the Redeemer's Kingdom, and an. . . offence against God. . . . Christians are bound by the strongest and most sacred obligations to do all within their power to secure the immediate universal and permanent abolition of war."[106] A typical resolution referred to peace as the "prelude of millennial day" and as "indespensible to the universal rule of God's Kingdom."[107] Other statements expressed the belief that the great mission of the Prince of Peace could never be realized until the instruments of "butchery and death were utterly abolished."[108] One resolution noted that waging war was "calculated to destroy all confidence in the integrity of Christian nations", and thus raised "fearful barriers against the success of missionary operations."[109] As the military spirit grew more intense in the United States just previous to the Mexican War, the Franckeans' resistance to the war fever became more determined. They passed a resolution noting that, since the synod stood opposed to war as sinful, it was "inconsistent for any member . . . to act as chaplain in any military parade."[110] In the session of 1846, they denounced the war with Mexico as wicked and wrong.

---

[103]Ibid., 32, 22.

[104]S. S. Schmucker to his wife, 10 May 1847, Schmucker Papers.

[105]S. S. Schmucker, *Elements of a Popular Theology*, 347.

[106]*Constitution of the Franckean Synod*, Standing Resolutions, 55-56.

[107]*JFS*, 1857, 10.

[108]Ibid., 1850, 14; 1852, 21.

[109]Ibid., 1858, 19.

[110]Ibid., 1845, 22, 23.

The sermon that opened the convention of the Franckean Synod in 1847 again took up the subject of opposition to the war with Mexico. By this time the protest was filled with increased animation and fervor.

> The cry of the blood of slaughtered thousands upon the plains of Mexico . . . [ascends] to the God of justice, calling for vengeance. . . . The hands of this entire nation are red with the blood of murdered men. God will hold this nation guilty . . . professed Christians heap honors upon the heads of those who have been most expert in desolating cities, . . . while others are crying, Let us place the military hero into our chair of state, and make him our highest civil ruler.[111]

Some of the Franckean efforts to promote peace were not only piously sincere but characterized by careful thought and reflection. Even today, they carry a surprisingly relevant and prophetic note. For instance, they warned that "fond parents and Christian friends unconsciously contribute to the development of the war spirit in small children [by] presenting them 'war-like toys' . . . drums, guns, swords, soldiers, etc." They feared that school parades and anniversary celebrations, where military arms were always on display, inculcated in students the martial spirit. They lamented the fact that young people learned that military titles were often a prelude to official power, that "young aspirants for future fame" were encouraged to join the army or navy, rather than engage in more useful pursuits or enlist as soldiers under the banner of Christ. Furthermore, the Franckeans contended that the masses of people had been generally deceived by ambitious and scheming leaders who had "manufactured a pretence for war where no cause existed" and devised aggressive wars "under the cloak of self-defense." They were convinced that, if the true results of war could be clearly seen by the people as a whole, "they would raise their hands and voice against it."[112]

In like manner, the devastating costs of war and its adverse affect upon those most in need was adduced as an argument against waging it. The enormous expenditures of military operations were described as a "millstone around the necks of the people." The Franckeans even contemplated some form of tax resistance, inquiring, "Should not the people of our land,

---

[111]Sefferenas Ottman, "The Christian Ministry: The Divinely Appointed Agency to Reform the World," delivered at the Franckean Synod, 10th Session, at Richmondville, Schoharie Co., 3 June 1847, *Pohlman Collection* 206:12, New York State Library.

[112]*JFS*, 1857; 11; 1858, 18.

especially the tax-payers, stamp war with the seal of condemnation?"[113] Finally, they calculated that the money expended by the United States in the war against Mexico could have built and endowed "a college in every state of the Union . . . a schoolhouse in every district of the land, and educated all the children in the United States."[114] Samuel Schmucker likewise discovered the evils of war in wasteful expenditures that robbed the poor of their rightful due and perverted justice. He protested that "immense standing armies . . . produce nothing toward the support of life and thus must be supported by the labors of others as fully as paupers in the poor-houses. . . . This falls hard on the people."[115]

In spite of this vigorous opposition to armed conflict, neither Schmucker nor the Franckean Synod ever advocated any kind of absolute pacifism or ethic of nonresistance. Once the Civil War began, they, along with most other Lutherans in the North, gave wholehearted support to the Union cause. They considered it an act of self-defense in the struggle against the insidious evil of human slavery. But even then, they never spoke of war as something right or honorable. Only the cause was just. The war itself was described in Lincolnian terms as the judgment of God upon the entire nation. After it ended they made it clear that they were just as much opposed to it as ever. Just one year after Appomattox, the Franckean Synod called on the churches "to root out all bitterness and feelings of animosity and discord" and to give themselves once again to the work of peace.[116]

Throughout the antebellum period, American Lutheran Pietists under the leadership of Samuel Schmucker remained for the most part united in their dedication to the fundamental traditions of classical German Pietism. Their emphasis on a living faith and a hopeful view of the future, with its corresponding stress on missions, revivalism, conversion, and ecumenical endeavor, were vital aspects of this tradition that they sought to retain and refine to meet the needs of their own day. A resulting activist ethical theology expressed itself in a concerted commitment to the major current reform movements, particularly Sabbath observance, temperance, and peace. However, the seeds of disunion arising around the volatile issue of human slavery began to challenge the consensus that had united Lutheran Pietism since its arrival in North America.

---

[113]Ibid., 1858, 19. An article in the *Lutheran Herald* 4 (1 February 1842): 20, taken from the *New York Evangelist*, also analyzed the terrible cost of war, calling the army "an all devouring monster" and noting that all military expenditures are "attended with extravagant waste" because "everything is purchased at whatever price the seller seeks."

[114]*JFS*, 1858, 19.

[115]S. S. Schmucker to his wife, 6 June 1846, Schmucker Papers.

[116]*JFS*, 1866, 24-25.

C·H·A·P·T·E·R 4

Abolitionism

By the early 1830s, the movement to abolish human slavery was far and away the overriding moral reform of the day. It was "the question of questions," involving economic, political, moral, and religious issues that were explosively controversial and divisive. The discord that followed in its wake did not confine itself to geographical lines. During the decades preceding the outbreak of the Civil War, the divisions it created were experienced most strongly in the North. The variety of alternatives proposed to deal with this "peculiar problem," combined with the emotions and fears surrounding it, produced sharp conflicts among the members of political parties, community groups, families, and churches. The Lutheran church, like all other religious groups, did not pass through this period unscathed by the ensuing strife.

Abolitionism had not sprung suddenly into being. Long before the turn of the century, reformers in Britain and the United States had raised their voices against the evils of human servitude, directing their opposition for the most part to the slave trade and its perpetrators. During the first two decades of the nineteenth century, the antislavery impulse in the United States was actually strongest in the Southern states. But its aspirations there were moderated by lurking fears of revolt and anarchy. The racism that permeated the minds of white citizens throughout the United States, and whose seeds lay embedded in the Constitution, was a chief cause for the exaggerated character of these fears. As a result, many who favored abolition counseled that emancipation could be realized only in a very gradual manner, that any steps toward eventual freedom would have to be proceeded by pervasive programs of education that stressed, in particular, moral and religious training.[1] An even larger group believed that the only feasible solution was to remove the free slaves, whom they considered the most potent source of danger, to a distant land. In most cases the place designated for deportation was Africa, the homeland from which nearly all slaves in the United States had been so cruelly uprooted.

The concept of Negro colonization was first publicly proposed by Thomas Jefferson in 1784. In 1816, a group primarily composed of prominent Southern citizens organized a society dedicated to "colonizing . . . free people of color . . . in Africa" or other places.[2] It was opposed for the most part by its intended subjects, who looked upon the United States as their native land.[3] For white citizens, the appeal of colonization ranged all the way from rank racism to benevolent concern. Those in the latter category honestly believed that it could help eliminate racial fears, elevate the status of Negroes both in this country and in Africa, and lead gradually to the complete abolition of slavery.[4] Colonization was definitely a reform movement and, to the extent that it proposed a drastic solution to the slavery problem, a radical one. But in another sense, it was deeply conservative in nature, making no effort to alter or alleviate the racist attitudes upon which slavery subsisted, but choosing the simpler solution of eliminating its problems by exporting its victims.

In the early years the colonization movement met with considerable success. Mainline Protestant churches supported its efforts. The federal government contributed funds. Free blacks were recruited for emigration. By 1822, Liberia, the first black republic in Africa, was founded.[5] From the beginning, however, the colonizationists faced a problem that eventually

---

[1]David Brion Davis, "The Emergence of Immediatism in British and American Antislavery Thought," *Mississippi Valley Historical Review* 49 (September 1962): 217-18.

[2]Robert Baird, *Religion in the United States of America* (1844; reprint, New York: Arno Press and New York Times, 1969) 716.

[3]Louis Filler, *The Crusade against Slavery, 1830–1860,* New American Nation Series (New York: Harper & Brothers Pub., 1960) 21. One free Negro commented, "Colonizationists want us to go on to Liberia if we will; if we won't go there we may go to hell" (p. 21, quoting Carter Woodson, ed., *Mind of the Negro,* 142).

[4]The story of the colonization society, with its dreams of an African empire, an all-white America, and a peaceful obliteration of slavery, is a fascinating saga of antebellum history. It is most fully documented in P. J. Staudenraus, *The African Colonization Movement, 1816–1865* (New York: Columbia University Press, 1961).

[5]Filler, *Crusade against Slavery,* 20.

proved insurmountable. The transportation of large numbers of people from one country to another required ongoing federal support. But the decentralizing tendencies of the day rendered this necessary assistance a political impossibility. As a result the proposed solutions never materialized to anywhere near the extent envisioned by its founders. Although the colonization society continued to exist in a technical sense for many years, in reality it expired with the Civil War.

In contrast to colonization efforts, abolition societies were dedicated to breaking down the wall of racial prejudice. Early in the nineteenth century they founded schools for free Negroes. Their aim was to improve gradually the lot of blacks in this country until they reached a level where equal opportunity and integration became realistic possibilities.[6] By 1830, the antislavery movement had arrived at a crucial turning point. Under the leadership of William Lloyd Garrison, there developed a vigorous movement to renounce all gradualism and rally under the slogan *immediate emancipation*.[7] It was, perhaps intentionally, an ambiguous slogan. To its opponents it stood for an irrational and even fanatical insistence that the abolition of slavery be effected without preparation or delay. To its advocates it more often meant a sincere personal acknowledgment of the sinfulness of slavery and a commitment to work for its abolishment without compromise or undue delay, yet without abandoning necessary preparations. Its uncompromising tone guaranteed that it would lead to controversy and confrontation with all those who continued to advocate gradual methods of emancipation—in particular, colonizationists. Garrison and his followers declared war on colonization, castigating it as "odious and contemptible" and describing all who supported it as "apologists for the crime of slavery, . . . and tools of slaveholders."[8] The crux of the crusade for immediate abolitionism lay in its definition of slavery. Armed with the religious concepts of evangelical revivalism, it categorized slavery as always a

---

[6]Merton L. Dillon, *The Abolitionists: The Growth of a Dissenting Minority* (De Kalb IL: Northern Illinois University Press, 1974) 21.

[7]For further details on the movement of immediate abolitionism in addition to the citations in this paragraph, see especially Filler, *Crusade against Slavery;* Bertram Wyatt-Brown, *Lewis Tappan and the Evangelical War against Slavery* (Cleveland: Press of Case Western Reserve University, 1969); and Lewis Perry and Michael Fellman, eds., *Antislavery Reconsidered: New Perspectives on the Abolitionists* (Baton Rouge: Louisiana University Press, 1979).

[8]Staudenraus, *African Colonization*, 194-95.

sin that had to be abandoned at once, even if it meant that the federal union would be split asunder.[9]

Colonizationists could not accept these categorical assertions. They admitted that slavery was an evil and its abuses sinful, but they were dedicated to gradualism and unalterably opposed to any disruption of the union over the issue of slavery. As the gulf between the two groups widened, Garrison wrote that he looked "upon the overthrow of the Colonization Society as the overthrow of slavery itself . . . they both stand or fall together."[10] Antislavery societies had already begun to diminish in the South by the early 1820s with the discovery that Denmark Vessey had plotted a slave insurrection. Garrison's actions speeded up this process. Angered by his all-out offensive and connecting its preachments to the bloody uprising of Nat Turner in August 1832, the South's attitude toward slavery shifted in a more drastic fashion. Feeling cornered and frightened, Southerners for the first time went on the attack, lashing out at their tormenters, upholding slavery as a God-given right and defending it on the grounds of biblical teaching.

In the North, too, the immediate abolitionists aroused the ire of the gradualists, and the result was an outbreak of violence in the form of antiabolition mobs. These riots occurred mainly between 1833 and 1838 and reached their peak in 1835. In many cases the participants were prominent members of the colonization societies.[11] This involvement in acts of violence contributed to the swift decline of their movement. By 1837, the forces favoring immediate abolition had gained an advantage that they never lost. Both groups still persisted, however, in the pursuit of their now almost totally separate strategies. Throughout the Northern states tremendous pressures were exerted to choose between gradualism and immediacy. Even the ranks of those who favored immediate abolition were riddled with serious internal divisions. When William Garrison witnessed the hesitancy of the Christian churches and their clergy to take a strong abolitionist stand, he directed his fury against them as well.[12] Meanwhile, men like Theodore Weld followed in the tradition of Charles Finney, preaching abolitionism as a great moral revival and continuing to identify its cause with that of religion. Weld and his colleagues argued that, because slavery was a sin,

---

[9]Bodo, *Protestant Clergy and Public Issues,* 37.

[10]Staudenraus, *African Colonization,* 194-95.

[11]Leonard L. Richards, *Gentlemen of Property and Standing: Anti-Abolition Mobs in Jacksonian America* (New York: Oxford University Press, 1970) 15.

[12]Smith, *Revivalism and Social Reform,* 183.

it must be immediately abandoned.[13] Finney, in turn, disagreed with Weld's growing determination to pursue the cause of abolition through legislative and political channels. After Garrison had turned antichurch and also antipolitical, another prominent abolitionist, Arthur Tappan, along with Weld, broke all ties with Garrison's leadership. In 1840, they formed the strongly evangelical American and Foreign Anti-Slavery Society. It continued to preach immediatist goals while seeking ecclesiastical and legislative support.

Not surprisingly, this growing divisiveness over an issue fraught with fundamental moral and religious questions soon began to surface within the various church bodies of the land. It is possible, as one historian has recently argued, that the consequent denominational schisms gave a powerful impetus to the secessionist movement and the eventual outbreak of the Civil War.[14] In 1837–1838, the Presbyterian church separated into New and Old School factions, which divided the church generally (but not entirely) into Northern and Southern groups. This split marked the first division of a major national church body involving slavery as a major issue. The quarrel leading to this separation was waged ostensibly over differing doctrinal opinions, and the embarrassing matter of slavery was carefully kept out of open debate on the floor of the assembly and from the minutes that recorded these proceedings. However, some historians now contend that slavery was an extremely important contributing cause and may well have been the determining reason for the schism.[15] The dispute that led to a North-South rupture of the Methodist Episcopal church in 1844 took the form of an argument over polity and procedure, even though the fundamental issue was obviously slavery. The schism of the National Baptist Societies just a year later was more openly and explicitly caused by internal divisions over slavery. The same was true for a further split that took place within the New School faction of the Presbyterian church in 1857. Thus nearly fifteen years before the political and military confrontation over slavery occurred, the three largest church groups in the nation had already divided over the issue.[16] The Protestant Episcopal, Roman Catholic, and

---

[13]Gilbert Hobbs Barnes, *The Anti-Slavery Impulse, 1830–1844* (Gloucester MA: Peter Smith, 1957) 103-104.

[14]See C. C. Goen, *Broken Churches, Broken Nation* (Macon GA: Mercer University Press, 1985).

[15]C. Bruce Staiger, "Abolitionism and the Presbyterian Schism of 1837–1838," *Mississippi Valley Historical Review* 36 (December 1949): 391-414.

[16]Goen, *Broken Churches, Broken Nation*, 66-67.

Lutheran churches were the only major denominational groups that managed to maintain a semblance of unity in the face of the divisions exerted by the slavery issue, up until the outbreak of war.

The single cross-sectional or national body of Lutherans in existence throughout the antebellum period was the General Synod. While it remained officially united until 1862, its internal affairs after 1830 were by no means isolated from the reverberations and agitations emanating from the controversial crusade to abolish slavery.

SCHMUCKER'S ABOLITIONISM:
BIBLICAL VIEWS

The titular head of the General Synod, Samuel Schmucker, was from beginning to end a persistent and outspoken opponent of slavery. No other individual Lutheran leader was more consistent or influential in the promotion of the abolition of slavery, both in public and private, in church and community, by legislative effort and moral persuasion, than the acknowledged leader of the American Pietist constituency. Schmucker's biblical and theological convictions on the subject of human slavery and its abolition are contained primarily in his textbook *Elements of a Popular Theology*, first published in 1834.[17] They are also recorded in various sermons, addresses, lectures, and letters. These viewpoints, expressed during the early years of his career, did not change appreciably throughout his entire life.

From a theological and biblical point of view, Schmucker believed that slavery, as an institution, contained elements so immoral that it was opposed to the very character and nature of God and could not therefore possibly find any sanction in the Scriptures.[18] He was convinced that, in violating the fundamental precepts of the Christian religion, slavery also denied the most basic of human rights as well. These antislavery sentiments were grounded in a profound respect for humanity and belief in the divinely ordained unity of the human race.

Schmucker refused to admit that slavery in the American sense of the term had any existence in the Old Testament era. He argued that the Hebrew word sometimes translated "slave" actually meant "servant" and that

---

[17]S. S. Schmucker, *Elements of a Popular Theology*, 332-36. This section on American slavery is contained in all nine editions from 1834 to 1860, with only minor changes in content through the years.

[18]S. S. Schmucker, "Of Slavery: Propositions on the Subject of Slavery," March 1840, 2, Schmucker Papers, 3750.00003.

the type of servitude referred to was different from American slavery.[19] He claimed, among other things, that the servitude practiced in the Old Testament was in all cases temporary and, to a great extent, voluntary, that the marriage relationship was acknowledged and respected, and that the religious privileges of servants were equal to those of their masters.[20]

With the exception of the Book of Philemon, Schmucker believed that the New Testament canon neither directly attacked slavery as an institution nor dealt with it as an abstract question. But he maintained that it categorically condemned the ingredients of which slavery was composed. It urged masters to treat their slaves with justice and equality (Col. 4:1), as no longer slaves but beloved brothers (Philem. 16), and to remember that they also had a Master in heaven.[21] Schmucker was certain that, if these and other core scriptural principles were put into practice, it would result in the abolition of human slavery.[22] He also provided a rationale for the absence of the open denunciation of slavery that one might expect in the New Testament. Such a stance, he claimed, would have been premature. Since the Roman government was powerful, despotic, and in favor of slavery's continuance, it would have retaliated with a persecution that would have drastically curtailed the progress of Christianity.[23] Given the historical circumstances, he believed the inspired writers pursued the path of prudence by laying down the principles that would eventually destroy slavery, while refraining from a direct attack upon its right to exist.[24]

In defense of this careful and cautious interpretation, Schmucker stated that the rule of wisdom is always to do the most good possible at the time. He used as an example the strategy of foreign missions, where the aim was never to condemn or attack immediately the civil institutions of the foreigners, no matter how oppressive they might be. Rather, the wise missionary allowed the maxims of the newly preached faith to have their natural

---

[19]Ibid., 2-3.

[20]Ibid., 3-4.

[21]Ibid., 4.

[22]S. S. Schmucker, Sermon manuscript no. 38, on 1 Timothy 6, delivered Seminary Chapel, 15 June 1833, Gettysburg College Archives.

[23]Ibid.

[24]S. S. Schmucker, "Of Slavery: Propositions on the Subject of Slavery," lecture delivered in August 1845 with some minor changes, plus a preamble and conclusion not included in the 1840 copy; ed. Douglas Stange, *Concordia Historical Institute* 40 (July 1967): 82.

wholesome effect, acting as "a fulcrum to sustain the lever of truth." But
Schmucker was quick to point out that, in his own day and in his own
country, this cautious prudence of the New Testament writers and of foreign missionaries with regard to slavery's evils, did not apply. "In the United
States . . . we enjoy the guaranteed liberty of debate . . . and ought to cry
aloud . . . there is a national conscience to call upon . . . an election poll
to act through."[25]

In his denunciation of human slavery, Schmucker turned again and again
to a single passage of Scripture that affirmed the unity of the human race:
that God "hath made of one blood all nations of men for to dwell on all the
face of the earth" (Acts 17:26). From the beginning, Schmucker's statements in regard to human slavery seemed invariably to find their source in
this verse. In a Gettysburg parish on 23 November 1833, he delivered a
powerful sermon on this text using as his theme "The Duties Resulting from
the Unity of the Human Family."[26] First, he challenged his listeners with
a question. "Are you willing to do justice to the oppressed of every nation,
or tongue, or complexion, and to aid in this vindication?" Then he stated
the thesis of his sermon:

> If God made all nations of the same blood, then all belong to the same family
> . . . and it is as sinful for one nation to enslave another or . . . portions of
> another, as for one individual of a family to enslave his brothers or sisters, and
> treat them as mere chattels, exacting labor without compensation. This is un-
> happily the degraded and cruel condition of nearly three million of our fellow
> creatures in this boasted land of republican liberty.[27]

In Schmucker's eyes, slavery was first and foremost a violation of the
"universal brotherhood of mankind,—of the fundamental unity of the human race, which Scripture affirmed."[28] He was so interested in this subject
that he devoted an entire chapter in his *Popular Theology* to the topic "Origin and Primitive State of Man."[29] Later he composed a carefully re-
searched and detailed lecture of some forty handwritten pages entitled, "On
the Origin of the Human Family," which he delivered to his seminary classes

---

[25]Ibid.

[26]S. S. Schmucker, Sermon manuscript no. 146, Gettysburg College Archives.

[27]Ibid.

[28]S. S. Schmucker, *Christian Pulpit, the Rightful Guardian*, 17.

[29]S. S. Schmucker, *Elements of a Popular Theology*, chap. 9, pp. 136-41.

throughout the 1850s and 1860s as a supplement to this chapter of his text.[30] His conclusion was that scientific evidence reinforced the biblical affirmation that all peoples of the world came originally from a single source and that differences of skin color, hair, body features, and culture were due primarily to human adaptation to conditions of geography and climate.

A second passage of Scripture that Schmucker frequently turned to in his condemnation of slavery contained the well-known words of Jesus, "All things whatsoever ye would that men should do to you, do ye even so to them!" (Matt. 7:12). He referred to this verse as the "fundamental ethical principle of Christianity."[31] In connection with this "Golden Rule," Schmucker also often alluded to the second portion of what Jesus referred to as the great commandment: "Thou shalt love thy neighbor as thyself" (Matt. 22:39). With these scriptural injunctions as a text, Schmucker raised questions that he directed with telling effect at those who participated in the practice of slavery. "Do ye unto others as ye would that they should do unto you. Would any slaveholders change conditions with their slaves? Love thy neighbor as thyself. Would he enslave even his own friend or family?"[32]

NATURAL AND CIVIL RIGHTS

In addition to his primary contention that the institution of slavery in the United States was incompatible with basic Christian principles contained in Scripture, Schmucker also argued that it was irreconcilable with fundamental human rights that the Creator had bestowed upon the crown of creation. Utilizing the philosophy and even the terminology of the American Revolution, but always within the framework of Christian ethics, he asserted that slavery was a gross contradiction to the political ideals of the American republic. In this connection it is interesting to note that the whole discussion of slavery contained in the *Elements of a Popular Theology* takes place within the context of a chapter on the subject of the proper role of civil government.[33] Schmucker quoted Article 16 of the Augsburg Confession, which states that Christians are to "yield obedience to civil officers and laws of the land, unless they should command something sin-

---

[30]S. S. Schmucker, "On the Origin of the Human Family," lecture no. 1, Schmucker Papers, 3420.2011.

[31]S. S. Schmucker, *Christian Pulpit, The Rightful Guardian*, 20.

[32]S. S. Schmucker, Sermon manuscript no. 38, Gettysburg College Archives.

[33]S. S. Schmucker, *Elements of a Popular Theology*, chap. 19 pp. 326-27.

ful."[34] From here he proceeded to the conclusion that the Lutheran confessions uphold the "justice of revolution" against governments that fail to accomplish the rightful purposes for which they were established.[35] Schmucker denied the constitutional right of states to nullify laws of the federal government or to secede from the union, but he granted the ultimate right of revolution.[36] Here Schmucker interpreted Romans 13:3 to the effect that rulers are commanded to be "a terror not to good works, but to evil; to be ministers of God for good; not to shed innocent blood, . . . obedience to civil officers ceases to be a duty, when their demands . . . are inconsistent with what is right."[37]

While Schmucker went well beyond Luther in upholding the right to revolution, he was nevertheless careful to note that the "worst government is better than anarchy."[38] Furthermore, he constructed a somewhat curious distinction between rebellion and revolution. He maintained simply that revolution is rebellion brought to a successful conclusion. Always the pragmatist, Schmucker advised that any resistance to unjust governments should be carried on in a manner promising success. Organization "among the oppressed is necessary to a successful resistance, . . . and therefore proper." Simple resistance to oppression might be condemned and punished as rebellion, while only its victorious termination could rightfully be called revolution. The great example of rightful revolution he saw in America's revolt against British oppression. Our fathers drew the sword against tyranny and "a righteous God smiled upon their efforts. . . . No other land can be found, in which the great mass of the people enjoy so large a share of liberty and security for their equal rights."[39]

At this point in his discussion of civil government (that is, in considering the right to revolt against unjust rule, as illustrated in the American Revolution), Schmucker inserted his lengthy comments on the subject of slavery. "When these words about liberty and equal rights are recited there rises up the image of a portion of the population to whom they represent the keenest irony . . . the poor enslaved African who after the lapse of half of a century, yet groans in bondage among us, a reproach to our political

---

[34]Ibid., 326.

[35]Ibid., 330.

[36]Ibid., 342.

[37]Ibid., 331.

[38]Ibid., 329.

[39]Ibid., 332.

system, and a violation of the rights of 'equal man.' "[40] Schmucker described slavery as creating fiction out of what the "revolutionary fathers" affirmed as a self-evident truth, that "all men are created equal and are endowed by their Creator with certain inalienable rights, among which are life, liberty, and the pursuit of happiness." For this reason, Schmucker believed, the Christian pulpit was required to hold up before the present rulers and citizens of the nation the duty to recognize the "universal brotherhood and equality of man in civil rights . . . and enact such laws as bear equally on the whole population."[41] Every article of legislation that withheld equal rights from blacks or stripped them of personal liberties and deprived them of inalienable rights was, he insisted, offensive to God.[42]

Furthermore, Schmucker claimed that the Christian faith upheld the truth not only of inalienable human rights but of obligations as well. He described in detail how slavery violated persons' right to carry out what they believed to be their religious duties.[43] It did so by destroying the matrimonial and familial relationships that God instituted and that were necessary aspects of a religious life. Finally, the institution of slavery restricted the obligation of every Christian to "search the Scriptures" by making it a crime to teach slaves to read and write.[44] Schmucker was convinced that slavery stripped its victims "of all personal rights and places it in the power of [the] master in practice to deny . . . the enjoyment of inalienable rights which God bestowed, and to prevent [the] performance of those inalienable obligations which God has imposed."[45] Finally, Schmucker condemned slavery as evil because it "converts the moral agent of God into mere Chattel, the person into a mere thing, the immortal being into a mere article of property."[46] The right of property, he asserted, can apply only to things, not to persons.[47] And he protested that, before an immortal being can be converted by human law into a mere thing, "men must possess the power to supercede or annul the laws of God."[48]

---

[40]Ibid.

[41]S. S. Schmucker, *Christian Pulpit, The Rightful Guardian*, 17, 19.

[42]Ibid., 19.

[43]S. S. Schmucker, "Of Slavery," 1840 version, 1.

[44]Ibid., 2.

[45]Ibid., 1.

[46]Ibid.

[47]S. S. Schmucker, "Of Slavery," 1845 version, 82.

[48]S. S. Schmucker, *Christian Pulpit, The Rightful Guardian*, 16.

Schmucker refused to accept any blatant appeal to the Negro's supposed inferiority as an excuse for the continuation of slavery. Many defenders of slavery contended that Negroes were degraded and incapable of providing for themselves and therefore in need of the protecting hand of the slave master. Schmucker called this a futile argument, for, he said, "the very degradation and incapacity, so far as they exist, are the results of the oppression" that slavery itself imposed.[49] In the end Schmucker did not flinch from the conclusion that all voluntary slaveholding was sinful. There can be little question that he deliberately used the term *sinful* rather than *moral evil*, for in another place he says, "There are many evils which are not sins, but no sin which is not an evil."[50] Schmucker concluded that it became the duty of individuals to abstain immediately from all violation of human rights and obligations and to emancipate their slaves.

Schmucker also advocated certain practical considerations. He believed that financial compensation should be granted to the extent that the price paid for the slaves exceeded their earnings. While advocating immediate emancipation in principle, he cautioned that the full bestowal of liberty should be gradual.[51] Following their emancipation, Schmucker advised that the former slaves be required by law to work. He suggested however, that they be allowed to choose their own employer, change employers, bargain for wages, and enjoy the same protection of laws as white citizens.[52]

COLONIZATION AND IMMEDIATISM

The gap between gradualists and immediatists widened during the early 1830s, and their attitudes toward each other hardened into hostility, a course of events that Samuel Schmucker viewed with intense concern and alarm. He tried to sail between the Scylla of colonization and the Charybdis of immediatism, between the inclusive moderation of the one and the exclusive radicalism of the other. Schmucker was personally convinced that both colonization and immediate abolition had positive contributions to offer. He repudiated the pressure to choose one side over the other. He did not hesitate to denounce the weaknesses of both.

From the outset Schmucker had supported the basic aims of African colonization, and throughout his entire career this conviction was never

---

[49]Ibid., 20.

[50]S. S. Schmucker, "Of Slavery," 1845 version, 82.

[51]Ibid.

[52]Ibid., 83.

altered. For years he was a member of the society, contributing on many occasions to its appeal for funds.[53] During the time of his parish ministry in Virginia, a resolution of support for the American Colonization Society was passed at the 1824 session of the Maryland and Virginia Synod, to which he belonged. It recommended that "all persons within the jurisdiction of this Synod, aid, according to their ability, in the promotion . . . of the [Colonization] Society."[54] Both of Schmucker's biographers record that, during the debate on this resolution, he pleaded "for its adoption,"[55] and it seems probable that it actually came from his pen.

Schmucker earnestly believed that the concept of colonization contained much that was conducive to the eventual eradication of slavery. He viewed its chief value to America as a "means of calling the 'deliberate and calm' attention of Southern slaveholders to the subject of slavery . . . its abstract injustice and criminality in the sight of God."[56] His exuberant missionary outlook also enabled him to view it as "the source of much good to Africa."[57] On the other hand, Schmucker had never envisioned colonization as the primary remedy for slavery, let alone the total answer. He was aware of its shortcomings and noted them in his *Popular Theology*.

> This inadequacy of foreign colonization will appear clear. Many will be unwilling to remove across the Atlantic, to an unknown land; and coercion would be unjust. If there is any truth in the argument that the descent of the negro from Africa requires his removal hither [this] . . . reasoning would send us back to Europe . . . it would appear to be the duty of . . . Christians to advocate the cause of colonization in Africa and elsewhere, but at the same time to advocate the justice and necessity of universal abolition.[58]

Only after freedom had been granted to the slave and blacks had gained the education and self-respect necessary to govern themselves did Schmucker believe that inducements to emigrate should be increased. If blacks themselves favored it, colonization might then serve an even greater

---

[53]S. S. Schmucker, Letter to *Colonization Herald*, 6 June 1838.

[54]*Evangelical Lutheran Synod of Maryland and Virginia, Minutes of the Session*, Oct. 17–20, 1824 (York PA: Henry C. Neinstedt, 1825) 11. This smaller district synod was affiliated with the General Synod.

[55]Anstadt, *Life and Times of Samuel Schmucker*, 293.

[56]S. S. Schmucker, *Elements of a Popular Theology*, 334.

[57]S. S. Schmucker, Letter to *Colonization Herald*, 1.

[58]S. S. Schmucker, *Elements of a Popular Theology*, 335.

purpose.[59] He understood it as "merely as introductory to a general system of emancipation . . . capable of its utmost extension only after general emancipation should have elevated the character and stimulated the enterprise of the colored race."[60]

Schmucker's position was consistently clear; it was never a matter of either/or but of both/and. Therefore when colonizationists and abolitionists became bitter enemies, Schmucker found it necessary to withdraw from his long-standing association with the colonization society. His reasons for doing so are succinctly stated in a letter written on 6 June 1838 and published in the *Colonization Herald*. In it he recorded his reasons for refusing to accept an appointment as a vice-president of the Pennsylvania Colonization Society. While he still believed that colonization had value, he found it impossible to affirm the principle that "expatriation and emancipation must . . . go together." He rejected this thesis because it "binds down the process of emancipation to the tardy progress of colonization, virtually admits . . . that justice, which is always a duty, cannot now be done . . . and consigns at least the present generation of slaves to the hopeless doom of . . . their present grievous privations."[61] This state of affairs he believed to be "entirely at variance with the law of Christian love, and the principles of our holy and benevolent religion."[62]

In this same letter Schmucker went on to state why he felt no compulsion to join the Anti-Slavery Society. He did not object to any of its stated goals and principles but disagreed with the use of exaggerated rhetoric and the indiscriminate denunciation of slaveholders as "robbers and manstealers."[63] He was inherently opposed to the strategy of confrontation and denunciation employed by many of the advocates of immediate abolition, including Garrison and his colleagues. He believed it to be counterproductive. In a sermon on 1 Timothy 6, delivered in 1833, Schmucker had described how a direct command against slavery in the New Testament times would have produced no effect on non-Christians and brought severe persecution from the Roman government, thus preventing the introduction of the very faith that in the long run would destroy slavery. He then commented, "How different from those who think the most impalat-

---

[59]S. S. Schmucker, Letter to *Colonization Herald*, 1.

[60]Ibid.

[61]Ibid.

[62]Ibid.

[63]Ibid., 1-2.

able truths should be unhesitantly preached everywhere at all times . . .
how different from many publications of our day."[64]

In the first edition of his *Popular Theology*, Schmucker had stated that
"those who advocate entire immediate abolition, do not understand the
subject."[65] He had also noted that, "in justice to the master and in mercy
to the slave," the accomplishment of abolition "must be gradual."[66] The fact
that both of these statements were eliminated in later editions indicates that
Schmucker moved toward a fuller acceptance of immediate abolition. He
continued to insist, however, that this "great work has difficulties more
formidable than some Christians in non-slave holding states suppose."[67] He
held to his conviction that many slaveholders who admitted slavery was an
evil still felt themselves "innocent of its introduction" and honestly believed that "emancipation on the soil . . . [is] inconsistent with the safety
of the white population and the welfare of the slave."[68] Such persons,
Schmucker concluded, could be convinced that abolition was in the best
interests of all concerned only by admonition, not by abuse. He viewed
this task of education as difficult and sensitive, requiring much in the way
of understanding and tact. "What is needed," he pleaded, "is light, presented in the spirit of Love."[69] While admitting that the difficulties in the
way of abolition were great, Schmucker remained incurably optimistic regarding the outcome.

MODERATING INFLUENCES:
SOUTHERN TIES

Schmucker's inveterate optimism that the days of slavery were definitely limited led him to moderate his abolitionism in some respects and
to reject the more radical strategies of the immediatists. This optimism appears to have received some support from Schmucker's intense millennial
hope. He believed not only that slavery in America would soon end but
that it would be abolished peacefully, as a part of God's predestined plan.
In the letter to the *Colonization Herald* of 1838, he had described the "sub-
lime spectacle . . . [of] the great and growing tide of reformation . . .

---

[64]S. S. Schmucker, Sermon manuscript no. 38, Gettysburg College Archives.

[65]S. S. Schmucker, *Elements of a Popular Theology*, 1st ed., 277.

[66]Ibid.

[67]S. S. Schmucker, *Elements of a Popular Theology*, 9th ed., 333.

[68]S. S. Schmucker, Letter to *Colonization Herald*, 2.

[69]Ibid.

gradually meliorating the condition of the laboring classes and the oppressed portions of our race."[70] Among these meliorating influences, he
pointed to colonization. In this case, Schmucker's millennialism operated
as a two-edged sword. It led him to view the elimination of slavery as a
precondition to the arrival of God's kingdom on earth and thus helped to
motivate his abolitionism. But at the same time, his sense of the closeness
and certainty of the millennium allowed him to remain somewhat sanguine
as to the struggle still required to eradicate slavery.

A far more significant element, which also contributed to Schmucker's
optimism and exerted a moderating influence on his abolitionism, was his
close personal ties to the South. After his ordination Schmucker had served
several parishes in Virginia. They were located in the general area where
his father had grown to manhood and where his Uncle Nicholas was still
a clergyman. Some of the members of his congregations owned slaves.[71]
Two and a half years after the tragic death of his first wife in 1823,
Schmucker married a Virginian, Mary Catherine Steenbergen, the cul-
tured daughter of a wealthy Dutch family who were members of his parish.
Through his marriage, this outspoken opponent of slavery found himself
an owner of slaves in a state that did not allow them to be set free. Under
the circumstances, he did the best he could. He treated his slaves with
kindness, provided them with a Christian ministry, and arranged for their
education.[72] When he was called to Pennsylvania as a seminary professor,
his desire was to leave the "servants" behind.

However, Schmucker's new wife had different views on the subject. She
was determined to retain her slaves, even though the laws of Pennsylvania
allowed for their freedom at a certain age or after an allotted time. A letter
from Schmucker to his bride, who still remained in Virginia, shortly after
he arrived in Gettysburg indicates that he had discovered a way to satisfy
her desire. "I am . . . delighted . . . that the difficulty with regard to servants may be obviated effectually by some little pecuniary sacrifice. Many
persons I am told here have black servants, and they are precisely situated
as in Virginia until they are twenty-eight years of age." Schmucker then
counsels his wife to exchange her present servants for two others, about
ten years of age, who could be trained by her mother before coming to
Pennsylvania. In this way, his wife would be assured of servants just "as in
Virginia, for twelve or thirteen years. Should we . . . let these go free [we

---

[70]Ibid., 1.

[71]Wentz, *Pioneer In Christian Unity*, 317.

[72]Ibid., 317.

could] procure several again by a similar arrangement for twelve years more etc."[73] A few months later Schmucker wrote to his wife that he had consulted with a lawyer in regard to the "servants." He had learned that they could have them legally indentured, or bound over to their service, for a specific number of years or, if the slaves were minors, until they were twenty-eight, on the promise that they would then be manumitted. But, Schmucker warned, "Unless this formality is observed they will go free." He was agreeable to any arrangement that his wife wished to make. The ardent husband was most eager to please, signing his letter, "your most *affectionate* and *unalterable* and *devoted* and *loving, dear old man.*"[74]

As time passed, Schmucker's mate apparently became more willing to adjust to her husband's wishes, and the slaves were offered their freedom. At any rate, Schmucker later testified that, "in two of the three cases, in which slaves were under his control," he set them free "and offered it to the third who refused and preferred to remain in slavery."[75] Schmucker's youngest son later recalled that his father supported his former slaves in their old age and until their death, although this support was assisted in part by a legacy from Schmucker's mother-in-law, who was probably the original owner.[76]

There is a humorous aspect to Schmucker's unwanted role as a slaveholder and his ardent efforts to find a solution satisfactory to his wife. Yet it had serious implications. His intimate experience with slaves and with slave owners helped to shape some of his developing attitudes. For this reason he could never bring himself to place all slaveholders into a single mold or to castigate them as a group. Since he remained, at least technically, a slaveholder for the better part of his life, it is little wonder he shrank from the shrill and indiscriminate denunciation that often characterized the abolitionist rhetoric. Up to the very outbreak of civil war Schmucker expressed the optimistic opinion that the majority of Southerners were in favor of emancipation but had just been unable to form a definite opinion concerning how it could best be accomplished.[77] He frequently voiced his belief that there were "thousands of humane and Christian masters who treated their slaves with kindness and worked them moderately,"[78] and he consid-

---

[73]S. S. Schmucker to his wife, 3 March 1826, Schmucker Papers.

[74]Ibid., 12 September 1826.

[75]S. S. Schmucker, "Of Slavery," 1845 version, 82.

[76]Anstadt, *Life and Times of Samuel Schmucker*, 293.

[77]S. S. Schmucker, *Elements of a Popular Theology*, 332-33.

[78]S. S. Schmucker, "Of Slavery," 1840 version, 1.

ered these owners far less guilty in the eyes of God than those who treated them with neglect or cruelty. Schmucker's personal experience and perhaps some sense of guilt found expression in his contention that only voluntary slaveholding was sinful. Among those whom he placed into this nonsinful and involuntary type were "persons, convinced of the evils of slavery, but on whom slaves have been entailed by inheritance or marriage." With obvious empathy, Schmucker lamented the fact that these "persons may become slaveholders in their sleep." He added, however, that the innocence of involuntary slaveholding lasted only until there was "time to execute legal deeds of manumission."[79]

Like Abraham Lincoln, who was born in a slave state and married to a woman born and reared there also, Schmucker had an innate empathy with the South. It led him, like Lincoln, to minimize the danger of secession, refusing to interpret the crisis over slavery in sectional terms.[80] Schmucker consistently declined to make any one-sided accusations against the South. He respected the opinions of those who opposed him. He believed in compromise rather than confrontation. He shunned the role of the radical reformer and the shrill rhetoric that accompanied it. He insisted that the North must bear a large portion of the guilt of slavery, since the greater part of the slave traffic had been carried on by Northern vessels.[81] In 1833, he called on his fellow church members and citizens of Gettysburg to register their protest against a technical reestablishment of slavery in their own state.[82] He deplored the unjust laws that "in our own and other free states" denied the right to vote to the colored population, "although they were required to contribute their full share of taxes."[83] Time and again he cautioned his fellow Northerners against simply washing their own hands, while blaming the South for slavery's sin. "Until we have used our utmost efforts to purify our own statute book, and to have slavery abolished in the District of Columbia, . . . as well as prevent the influence of the Federal government . . . to favor this unjust system, we must stand guilty at the bar of heaven of participation in this sin."[84]

---

[79]Ibid., 4.

[80]George B. Forgie, *Patricide in the House Divided* (New York: W. W. Norton, 1979) 260.

[81]S. S. Schmucker, *Elements of a Popular Theology*, 336.

[82]S. S. Schmucker, Sermon manuscript no. 146, Gettysburg College Archives.

[83]S. S. Schmucker, *Christian Pulpit, The Rightful Guardian*, 30.

[84]Ibid.

Schmucker's close ties to the South, along with his intimate connections with its people, would simply not allow him to make incendiary statements regarding slaveholders or blanket condemnations of their Christian character. He continued to believe that, if Southerners could be led to see the error of their ways in a clear and calm fashion and not be further angered by the indiscriminate denunciation of Northern abolitionists, they would eventually dismantle the system of slavery on their own.

In spite of his optimistic view of Southern flexibility and his unwillingness to adopt confrontational tactics, Schmucker's views in many respects remained similar to those of the immediate abolitionists. As a result it is understandable that he was urged to unite officially with their organizational activities. Among those who wrote to him in this regard was the noted New York philanthropist and abolitionist, Geritt Smith, who himself had once been a supporter of colonization. In a lengthy letter to Schmucker published in the *Pennsylvania Freeman*, Smith agreed with Schmucker that "to charge all American slaveholders with the consciousness of their enormous wickedness" was neither reasonable nor charitable, but Smith did not believe the Anti-Slavery Society had done this. Smith was also sure that Schmucker was not really against calling slaveholders "hard names," as long as it was done truthfully and without malice. Admitting that members of the Anti-Slavery Society had at times spoken with unwarranted harshness, Smith said that, on the whole, they tried to "speak the truth in Love."[85] In general, he agreed that Schmucker's criticisms of the society had been valid but that they applied only to a minority of its members. Therefore, he urged Schmucker to show toleration for occasional errors of "judgment or temper" and to lend the "much needed and much desired influence of your good name."[86] There is no evidence of any reply. Schmucker remained aloof from both colonization and abolition organizations, content to "remonstrate against the violence of both parties" and to advocate "what appears to be the truth," hopeful behind the armor of his unconquerable optimism that "the violence will subside, the motives of all parties [be] duly appreciated, [and] the erroneous position of those who would justify slavery . . . eventually abandoned."[87]

Although Schmucker never rejected the values of colonization, believing it might still become the wave of the future, he was even more certain

---

[85]Gerrit Smith, Reply to the Rev. Dr. Schmucker, *Pennsylvania Freeman*, 19 June 1838, 7.

[86]Ibid.

[87]S. S. Schmucker, Letter to *Colonization Herald*, 2.

that abolitionism was the order of the day and gave it his wholehearted support privately and in public. While refusing to accept the bombastic aggressiveness of immediate abolitionism, he supported its basic philosophy and aims, remaining steadfast in his dedication to the complete eradication of slavery and to the belief that it was feasible to accomplish that goal in the United States. In this vein he wrote, "Reason and religion teach alike that to do right is always *practical* and always *salutary*. Although the path of duty and right . . . is connected with difficulties, as in the case [with slavery] they are never insuperable."[88]

A LUTHERAN ABOLITIONIST SYNOD

Of all the various district synodical groups of Lutherans scattered throughout the country, only the Franckean Synod subscribed without reservation to Samuel Schmucker's abolitionist agenda. Unencumbered by the strong Southern ties that contributed to Schmucker's moderation, the Franckeans took a more radical approach. They were, in fact, the only group of Lutherans in the entire country who during the antebellum era dealt openly, earnestly, and consistently with the most critical moral issue of the day. Its organization in 1837 took place at the very time when the dark specter of division over the issue of human slavery threatened to erupt into violence.

The Franckean Synod was conceived in the conviction that slavery was a sin and dedicated to the proposition that the church of Christ was obligated to root it out and wipe away every vestige of its image from the face of the earth. Opposition to slavery was, according to the Franckeans' own testimony, "among the prominent causes which led to its organization."[89] The tabling of a strong antislavery resolution at the Hartwick Synod Convention in 1836 proved to be the "last straw," leading the way to open schism. The militant abolitionism of the Franckean founders was not confined to resolutions but was incorporated into the body of their constitution, an action without precedent in the history of the Lutheran church. The original constitution of 1837 stated that no layperson who was a slaveholder was entitled to a seat in the synod's meetings, either as a delegate or a commissioner.[90] In addition, no minister could be a member of the synod who was a slaveholder or who engaged in the traffic of human beings or who advocated the system of slavery

---

[88]S. S. Schmucker, *Elements of a Popular Theology*, 5th ed., 333.

[89]*JFS*, 1856, 13.

[90]*Constitution of the Franckean Synod*, Art. 7, Sect. 3, p. 9.

as it then existed in the United States.[91] Furthermore, a standing resolutio
on American slavery was incorporated into the constitution and adopted wit
it. This resolution repudiated "the whole system of American slavery as equall
opposed to civil and religious liberty . . . as an offense to God," and any ju
tification or support of slavery, either by "precept or example," was cor
demned as sinful.[92]

While the Franckeans never went so far as to refuse to accept int
membership (except for clergy) even those who were actively involved i
the system of slavery, they did pass a resolution in 1841 recommendir
that "any person who is a slaveholder or traffics in human beings" be denie
admittance to the sacrament of the Lord's Supper.[93] At this same conver
tion a resolution was passed unanimously that affirmed "the duty of Chri
tian ministers and all Christian Churches" to rebuke the "accursed syster
of slavery, with its "unblushing advocates and apologists among professo
of religion and ministers of the gospel of peace!"[94]

The Franckean opposition to slavery grew more stringent with tl
passing years. In 1843, they passed a resolution which held that, sin
slaveholding was opposed to the gospel of Christ and "inconsistent with
Christian profession," all ecclesiastical associations that continued to su
port slavery "either by holding slaves or property or defending its righ
fulness, or refusing to plead the cause of the oppressed" could not be tr
representatives of Christ. They themselves, furthermore, felt duty bour
to withhold their Christian fellowship and communion from all su
groups.[95] In 1844, another resolution specifically requested a dissoluti
of all "Christian connection with slave traffickers and slaveholders."[96]]
nally, in 1848, the original constitutional requirements were amended a
extended so as to exclude from service as delegates to the synod conve
tion not only those laypersons who were slaveholders but any who justifi
"the sin of slavery."[97] Likewise, the reasons for the rejection of ministers
members of the synod were broadened to include any who did not "oppc
the system of American slavery."[98]

---

[91]Ibid., Art. 8 Sec. 6, p. 11.

[92]Ibid., "Standing Resolutions," Art. 2, p. 53.

[93]*JFS*, 1841, 24.

[94]Ibid.

[95]Ibid., 1843, 20.

[96]Ibid., 1844, 18.

[97]*Constitution of the Franckean Synod*, 1848 Revision, Art. 8, Sec. 2, p. 13.

[98]Ibid., Art. 7, p. 13.

BIBLICAL AND THEOLOGICAL BASIS

The biblical basis of the Franckean abolitionism was never compiled in any systematic fashion. It can, however, be gleaned from synodical reports, articles in their paper (the *Lutheran Herald*), and items of correspondence. In 1842, the Franckeans did publish a manifesto called "A Fraternal Appeal,"[99] which provides a fairly comprehensive biblical and theological rationale.

The primary reason put forward by the Franckeans for their denunciation of slavery as a heinous sin was that it denied, both in theory and practice, the biblical affirmation that all persons are created in the image of God and redeemed by the blood of Christ. The Franckeans maintained that slavery flew directly in the face of this biblical truth by its "reduction of immortal and godlike man, the crowing glory of this created world, into a thing or a chattel."[100] The "abhorrent principle of Chattleship" and "the denial of personhood" in their eyes constituted the heart of slavery's sinfulness. "Never did the all wise Creator ordain that one man should hold his fellow as his property . . . but all were created in the image of God."[101] This reference to Genesis 1:26-28 was the cornerstone of the Franckean attack on slavery and was referred to frequently.[102] They found it difficult to comprehend how any body of Christian believers could hold to a different opinion or could conceive of slavery as anything other than sinful, because it "converts man, made in the image of God, into an article of merchandise."[103] While admitting that "tortured arguments" could be torn from the Bible in its support, the Franckeans insisted that they were only a "perversion of Scripture,"[104] since slavery "barters the children of God, the price of the Redeemer's blood, for money, and sets at naught all the laws of human and Christian equality enjoined in the Bible."[105] As a result, the Franckeans were certain that "if there is a wrong in the universe . . . that

---

[99]"A Fraternal Appeal," adopted by the Franckean Synod at its convention on 3 June 1842, was a statement on slavery designed for presentation to other Lutheran synods and published by order of the synod in the *Lutheran Herald* 4 (1 July 1842): 81-82.

[100]"Fraternal Appeal," 81.

[101]Ibid.

[102]*Lutheran Herald* 2 (2 November 1840): 82.

[103]*JFS*, 1858, 28. See also the *Lutheran Herald* 2 (2 November 1840): 42.

[104]*Lutheran Herald* 2 (1 May 1840): 35.

[105]*Constitution of the Franckean Synod*, Standing Resolutions, Art. 2, p. 52.

wrong is slavery . . . if there is a single sin compounded of the quintess-
ence . . . of what is hateful in the eyes of a holy God . . . that sin is slavery."[106]

Closely connected to the Franckean view that slavery denied the doctrine
of the image of God was the contention that slavery deprived its victims of
universal God-given natural rights and privileges. These rights were also attributes of the divine image. For the Franckeans, the concept of equal justice
for all was in the forefront of these divine prerogatives. Oppression of one
human being by another was a violation of this sovereign right. Slavery was
described as a system of "unmingled injustice" because it robbed persons of
their "indisputable right" to themselves.[107] No slave could say, "My soul, my
will . . . my body, my affections," for all these things belonged to the master.[108] Another divine right that the Franckeans believed to be severely curtailed by the system of human slavery was that of equality, with its corollary
of universal brotherhood. Because all human beings shared an equal portion
of God's image, they were also entitled to equal rights, privileges, and opportunities.[109] This basic human equality had nothing to do with worldly distinctions of race or color or class. As the Franckeans put it in their manifesto
on slavery, "All humanity constitutes one common brotherhood, rich or poor,
high or low, honored or dishonored."[110]

The biblical emphasis on a divinely bestowed human equality led the
Franckeans to seek support from the words of the Declaration of Independence, with its assertion that "all men are created equal and endowed by
their Creator with certain inalienable rights." A petition presented by parish members to the synod convention in 1839 announced that "slavery is
. . . hostile to the proclamation of the Gospel" because it is "diametrically
opposed to the Declaration of Independence."[111] The Franckeans tended
to view slavery as a violation of both natural and revealed religion. They
conceived both as parts of a single whole and took it for granted that, since
they sprang from a common source in God the Creator, there was rarely,
if ever, any real conflict between the two. This view is evident in a state-

---

[106]*JFS*, 1857, 16.

[107]"Fraternal Appeal," 81.

[108]Ibid.

[109]Ibid.

[110]Ibid.

[111]Handwritten petition from fourteen members of the Evangelical Lutheran
Church of Summit, Franckean Papers.

ment attributed to one of their founders, William Ottman, in defense of the proposition that abolition enjoyed divine support. "Slavery," he said, "deprives of rights which all who breathe the vital air have a right to enjoy. Therefore it is a sin, and if a sin, its destruction is God's cause."[112] In January 1837, John Quincy Adams had read a petition in the House of Representatives that he stated had come from "fifty ministers and members of the Lutheran Church in the State of New York." The petition, which simply asked that the protection of the laws might be extended to all citizens of the District of Columbia according to the Declaration of Independence, was almost certainly composed by persons who only a few months later organized the Franckean Synod. Adams, noting that the petition contained "not a word about slavery," cleverly utilized it (as its framers had undoubtedly intended) to evade the famous "gag rule," which at that time forbade any discussion of abolition in Congress.[113]

While the Franckeans occasionally based their case for human equality on the Declaration of Independence or on natural rights, they most frequently founded their arguments on biblical grounds. A common bond of humanity was, according to the Franckeans, strongly asserted in the Scriptures. In this connection they were quick to quote Samuel Schmucker's favorite text (Acts 17:26), with its testimony that God "hath made of one blood all nations of the earth."[114] They were convinced that this "equalizing principle of the Gospel"[115] was absolutely demolished by the institution of slavery. Loud and long, the Franckeans tolled the litany of the God-given human rights that were denied to the slave. The relationship of marriage and the family was subject to the brazen intrusion of the slave master.[116] Slaves were denied the opportunity to read the Bible and worship God according to their own conscience. They were disenfranchised, debarred as witnesses in the courts, and excluded from the protection of the civil laws, including trial by jury. They were robbed of the rewards of their work and the privileges of citizenship in the very land they had labored to build with their muscle and sweat. Thus was slavery condemned as "a system of theft and unparalleled robbery."[117] The Franckeans also

---

[112]*Lutheran Herald* 2 (16 June 1840).

[113]Incident quoted from the newspaper *Friend of Man* 1 (8 February 1837): 135; (1 March): 147; William Goodell, editor.

[114]*Lutheran Herald* 2 (1 July 1840): 50.

[115]"Fraternal Appeal," 81.

[116]*JFS*, 1838, 15; *Constitution of the Franckean Synod*, Standing Resolutions, Art. 2, p. 52.

[117]"Fraternal Appeal," 81.

noted how slavery robbed not only the oppressed but the oppressor as well, denigrating the image of God in the slaveholder as well as the slave. According to synod report, slavery "renders the master helpless, imbecile, petulant, overbearing and tyrannical, thereby preventing him from a full development of himself into a noble manhood. It fosters . . . the baser passions of his nature . . . reducing the immortal into bondage to corrupt appetite. . . . It debases him in body, soul and spirit and casts him upon Eternity's strands, having the form of man but destitute of his power and excellence."[118]

The Franckeans' millennial hope contained the vision of "a common brotherhood, . . . the grand aim of the law and gospel." Here all would equally enjoy their God-given and inalienable rights. What was right for one person would be right for every other, for all would be recognized as the children of God. The dedication of these Lutheran abolitionists to this millennial goal knew no bounds. They issued forth the call to work for its realization in words that soared with an emotional eloquence.

> For the practical establishment of this equalizing principle we should toil and pray. . . . Sound abroad this sentiment of inspiration with the pealing notes of Sinai from every hill top and through every valley; let it mingle with every breeze and sweep over every plantation down to the gulf stream; and along the winding Sabine, re-echoed from the Rocky mountains and the growling surges of the Atlantic, till the whole land becomes tremulous with the blessed truth, that in the scale of humanity, all . . . are brethren.[119]

The Franckeans used another major scriptural concept in their abolitionist theology: the theme of liberation and freedom. Here the Franckeans turned especially to the Old Testament theme of the Exodus. "Has God said, 'Let my people go,' while enduring a relatively mild system of oppression in Egypt . . . and shall not the people of this country obey the command of God 'to let the oppressed go free'?"[120] The Franckeans seldom if ever used proof texts to uphold their attack on slavery.[121] The defense of

---

[118]*JFS*, 1860, 15.

[119]"Fraternal Appeal," 81.

[120]Ibid.

[121]The Franckeans, like other Lutheran Pietists and other Protestant evangelicals of their day, were not literalistic in their interpretation of Scripture. In this sense they have little if any connection with what was later called 'fundamentalism.' Today, however, the terms *evangelical* and *fundamentalist* are often lumped together, confusing the fact that these two groups have different histories and various understandings of the Christian faith.

slavery by an appeal to the Holy Scriptures they considered as "blasphemy against God, and a shocking prostitution of His Word."[122] They were confident that the "prominent, fundamental and all-wise principle of the gospel" was one of liberation, "to raise up those who are bowed down, to abase the proud and elevate the humble."[123] They viewed Christ's ministry on earth as designed to free humankind from every bondage of mind, body, and spirit. The whole object of the gospel, wrote H. L. Dox, "is to set free those who are enslaved."[124] In addition, the Franckeans emphasized that freedom is God's greatest gift to humankind, constituting the essence of what it means to be human. "God made man free in mind and body, but slavery deprives him of that liberty."[125] They concluded that slavery was opposed to the most basic themes of the Bible and the most fundamental purposes of God.

MODERATE IMMEDIATISTS

Unlike Samuel Schmucker, the Franckeans had no problem at all in choosing between the colonization and antislavery societies. Colonization was rudely rejected. Reporting in their paper on a request by the colonization society for churches of all denominations to receive an offering on 4 July 1841 to support its work, the Franckean editor scornfully commented, "Raise money for what? To drive war into Africa and exile freemen, and fatten up the enormous system of slavery by removing free labor? Astonishing that men of intelligence should try to impose upon . . . Churches and ministers with such humbugism . . . to raise money on the fourth of July to carry into operation a system of oppression? We go no such recommendation."[126] Two years later the synod passed an official resolution in which it expressed the view that the colonization society had originated in "sheer selfishness" and stood in opposition to "universal and impartial emancipation." The resolution concluded that the synod could not "exercise any sympathy for its measures."[127]

The Franckeans, rather, from their earliest years, united themselves with the efforts of the Anti-Slavery Society and its announced goal of imme-

---

[122]JFS, 1845, 18.

[123]Ibid.

[124]Lutheran Herald 2 (16 June 1840): 47.

[125]JFS, 1838, 15.

[126]Lutheran Herald 3 (1 July 1841): 101.

[127]JFS, 1843, 20.

diate emancipation. At its synodical meeting in 1839, they appointed all of the ministers and delegates of their synod as official representatives to the National Anti-Slavery Convention, which was held in the city of Albany later that month.[128] A number of the Franckean members not only attended meetings of the Anti-Slavery Society but held positions of leadership in them. Thomas Van Alstine, a relative of one of the synod's outstanding leaders (who himself was a member of the synodical Board of Missions), served as president of the Schoharie County Anti-Slavery Society.[129] On the controversial issue regarding immediate abolition, the Franckeans never wavered. A front-page article in their synodical paper early in 1841, entitled "Would it be safe to abolish Slavery?", asserted that the answer to that question depended on another, more vital one. "Is the immediate abolition of slavery right?" The answer to this question was an unequivocable "Yes . . . because man has no moral right to hold other persons as property. The divine law does not grant such a right. . . . Immediate abolition is undoing wrong without compromise. In a work like this, delay is dangerous, but the immediate discharge of duty both safe and right." The question of financial compensation to the slave master received a curt reply. "Slaves have more than paid their owners for their investment. They are *owed their freedom.*"[130]

In spite of this strong immediatist stance, the Franckeans were quick to reject the leadership of William Garrison when he turned against the church. Soon after the American and Foreign Anti-Slavery Society was organized in opposition to Garrison's group, the synod took action approving it.[131] At the same time, the Franckeans began to take issue with Garrison's position. In 1841, an article appearing in the *Herald* made reference to a certain magazine that was "ultra radical" in its ecclesiastical views, and the Franckean editor then commented, "It appeared to us that on the subject of Church government it held the same position that the reckless pioneering of . . . William L. Garrison does to civil government."[132]

Several years later, Henry Dox, in an opening sermon to a synod convention, designated Garrisonianism as an enemy of the church.

[128]Ibid., 1839, 22.

[129]Ibid., p. 23; see also *Friend of Man* 3 (21 August 1839); 4 (10 June 1840); 5 (23 February, 14 August 1841) for reports of Franckeans' antislavery activity.

[130]*Lutheran Herald* 3 (15 January 1841): 9.

[131]*JFS*, 1840, 19.

[132]*Lutheran Herald* 3 (1 September 1841): 68.

Although he did not mention the name specifically, his references were clearly to Garrison's criticisms of the church. Dox admitted that "the Church has been criminally tardy" in speaking out against slavery, but this delay was no reason for "unbelievers" to attack its preaching and its purpose. He implored the church to become "what her great Founder intended her to be, a spiritual . . . reformatory organization," and then those who disputed her right to the confidence of humankind would be silenced.[133] But the Franckeans did not oppose Garrison just because of his scathing attack upon the church and its ministry. To a certain degree they reluctantly admitted the accuracy of this criticism. Their abolitionism was simply not as radical as that of Garrison and his follows.

The Franckeans never came to the outright conclusion that one had to be an abolitionist in order to be a Christian. Such a stance, they believed, might result in their "unchristianizing" those "whom God has accepted." An editorial on this subject stated, "If we believe that no one can be a child of God unless he embraces . . . earnestly the principles of abolitionism, then we are guilty of . . . bigotry and illiberality . . . then all professed Christians before the days of abolitionism were deceived and . . . children of the devil. . . . We cannot as yet subscribe to such doctrine."[134] Yet as the years went by, the Franckeans moved closer to an endorsement of Garrison's original position. As noted earlier, they even recommended that those who defended slavery be refused admission to the Lord's Supper. But they never went as far as to make abolitionism a direct test of membership, except for the clergy and delegates of the synod.

The Franckeans' moderation expressed itself in a number of ways. In spite of their harsh denunciation of slavery, they not only mailed all of their papers, synod minutes, and other publications to synods in the South but encouraged a dialogue on the subject with their opponents. Throughout the entire year of 1840, the *Lutheran Herald* carried in full, and often on its front page, lengthy letters from the Reverend J. C. Hope, a Southern Lutheran clergyman who offered a vigorous biblical defense of slavery. Over the months the *Herald* devoted a great deal of space to Hope's regular epistles and to the Franckean editor's meticulous replies and

---

[133]H. L. Dox, "Christ the Foundation," a synodical and dedicatory discourse at Gardnersville, Church of the Reformation, Schoharie County, New York, 7 June 1849, *Pohlman Collection*, vol. 161, pp. 35-36, New York State Library, Manuscripts and Special Collections.

[134]*Lutheran Herald* 3 (1 October 1841): 150.

counterarguments.[135] J. C. Hope was a leader of the South Carolina Synod, serving as its president and as an official delegate to meetings of the General Synod.[136] These articles constitute one of the few public debates on the subject among Lutherans in the years before the Civil War. Though often lengthy and somewhat tedious, they were informative and educational. Nearly every important text relating to the subject of slavery in the entire Bible was taken up at one time or the other and its interpretation debated pro and con by Hope and the editor of the *Herald*.

The publication of these letters indicated that the Franckeans were at least willing to listen to the other side of the question. They never issued any blanket condemnation of the South. In 1857, the synod passed a resolution praising the "noble efforts of [those in the Southern states] . . . and we believe the number not inconsiderable, who at the hazard of their reputation, . . . property and . . . lives dare to lift up their voices against this sin [of] slavery."[137] At the same time, the Franckeans had little sympathy for slaveholders who defended their continued involvement in the system of slavery by treating their slaves with comparative kindness. They believed that such action only helped impart some modicum of respectiblity to a system essentially evil. While conceding that many persons who admitted the evils of slavery were overwhelmed by the practical problems that stood in the way of its eradication, the Franckeans insisted that "however difficult the task and self-sacrificing the demand, the path of safety and righteousness lies in the imperative instructions of God 'cease to do evil, and learn to do good.' "[138]

OTHER LUTHERAN SYNODS RESPOND TO THE SLAVERY ISSUE

For a time after their organization in 1837, the Franckeans remained the only Lutheran synod in the United States to have gone on record as opposing the system of American slavery and favoring its abolition. They were not content, however, to keep this conviction to themselves. Imbued with the missionary spirit characteristic of their Pietist heritage, they felt themselves called by God to spread the gospel of abolitionism among their fellow Lutherans.

---

[135]Ibid. 2 (1 May 1840): 34-35; (16 May): 38-39; (1 July): 50-51; (1 August): 58-59; (1 September): 63; (1 October): 71, 74; (16 October): 82; (2 November).

[136]Bost, "Rev. John Bachman," 307, 412.

[137]*JFS*, 1857, 18.

[138]Ibid., 1858, 18.

In July 1842, the Franckeans ordered copies of their antislavery manifesto "A Fraternal Appeal" sent to "every Evangelical Lutheran Synod in the United States."[139] Taking the same title that Samuel Schmucker had used four years earlier in his appeal for Christian unity, the Franckeans called on their "beloved brethren" in the Lutheran synods and congregations throughout the United States to take "decisive action" on the subject of slavery.[140] The "Appeal" has been called a "powerful indictment of slavery from a theological perspective"[141] and the "most explosive anti-slavery document ever to come forth from a Lutheran body."[142] Its opening paragraphs made it clear that the Franckeans did not approach their sister synods under any illusion that they had a right to "prescribe rules of binding obligation" but that they spoke from a sense of Christian duty. "Our relation to God, our destiny as blended with the destiny of the human race, and the responsibility of this synod, most preemptorily urge us to address you . . . in love, yet with the final day solemnity."[143] A lengthy description of the curse of slavery, its causes, and its remedies was followed by the call for a definite response to the "voice of kind entreaty and well-designed admonition." The Franckeans wanted undeniable evidence of some tangible resistance to slavery. They insisted that faith be given an explicit expression. "Faith without works is dead—we wish for action. The slave in chains . . . prays for decisive action. The God . . . of justice sternly demands uncompromising action. . . . Brethren, having discharged our duty, we roll the responsibility on you . . . to consider the poor and . . . labor by prayer and direct effort . . . for emancipation."[144]

This stirring call resulted in an almost complete lack of positive response. At their convention in 1843, the Franckeans took notice of the few replies that had been received. The Maryland Synod had tabled the matter, since they could not "entertain any subject not immediately connected with . . . synodical business." The Franckeans commented with

---

[139]Ibid., 1842, 12.

[140]"Fraternal Appeal," 81.

[141]Douglas Stange, "The 125th Anniversary of a Fraternal Appeal," *Concordia Historical Institute Quarterly* 40 (1967): 43.

[142]Milton C. Sernett, "Lutheran Abolitionism in New York State: A Problem in Historical Explication," in *Essays and Reports, 1982* (St. Louis: Lutheran Historical Conferences, 1984) 7.

[143]"A Fraternal Appeal," 81.

[144]Ibid.

a tinge of sarcasm that, since the Maryland Synod had previously considered the evil of intemperance as connected with their synodical business but had refused to express themselves on the subject of human bondage, they were forced to regard "this synod as pro-slavery." They further noted that the Hartwick Synod, which had "heretofore refused to express disapprobation of the sin of . . . slavery," had "also refused to consider or respond to our 'Fraternal Appeal.'" The same was true for the Virginia Synod, even though it had adopted "a very excellent resolution on the Temperance Reformation." The Lutheran Synod of the West had taken cognizance of the "Appeal" but made a rather enigmatic reply, thanking the Franckeans for their "well-meant attempt" at enlightenment but at the same time recommending to them "the propriety of considering well the measures of the Abolitionists in the present day, *before they act.*" To this the Franckeans replied that they could "scarcely believe" that the members of that body could still remain unconvinced that slavery was "one of the greatest evils that curses our land." They expressed the hope that the Synod of the West would soon "obtain more light, and act accordingly." Surprise was expressed over the fact that the East Ohio Synod, "a very active and zealous body of ministers," should have remained silent on the whole subject. It was noted that the Allegheny Synod of Pennsylvania, which had recently organized and adopted a constitution very similar to that of the Franckeans, had also not responded.[145] The net result was that not a single synod had commented favorably or acted positively on the matter of the "Fraternal Appeal."

A year later, at their convention in June 1844, the Franckeans were at last able to report on a smattering of affirmative responses. The Allegheny Synod had passed a resolution stating "that the time had arrived when ecclesiastical associations are in duty bound to express their views on the system of American Slavery."[146] This long-awaited show of public support brought from the Franckeans a word of thanks, coupled with the challenge to go even further by refusing to "hold fellowship with slaveholders in their churches." The Franckeans wished their friends Godspeed, but they could "indulge in no eulogistic extravagance," since the Alleghenians had only done their duty, "no more than they ought to have done before, nor more than ought to have been done by every Evangelical Lutheran Synod in the

---

[145]*JFS,* 1843, 21.

[146]W. H. Bruce Carney, *History of the Allegheny Evangelical Lutheran Synod of Pennsylvania, Together with a Topical Handbook of the Evangelical Lutheran Church: Its Ancestry, Origin, and Development,* vol. 1 (Philadelphia: Lutheran Publication Society, 1918) 189.

United States years ago."[147] During this same year the East Ohio Synod had also taken a stand against slavery. The resolution read, "This synod regards slavery as an evil, which all Christians should deplore."[148] Undaunted by lack of further support, the Franckeans rejoiced over the fact that three synods had now spoken on the slavery subject and expressed the hope that Lutherans might yet stand among the first in this glorious reformation.[149] The year 1846 saw yet another ally join the ranks of the abolitionist cause. The Pittsburgh Synod, organized a year earlier, came out strong with words reminiscent of former Franckean statements, but with no explicit reference to the "Fraternal Appeal." Their resolution read in part that the practice "of buying and selling men, women and children . . . is . . . a moral and national evil, and an offence condemned by the principles of humanity and the Word of God."[150]

A number of western synods, organized in the mid-1840s and early 1850s, including Miami of Ohio, Olive Branch of Indiana, Northern Indiana, and Northern Illinois, while strongly Pietist and inclined to speak out on other moral reforms, including temperance, chose to remain silent on the subject of slavery.[151] By 1852, the Wittenberg Synod, headed by Schmucker's brother-in-law and colleague Samuel Sprecher, stated that its members regarded "slavery as a great national evil and an abomination in the sight of God." The resolution also urged its members to "pray for those who legislate, . . . that a plan may be devised for its speedy extinction" and to use their "influence for its removal." The following year, however, a more cautious statement reflected the Wittenbergers' concern over the antichurch tone of some abolitionists, warning its members to exercise care in their promotion of the antislavery crusade, "lest the cause of truth be compromised."[152] Finally, in 1859, the Northern Indiana Synod denounced both intemperance and slavery as "crying sins" and dedicated themselves to "labor and pray for the abolition and destruction of these great evils."[153]

---

[147]*Lutheran Herald* 1 (30 October 1844): n.p.

[148]Fortenbaugh, "American Lutheran Synods," 82, referred to in the report by the Franckeans as the "English Lutheran Synod of Ohio and Adjacent States." It was in reality the East Ohio Synod, organized in 1836.

[149]*JFS*, 1845, 10.

[150]Fortenbaugh, "American Lutheran Synods," 85.

[151]Ibid., 87.

[152]Ibid., 85.

[153]Wentz, *Basic History of Lutheranism in America*, 166.

In the end, only five small district units of the General Synod out of over twenty, representing a tiny proportion of its total membership, expressed themselves as opposed to the system of slavery in the United States and in favor of its abolition. However, most of these expressions were apparently in response to the inquiries of the Franckean Synod, and none of them came close to rivaling the Franckeans' aggressive stance.

Next to the Franckeans, the Pittsburgh Synod expressed itself most boldly on the slavery subject. One of the reasons they gave for their hesitancy to join the General Synod was its policy of admitting slaveholders as delegates. Although there was considerable division among the members of the Pittsburgh Synod, the majority was unwilling to become thus "implicated in the sin of slavery." When they affiliated with the General Synod in 1852, a resolution was first passed to safeguard their own position on slavery "as defined in their printed minutes."[154] The leadership of Rev. William A. Passavant was undoubtedly a major factor in the antislavery position taken by the Pittsburgh Synod.

William Passavant was by far the most prominent of the very few leaders in the conservative, or Old Lutheran, group who exhibited an activist ethic. Passavant had been a student of Samuel Schmucker at the seminary in Gettysburg in the early 1840s, at which time he was in full accord with Schmucker's emphasis on revivalism, moderate confessionalism, and social action. In his early ministry he remained thoroughly within this Pietist tradition. He was "imbued with the New Measure Spirit," preaching revivals, and "urging mourners to come forward for prayer that they might be immediately converted."[155] A few years later Passavant experienced a conversion to the more strict confessionalism that was fast gaining ground throughout the United States.[156] However, the concern for the poor, the sick, and the needy, an aspect of his Pietist upbringing that had been encouraged by Schmucker's teaching and example, continued to burn deeply within Passavant's heart throughout all of his life. In opposition to most of his conservative colleagues, he refused to believe that a ministry to relieve physical suffering was less spiritual than any other. When accused of departing from "the appropriate sphere of the ministry," he replied, "The gospel must be lived as well as told, or men disregard it as an idle dream.

---

[154]Fortenbaugh, "American Lutheran Synods," 86.

[155]G. H. Gerberding, *Life and Letters of W. A. Passavant* (Greenville PA: Young Lutheran, 1906) 83.

[156]Ibid., 159-60.

. . . What wonder that reflecting men are disgusted at the religion of our pewed city Churches with their awful want of mercy and charity."[157]

In time Passavant became Lutheranism's chief pioneer in organizing hospitals and charitable institutions to serve the poor and handicapped. He was also a lifelong opponent of human slavery and never hesitated to speak out against it. After the war he lent his efforts to programs aimed to aid free blacks and to bring them into the Lutheran church. William M. Reynolds, another of Schmucker's former students, who later joined him on the Gettysburg faculty and became one of his most caustic and implacable foes on the confessional issue, also took a position against slavery. But these men were exceptions to the rule. Their abolitionism did not represent an integral aspect of their otherwise conservative theology. In fact, their social activism appears to have been a holdover from an earlier attachment to Pietism.

SCANDINAVIAN IMMIGRANTS
RESPOND TO ABOLITION

The abolitionist movement received strong Lutheran support from the growing stream of Norwegian and Swedish immigrants who began arriving in the states of Illinois, Wisconsin, and Minnesota during the early 1840s. A large number of these new arrivals from Scandinavia were Pietists who had been influenced by lay leaders like the Norwegian Hans Nielsen Hauge (1771–1824). Most of them had been taught the essentials of the faith from an explanation of Luther's catechism written by the Danish Pietist theologian Eric Pontoppidan (1698–1764). This work had in turn depended heavily on an earlier catechism of Philipp Spener. Hans Hauge's emphasis on revivalism, a living faith, lay participation, and social and political reform followed closely in the footsteps of the earlier German Lutheran Pietism.[158] Haugean followers in Norway became politically active in the parliament,[159] in the temperance movement, and in other moral reforms. To a lesser degree, the impact of German Pietism was also experienced in Sweden.

The first nineteenth-century Norwegian Lutheran leader in the United States was Elling Eielsen, who arrived in 1839. He was a follower of Hauge

---

[157]Ibid., 284.

[158]Andreas Aarflot, *Hans Nielsen Hauge* (Minneapolis: Augsburg Publishing House, 1979) 48-49.

[159]Eugene L. Fevold, "The Development of Norwegian-American Lutheranism in the Upper Midwest," in *The Lutheran Historical Conference: Essays and Reports, 1984,* 101.

and a strong opponent of slavery. Eielsen's young associates who arrived on the scene a few years later were likewise Haugeans. Because of their antipathy to slavery, a number of these men associated themselves with the Franckean Synod, through one of its midwestern missionary pastors, Marcus Empie. Ole Andrewsen was licensed by the Franckeans in 1847,[160] and Paul Anderson received ordination from their hands in 1849.[161] Later a third Norwegian, Ole J. Hatlestad, also threw his lot in with them.[162] When these three along with Eielsen organized a synodical group at Jefferson Prairie, Wisconsin, in 1846, they inserted a clause into their constitution repudiating the sin of slavery.[163] Outside of the Franckeans, they were the only Lutheran synod ever to do so.

Lars P. Esbjorn, the first of the nineteenth-century Swedish Lutheran leaders, arrived in the United States ten years after Eielsen. He also was a product of the Pietist revival movement and a crusader for temperance. He was intensely opposed to slavery and believed it to be antithetical to Christianity.[164] Esbjorn formed a close friendship with the Franckean pastor Paul Anderson. As a result, around 1850 his historic pioneer parish in Andover, Illinois, was for a short time connected with the New York abolitionist synod.[165] Esbjorn's Swedish colleague Tuve N. Hasselquist, also a Pietist, gave political issues a prominent place in his paper *Hemlandet* and based his advocacy of abolition on theological and biblical grounds.[166] Along with their Norwegian counterparts, Esbjorn and Hasselquist took stands similar to those of Samuel Schmucker and the Franckean Synod in regard to the crucial public moral issues of their day, and for essentially the same theological reasons. This involvement with social and political

---

[160]*JFS*, 1847, 7.

[161]Ibid., 1849, 22. See also J. Magnus Rohne, *Norwegian American Lutheranism up to 1872* (New York: Macmillan, 1926) 101.

[162]O. Nothstein, "The History of Lutheranism in Illinois," *Augustana Quarterly* 27 (July 1948): 241.

[163]Rohne, *Norwegian American Lutheranism*, 109, 207; E. Clifford Nelson and Eugene L. Fevold, *The Lutheran Church among Norwegian-Americans* (Minneapolis: Augsburg Publishing House, 1960) 340.

[164]George M. Stephenson, *The Religious Aspects of Swedish Immigration* (Minneapolis: University of Minnesota, 1932); reprint (New York: Arno Press and New York Times, 1969) 20, 53.

[165]*JFS*, 1850, 6.

[166]Wentz, *Basic History of Lutheranism in America*, 171.

reforms, including abolition, did not rest upon the rejection of any fundamental Lutheran doctrines or confessions. It resided, rather, in the conviction that the improvement of human affairs in the historical realm was a necessary result of an inner or spiritual reform of the heart.[167]

The influx of Scandinavian Pietists in the Midwest occurred at just the time when the battle lines were being more tightly drawn between the American Lutheran Pietism of Samuel Schmucker and the Old Lutheran orthodoxy advocated by more strict confessionalists. In addition to having a benevolent concern for these newly arrived immigrants, the conservative leaders viewed the Scandinavians as possible allies in the burgeoning struggle. William Passavant was an ideal ambassador in the effort to win them to the Old Lutheran cause. He was deeply alarmed at the missionary inroads that the Franckean Synod had so quickly made among these people.[168] He had the ability to open doors to financial aid, which the Scandinavians desperately needed to keep their struggling missions alive. Through his magazine the *Missionary* he was able to publicize their needs widely.[169] Most of all, Passavant, more than any other conservative leader, maintained the vigorous social concern and opposition to slavery capable of assuring the Scandinavians that they need not desert this vital aspect of their Pietist heritage.

The early nineteenth-century Scandinavian Pietist immigrants did not bring with them an especially strict tradition of adherence to the Lutheran Confessions. They found themselves, however, caught in the midst of a confessional controversy in which strong pressures were exerted to opt for one side or the other. They chose the more strict confessionalism only partly because of the encouragement and aid received from the Old Lutheran party. Perhaps even more important was the disturbing numbers of radical sectarians on the midwestern frontier who threatened to steal the Lutheran immigrants away from their fledgling churches. The same reason had moved Henry Muhlenberg in the direction of more confessional concern a century earlier, at the time the eastern colonies represented the American frontier.

---

[167]Stephenson, *Religious Aspects of Swedish Immigration*, 6, 18; Rolph A. Syrdal, "Hauge's Lay Evangelism Builds a Missionary Church: What Is the Proper Role of Lay Activity?" in *Church Roots: Stories of Nine Immigrant Groups That Became the American Lutheran Church* (Minneapolis: Augsburg Publishing House, 1985) 66-67.

[168]Gerberding, *Life and Letters of Passavant*, 207-208.

[169]Ibid., 218-20. Also Dorris A. Flesner, "The Beginning of English Lutheranism in the Upper Midwest," in *The Lutheran Historical Conference: Essays and Reports, 1984*, 46-47.

When Paul Anderson withdrew from the Franckean Synod and, along with his colleagues Andrewsen and Hatlestad, helped to organize the Northern Illinois Synod in 1851, the assumption arose that it was done in "direct protest against the loose confessionalism of the Franckean Synod."[170] Yet, in a letter to the Franckeans dated 28 May 1851, Anderson thanked them profusely for "the blessings" their synod had "been instrumental in conferring upon our people" and assured them that the organization of the new synod arose not out of any dissatisfaction with the Franckeans but from the need for an association in their own region.[171] In fact, two of the Franckean leaders made the long trip to Illinois in September 1851 to be Anderson's honored guests and to take part in the ceremonies marking the organization of the new synod.[172] Though Scandinavian Lutherans moved in the direction of a strict confessional allegiance, yet, in their views on the nature of the church and the ministry, the importance of the congregation and the laity, and the direct relationship of faith to matters of social and political concern, including abolition, they held fast to their Pietist heritage.

GERMAN IMMIGRANTS
RESPOND TO ABOLITION

Unlike the Scandinavians, the rapidly rising tide of Lutheran immigrants from Germany during this period was not predominantly Pietist but orthodox. This surge of German emigration from largely conservative Lutheran areas became a definite factor in the shift from Pietism to strict confessionalism that took place during the antebellum period. Due to famine conditions in 1816–1817, the heaviest influx of German migrants in the early part of the century had come from Pietist Württemburg. Beginning in 1838, many of the newcomers came from areas where Lutherans were strongly opposed to the state-imposed merger with the Reformed church. It has been estimated that about 7,000 Germans of the Old Lutheran persuasion had emigrated by 1854, most of them arriving before 1846.[173] There were few if any abolitionists among them, although most were at least nominally antislavery. Those who arrived in St. Louis from

---

[170]Rohne, *Norwegian American Lutheranism*, 104.

[171]Paul Anderson to Nicholas Van Alstine, Franckean Papers.

[172]*JFS*, 1852, 10-12.

[173]Mack Walker, *Germany and the Emigration, 1816–1885* (Cambridge: Harvard University Press, 1964) 79, 161, 174.

Saxony in 1839 and later formed the Missouri Synod had been exposed to strong elements of Pietism in their homeland under their original leader, Martin Stephan. But following his banishment on charges of "gross wickedness" soon after arriving in the United States, C. W. F. Walther assumed the chief position of leadership.

While retaining the Pietist emphasis on congregational autonomy and lay participation, Walther led the Missouri Synod to become by far the most staunch and rigid confessionalists of all Lutherans in North America. [174] With regard to the issue of abolition, Walther became the only notable Lutheran leader in a Union state to take a decided and public proslavery position. His rigid orthodoxy led him inevitably toward a preservation of the political status quo, a position typical of Lutheran conservatism since the time of the Reformation. Walther was convinced that the Scriptures upheld the American system of servitude, and he published several articles in his magazine, *Der Lutheraner*, by Dr. Wilhelm Sihler of Fort Wayne containing a definitive defense of slavery as an institution. [175] The official position of the Missouri Synod, typical of orthodoxy, was to remain silent on the subject, maintaining that the consideration of "secular" matters by ecclesiastical bodies was improper. [176]

SOUTHERN LUTHERANS
RESPOND TO ABOLITION

The majority of Lutherans in the South, as was noted, possessed a Pietist heritage. It is not surprising, then, that Southern Lutherans took the first initiatives in regard to the problems of slavery. As early as 1809, the North Carolina Synod authorized its pastors to baptize slaves, provided their masters did not object. In a subsequent resolution just five years later, they urged owners to permit slaves to receive instruction and baptism. In 1815, a plan for the reception of slaves into the church was devised by the South Carolina Synod by which relatively large numbers of blacks became members of its parishes.

The Reverend John Bachman, a prominent leader of the South Carolina Synod and dominant figure in the life of Southern Lutheranism during

---

[174]Wentz, *Basic History of Lutheranism in America*, 117-19.

[175]Ibid., 168-69. During the Civil War and up until 1868, the Norwegian Synod carried on a controversy with the Missourians over their proslavery stance, which dashed any hopes of organic union between these two groups.

[176]Robert Fortenbaugh, "The Representative Lutheran Periodical Press and Slavery, 1831–1860," *Lutheran Church Quarterly* 8 (1935): 171.

the entire antebellum period, greatly expanded this ministry to blacks. Bachman's Swiss-German parents had religious roots in Anabaptism. They had migrated first to Pennsylvania and then to Rhinebeck, New York, where Bachman was born in 1790. He grew up on a farm just north of Albany in an area where several thousand slaves and free blacks resided. His father was a slave owner. After a study of theology under several private tutors, including Frederick Quitman, Bachman was licensed by the New York Ministerium and served his first congregation near his home area in a parish composed largely of Pietist descendants of the Palatine emigrants. He then moved to Charleston, South Carolina, as pastor of St. John's Lutheran Church, where he served until his death in 1874, a pastorate of nearly sixty years.[177] During his long and distinguished career he served as president of both the South Carolina Synod and the General Synod. In addition to his role as a church leader, Bachman became a celebrated naturalist. His scientific works were known and read throughout the world. He collaborated with James Audubon in *The Birds and Beasts of America*, and both of his daughters were married to sons of Audubon.[178]

Bachman's theological position, which was shared by nearly all of his Southern colleagues, with the exception of those in the Tennessee Synod, was that of American Lutheran Pietism. His theology led him to engage in an extended controversy with the Tennessee Synod, during which he made explicit his identification with Samuel Schmucker and the General Synod. In presenting his views on baptismal regeneration and the presence of Christ in the Lord's Supper, he quoted extensively from Schmucker's *Elements of a Popular Theology* and noted his complete accord with its author on all these subjects.[179] He stated without any equivocation that he "read the symbolic books with respect but I yield . . . assent to a much better guide . . . the Scriptures. . . . I have not adopted baptismal regeneration, consubstantiation, or auricular confession as any part of my creed."[180] Bachman was a founding father of the only Lutheran seminary in the South, and in 1834 he was influential in calling Ernest Hazelius, who, after leaving Hartwick Seminary, had also taught for a short time at Gettysburg, to its chair of theology. Hazelius fully supported Bachman's attack on Henkelite conservatism, castigating the Tennessee Synod for their opposition to "all the benevolent operations of the day" and for their "literal adherence to the

---

[177]Bost, "Rev. John Bachman," summary page, 1-30, and 381.

[178]Gerberding, *Life and Letters of Passavant,* 100.

[179]Bost, "Rev. John Bachman," summary page, 276-310; see especially p. 286.

[180]Ibid., 263-64.

Augsburg Confession."[181] Later, Schmucker identified both Bachman and Hazelius, as well as the earlier Southern leader, Gottlieb Shober, as representatives of Lutheranism whose views coincided with his own.[182]

The slavery issue alone drove a dividing wedge between Lutheran Pietists in the North and those in the South. The Southerners' social activist theology led them for a time to look upon human slavery as a moral evil that could gradually be abolished under the benevolent influence of the Christian faith. But after 1830, with the rise of immediate abolitionism and a series of slave revolts, that attitude rapidly changed. It was replaced by one that upheld slavery as a moral good, capable of being defended on biblical as well as social and political grounds. The all-out assault on slavery emanating from the North threatened too drastically the social and economic fabric of the Southern way of life. Even Peter Cartwright, the well-known evangelist and antislavery prophet, found that, after 1830, he did not dare to mention the issue of slavery in his sermons. When he attempted to oppose it in other ways, he was finally forced to give up his preaching in the South altogether.[183]

John Bachman and his Lutheran Pietist colleagues took up the Southern defense of slavery. Bachman was a careful, capable, and convincing spokesman on the subject. He had made a thorough scientific investigation regarding the unity of the human race and published a scholarly treatise on the subject. His findings challenged commonly held racist views and afforded scientific support to the very theology Samuel Schmucker utilized to champion abolitionism, namely, that God had created all people of one blood.[184] Yet, Bachman considered blacks to be better off under a system of "mild servitude." He maintained that the Bible did not condemn slavery as such, but only its abuses. He differed only in degree from Schmucker when he labeled as prejudice the tendency of Northerners to "condemn men in the masses for crimes committed by a few." Above all, he was convinced that agitation for immediate abolition produced only bitterness and strife and therefore should be left to civil legislation and kept out of the church.[185]

---

[181]Ibid., 308.

[182]S. S. Schmucker, *Lutheran Observer* 17 (9 and 16 November 1849).

[183]McLoughlin, *Revivals, Awakenings, and Reform,* 136.

[184]John Bachman, *The Doctrine of the Unity of the Human Race, Examined on Principles of Science* (Charleston SC: C. Canning, 1850).

[185]John Bachman, *Missionary* 2 (10 December 1857).

Not many Southerners were as moderate as Bachman in their reaction to abolitionism. In 1835, the Synod of Virginia declared it to be a combination of ignorance, fanaticism, and dishonesty. Four years later the Virginians expressed their decided disapproval of "the pretensions" assumed by the Franckean Synod, referring to its adoption of abolition as an "arrogant assumption of synodical censorship."[186] In 1835, Bachman's South Carolina Synod had reacted with strong words of condemnation directed at the Northern abolitionists and their "incendiary publications," labeling them as "enemies of our beloved country, whose mistaken zeal is calculated to injure the cause of morals and religion." They went on to express their "heartfelt pleasure that none of the ministers in our connection . . . have adopted the sentiments of the Abolitionists."[187] This pleasure was destined to be short-lived. The very next year word had reached the South Carolinians of "some person or persons, in all probability of our own creed, living . . . in the distant North," who had made "violent and unchristian attacks" upon some of their clerical members. Calling this "interference" both improper and unjust and labeling its perpetrators as "rotten-hearted benefactors of [a] . . . much commisserated race," the synod vowed never again to discuss the subject with the abolitionists.[188]

In spite of this vitriolic response to "abolitionary agitation," the South Carolina Synod was responsible for bringing more blacks into the Lutheran fold during this era than any of its sister synods. By 1850, one-third of all new members received by the forty-three parishes of the South Carolina Synod were black. Ten years later, blacks, both slave and free, accounted for one-fourth of its entire membership.[189] It has been noted as an ironic fact of history that Southern clergymen did more for the Christian instruction of slaves than ministers in the North did for free blacks.[190] The ministry of John Bachman illustrates this contention. Just a year after his arrival in Charleston, Bachman had served notice to St. John's governing board that he intended to engage in a ministry to blacks. Within two years he had already received 37 members. In 1818 and again in 1831 and 1845, the congregation had to enlarge the seating space in the gallery where black

[186]Wentz, *Basic History of Lutheranism in America*, 165.

[187]Bost, "Rev. John Bachman," 406-407.

[188]Ibid., 407.

[189]Bost, "Rev. John Bachman," 380-90. See also Jeff G. Johnson, "Black Lutherans in the New World," *Cresset* 47 (February 1984): 11.

[190]Bodo, *Protestant Clergy and Public Issues*, 145.

members were confined. Before 1850, the number of black communicants had peaked at around 200, and by 1860, a Negro Sunday school had an enrollment of 150, with 32 teachers. [191] Other Lutheran pastors in the South engaged in similar ministries, but none even approached the results of Bachman's efforts, as can be garnered from baptismal records. In 1829, Bachman baptized 29 blacks; all other pastors in South Carolina, 9. The following year he baptized 40, while all others baptized only 6. In 1835, he baptized 44; all others, 14.

In the light of this unique and extensive ministry, it is not surprising that the first blacks seeking to enter the Lutheran ministry came either through membership in St. John's Church or through a personal relationship with Bachman. The first two blacks to become Lutheran clergy were Jehu Jones and Daniel Alexander Payne. They were both freemen. Jones was a member of St. John's, and Payne a friend of Bachman. Later, another member of St. John's parish, who had assisted Bachman in his ministry to blacks, Boston Jenkins Drayton, also a free black, was commissioned and sent as a missionary to West Africa. Since ordination was both illegal and unthinkable in the South, Bachman sent these men to his friends in the Northern states to pursue further education in their quest for positions of leadership and service in the church.

In October 1832, Bachman directed Jehu Jones to his friend and former colleague, Rev. William D. Strobel in New York City. Jones carried with him letters of introduction, along with Bachman's request that he be ordained by the New York Ministerium as a Lutheran missionary to Africa. By the time Jones arrived the convention of the ministerium had adjourned. However, Strobel gathered together several of the pastors who still remained in the city to perform the ordination. [192] In this somewhat irregular fashion, in 1832 Jehu Jones became the first black man ever to be ordained in the Lutheran church. But even though the ministerium approved the action at their convention in 1833, Jones was not officially received as a member of the synod, and his name never appeared on the roll of the clergy. [193] He later established an independent Lutheran colored congregation in Philadelphia, apparently the first of its kind; but his fre-

---

[191]Michael Lee Cobbler, "What Price Inclusion," *Mt. Airy Parish Practice Notebook* 19 (Summer 1982): 3.

[192]Bost, "Rev. John Bachman," 390-92.

[193]Harry J. Kreider, "Negro Lutheran Work in New York," *Lutheran Church Quarterly* 20 (July 1947): 262.

quent appeals to his Lutheran brethren for funds were never answered.[194] In 1849, the New York Ministerium issued a stinging denunciation of Jones, accusing him of falsely representing himself as a Lutheran minister and noting his "inefficiency and general deportment."[195] Nothing was heard further of the Reverend Jehu Jones, and the question why he was never enrolled as a member of the ministerium or given support in his endeavors remains unanswered.

Boston J. Drayton likewise did not fare well as Lutheranism's first black missionary. After receiving financial aid and support from Schmucker's colleague Benjamin Kurtz, he was commissioned in 1845 to serve in the colony of Las Palmas in West Africa. Kurtz noted at the time that Bachman had made "notable efforts in behalf of the African race" and had been "instrumental in providing for the education and qualification for the Lutheran ministry of several colored brethren."[196] However, Drayton fell ill soon after arriving in Africa and later turned his interest toward government and law. A talented man, he became the third chief justice of the Liberian Supreme Court.[197]

THE REVEREND DANIEL A. PAYNE

The story of Daniel Alexander Payne deserves a fuller account because of his close and meaningful relationships with the most influential leaders of American Lutheran Pietism. It was an association that, without any doubt, fueled the fears of those who opposed both the church's involvement in the issue of abolition and the freedom of blacks in American society. It exposed the alarming ambiguity of both the timid openness and the resolute unwillingness of Lutherans to immerse themselves in the flesh-and-blood realities of the moral issue that lay at the heart of abolitionism, namely, the quest of black Americans for equality and freedom of opportunity.

Daniel A. Payne was the first black student ever to enroll in a Lutheran seminary, and also the first to be regularly ordained and placed on the clergy rolls of a Lutheran synod in North America. After a short stay in the Lutheran church, he returned to his original affiliation with the African Methodist church, where he became a distinguished bishop, historian, and

---

[194]*Proceedings of the General Synod*, Lutheran Theological Seminary Archives, Gettysburg PA, 1839, 19.

[195]Kreider, *History of the United Lutheran Synod*, 152-53.

[196]*Lutheran Observer* 13 (31 October 1845).

[197]Johnson, "Black Lutherans in the New World," 11.

educator. As president of Wilberforce University near Xenia, Ohio, Payne was the first black president of a college owned and operated by black educators. [198] He did more to shape the policies of the A.M.E. church body "than any other man of his time."[199] His influence on this denomination was tremendous, and a recent historian called him the St. Paul of the A.M.E. church. [200] Without a doubt he is the most influential black man ever ordained as a Lutheran pastor, and his brief membership left its passing mark on the history of Lutheranism in America.

Daniel Payne was born free in 1811 in Charleston, South Carolina. His father had been kidnapped and sold into slavery but later bought back his freedom. His mother was half native-American. Both of his parents died before he was ten, and he was reared in a religious home by his grandaunt. For a time he was enrolled in a school for free Negroes, but it was closed following the Denmark Vesey plot in 1822. [201] Payne's thirst for knowledge was insatiable, and he continued to study on his own and with the aid of a tutor. At the age of eighteen he joined the African Methodist Episcopal Church and shortly thereafter experienced a religious conversion in which he felt called to be an educator to his people. [202] The very next year he opened a school of his own and enrolled six pupils. Within a few years the number grew to sixty. Among other subjects Payne taught the natural sciences, and it was through this interest that he first met the Reverend John Bachman, whom he described as "the most distinguished naturalist in South Carolina." Payne was directed to Bachman when he sought to identify a

---

[198]The fascinating story of Bishop Daniel Alexander Payne is found in his autobiography, *Recollections of Seventy Years*, compiled and arranged by Sarah C. Bierce Scarborough, ed. E. S. Smith (Nashville: A.M.E. Sunday School Union, 1888; reprint, New York: Arno Press and New York Times, 1968). See also Saunders Jay Redding, *The Lonesome Road: The Story of the Negro's Part in America*, Mainstream of America Series (Garden City NY: Doubleday, 1958); Michael Lee Cobbler, "What Price Inclusion?"; Thomas R. Noon, "Daniel Payne and the Lutherans," *Concordia Historical Institute Quarterly* 53 (Summer 1980): 51-69; Kreider, "Negro Lutheran Work in New York," 261-71.

[199]Josephus Coan, *Daniel Alexander Payne: Christian Educator* (Philadelphia, 1935) 21, quoted by Douglas Stange in "Bishop Daniel A. Payne and the Lutheran Church," *Lutheran Church Quarterly* 16 (1964): 354-59.

[200]George A. Singleton, *The Romance of African Methodism: A Study of the African Methodist Episcopal Church* (New York: Exposition Press, 1952) 38.

[201]Bost, "Rev. John Bachman," 394.

[202]Payne, *Recollections of Seventy Years*, 17.

strange-looking caterpillar that a student had brought to school. He was cordially received, given the information he needed, and invited to return again. Payne described how on his second visit the "learned divine and naturalist . . . showed me his fine collection of insects. . . . He took me into his parlor and introduced me to his wife and daughters as the 'young philosopher'. There I sat and conversed with his family as freely though all were of the same color and rank; and by my request his daughter skillfully performed several pieces on the piano."[203]

Payne's days in Charleston, however, were limited. The Nat Turner revolt in 1832 resulted in the passage of oppressive laws in the state, which led to the closing of his school. Full of rage and despair Payne determined to leave Charleston and never return until the sting of slavery was removed. In his extremity he turned for aid to his friend, John Bachman. He was furnished with letters of introduction to friends of Bachman, including the Reverend William Strobel in New York. While visiting with Strobel, Payne carefully examined Samuel Schmucker's textbook *Elements of a Popular Theology*. The young black educator concluded from his reading that "the students at Gettysburg were not screwed down to the Procrustean bedstead" and that Schmucker was a teacher who "would be as liberal as he was Christian and learned."[204] He resolved to attend Gettysburg Seminary and arrived there in June 1835. An illness resulting in temporary loss of eyesight forced Payne to terminate his studies after a period of two years, but during that time he and Schmucker developed a close and lasting personal relationship.

Payne had only the highest praise for the man he referred to as his "venerable preceptor" and commented that Schmucker "was not only a kind instructor, but often exhibited the tenderness of a father by supplying my bodily needs."[205] The relationship established during Payne's Gettysburg sojourn did not languish when he left. He continued to address letters to Schmucker on numerous occasions, keeping him informed of his earlier educational endeavors[206] and seeking advice regarding administrative procedures as late as 1869, when Payne was serving as president of Wilberforce University.[207]

---

[203]Ibid., 24.

[204]Ibid., 45.

[205]Ibid., 59-60.

[206]Daniel A. Payne to S. S. Schmucker, 20 March 1841, Schmucker Papers.

[207]Daniel A. Payne to S. S. Schmucker, 30 March 1869, Schmucker Papers.

Before he left Gettysburg, Payne conferred with Schmucker concerning his future and recorded the advice of his teacher in these words: "We should be glad to have you operate as a minister of the gospel in the Lutheran Church, but I think you can find a greater field of usefulness in the A. M. E. Church; therefore I advise you to join that body of professing Christians."[208] Since Schmucker's advice was agreeable to Payne's "Methodistic predilections," Payne left Gettysburg for Philadelphia in May 1837, with the firm intention of becoming a minister in the A. M. E. church. He carried with him testimonials from both Schmucker and the man who had taught him Hebrew and Greek, Charles Philip Krauth. Krauth's letter, while somewhat paternalistic, was nevertheless filled with a spirit of genuine kindness and concern.[209] Schmucker appeared more intimately acquainted with Payne. His letter was brief, direct, and without any touch of condescension. He noted that "our daily intercourse, . . . has been in unwavering confidence in the integrity of your purposes and the excellence of your character, together with the conviction, that God who of one blood made all nations to dwell upon the face of the earth, will crown with his blessing your labors on behalf of your oppressed kinsmen after the flesh." Schmucker closed his letter, "Your friend and brother in Christ."[210]

Upon reaching Philadelphia, Payne was deterred from beginning his work in the A. M. E. church when he discovered that many of its clergy were strongly opposed to an educated ministry. He described how in their sermons they would declare that they had never "rubbed their heads against college-walls" or studied Latin, Hebrew, or Greek, and members of the congregation would respond with "Amen" and "Glory to God."[211] Payne wanted none of this and turned once more toward the Lutheran church. He had either heard about the Franckean Synod's dedication to abolitionist principles or was directed to it by Schmucker. At any rate, he determined to apply there for ordination.[212] Payne later revealed that he doubted whether any other synod in the Lutheran church would have entertained his application.[213] After traveling to the home of the Franckeans' newly elected president, John D. Lawyer, in Rensselaer County, New York, Payne

---

[208]Payne, *Recollections of Seventy Years*, 61.

[209]Ibid., 63-64.

[210]Ibid., 63.

[211]Ibid., 61.

[212]Ibid., 65. Payne referred to the synod as the "Franklin" Synod.

[213]*Lutheran Observer* 46 (17 May 1878).

requested admission into the synod. On 31 May 1837, exactly one week after the Franckeans' organization, he was issued an ad interim license, entitling him to perform all the functions and duties of a pastor of the synod. Under this licensure, Payne served a Presbyterian parish in Troy, New York, for two years.

In the spring of 1839, he attended the convention of the Franckean Synod, held in the chapel at Fordsbush, the site where the synod had organized. On Sunday, 9 June, he and another candidate, Henry L. Dox, received the solemn rite of ordination. "They kneeled and were duly set apart and ordained as Bishops and ministers of the gospel . . . the right hand of Christian love was then given . . . and they were welcomed to take part in our labors."[214] During the convention Payne served on the Committee on American Slavery. When the report was presented, he arose and delivered a remarkable and moving appeal on its behalf, which was received by the assembled members with "fixed attention and feeling."[215] First noting that the word *man*, "in its primitive sense," signified all persons, male and female, Payne began his appeal by stating:

> I am opposed to slavery, not because it enslaves the black man, but because it enslaves man. And were all the slaveholders . . . men of color, and the slaves white men, I would be as thorough and uncompromising an abolitionist as I now am. Wherever . . . I see a being . . . enslaved . . . without respect to complexion, I shall lift up my voice to plead his cause not merely from sympathy . . . but because . . . the living God, whom I dare not disobey, has commanded me to open my mouth for the dumb, and to plead the cause of the oppressed.[216]

Payne then went on to illustrate in detail just how slavery brutalizes its practitioner and victim alike. Calling on his twenty-four years' experience in the midst of slavery, Payne told his listeners how some Southern states had enacted laws that made it a crime punishable by death for a slave to read the Bible, to teach, or to receive instruction. Admitting that there were presently four Methodist missionaries and one Lutheran[217] laboring among

---

[214]*JFS*, 1839, 17.

[215]*Lutheran Herald* 1 (1 August 1839): 116.

[216]*JFS*, 1839, 15. The hint that Payne was in advance of his day with regard to views on the status of women is further borne out by the fact that the sole resolution that he offered during the convention was that "licentious men should be held by this Synod, in the same disrepute as licentious women" (*JFS*, 1839, 13).

[217]The reference here was undoubtedly to his benefactor, the Reverend John Bachman of Charleston.

the slaves in South Carolina, he nevertheless maintained that in most instances both preaching and instruction was prohibited to those in bondage. Reminding his audience that he spoke "not of what others have told me, but what I have seen and heard," he described how the slaveholders' profession of Christianity, coupled with human oppression, led the slave to "scoff at religion . . . mock their masters, and distrust both the goodness and justice of God. . . . I have heard the mistress ring the bell for family prayer and heard the servants . . . begin to sneer and laugh . . . I have seen colored men at the Church door, scoffing at the ministers while they were preaching, and saying 'You had better go home and set your slaves free.' "

Payne then related how the author of the very law that prohibited blacks from teaching and that resulted in his own flight from Charleston had given $20,000 to South Carolina College for the education of white youth. He closed his remarks with a stirring appeal to action on behalf of the battle against human slavery. "O Brethren of the Franckean Synod! Awake! *Awake!* to the battle, and hurl the hottest thunders of divine truth at the head of this cruel monster, until he shall fall to rise no more; and the groans of the enslaved are converted into the songs of the free!"[218] It was a message the Franckeans would not soon forget and undoubtedly deepened their dedication to the cause of abolition.

Payne waited in vain for an assignment to a Lutheran parish. He even volunteered to serve the synod as a missionary to the West Indies, but the necessary funds could not be raised. Within three years Payne had returned to the A.M.E. church, where he remained throughout a most distinguished and fruitful career. He never attended another convention of the Franckean Synod, although he was retained on the rolls of its clergy for ten years. Until his death in 1893, Bishop Payne held a strong attachment to the Lutheran church, following its affairs with interest.[219] Nearly fifty years after his ordination he wrote, "Oh, that the Lord Jesus would move the heart of the Lutheran Church to work among the colored people, according to their ability. Luther ought to be as widely and intimately known down South among the colored Christians as Calvin, Knox, or Wesley."[220]

---

[218]*Lutheran Herald* 1 (1 August 1839): 113-14. Payne's speech is printed in its entirety.

[219]*Lutheran Observer* 46 (19 April 1878): n.p.

[220]Gerberding, *Life and Letters of Passavant*, 531.

H. L. Dox, the Franckean leader who was ordained with Payne, recorded in later years his deep regret that the abilities of this brilliant black minister were lost to the Lutheran church. "He left [the Lutheran Church] . . . not because he did not love it. He left it because it had no place for him, because he felt that he had no right to expect . . . cooperation from the denomination at large in any movement he might make on behalf of the colored people."[221] The story of Daniel Payne throws light on the inability and the unwillingness of Lutherans to deal openly and forthrightly with the deep underlying issues of abolitionism. Potential black clergymen along with white activists found little "cooperation from the denomination at large."

John Bachman, the acknowledged leader of Southern Lutheranism, more than any other person encouraged the ordination of blacks in the Lutheran church. His action bears testimony to the fact that the Lutheran Pietism he represented was inherently activist and abolitionist in its theology. Yet the overwhelming economic and cultural pressures to preserve the system of slavery in the South kept its adherents there from opposing it. Lutheran Pietists in the North for the most part supported abolitionism in one degree or another. However, this approval was moderated or even severely curtailed because of the bitter divisiveness it entailed. In most cases the desire to maintain Lutheran unity or to realize the ecumenical goal of a united or cooperative Protestantism took precedence over their abolitionist convictions. The result was that the broad spirit of cooperation that had united American Lutheran Pietists around the causes of benevolent and moral reform began to crack apart under the pressures of abolitionism. During the 1840s and 1850s, the entire Pietist constituency of the South, along with those in the North who were most alarmed by the threat that abolitionism posed to Lutheran harmony, united with the conservative elements to implement a common policy with regard to the whole issue of slavery. The strategy pursued was one of silence and neutrality.

SILENCE AND NEUTRALITY

The growing number of strict confessionalists, or Old Lutherans, within the General Synod defended the policy of silence in regard to slavery on dogmatic grounds. They argued, on the basis of the traditional two-kingdom doctrine, that the slavery issue, along with most other moral reforms, was political in nature and therefore to be regulated by civil legislation. They relegated it to the realm of secular authority and refused to recognize

[221]H. L. Dox, *Lutheran Observer* 46 (17 May 1878): n. p.

it as a proper subject for either debate or action by an ecclesiastical body. This ethical approach was a fundamental aspect of conservative Lutheran theology.

Many Northern Pietists adopted a similar strategy but for a very different reason. They cooperated with the General Synod's policy of silence on practical grounds, not theological. They believed the issue of slavery was so loaded with emotion and so divisive in nature that to discuss it publicly or to take sides in regard to it would exacerbate internal strife and lead inevitably to schism. A few of the Northern judicatories made this reasoning explicit. The Hartwick Synod, having previously refused to deal with the issue of slavery, passed the following resolution in 1839: "Contention and strife in politics are inconsistent with the spirit of religion and dangerous to Christian principle." The statement went on to request its members "to abstain from party feelings which cause divisions among Christians."[222] Most district synodical groups, both Pietist and conservative, followed the pattern of the Hartwick Synod's original action and did nothing at all. For instance, when the matter of slavery was introduced at a meeting of the New York Ministerium, the matter was "laid on the table."[223]

Southern Pietists, led by John Bachman, were also deeply concerned that Lutheran unity not be marred by public feuding over the issue of slavery. Furthermore, they were fearful of the unsettling ramifications that ecclesiastical debate on the subject would have upon their entire community. When John Bachman accepted the office of president of the General Synod in 1835, he confided to members of his parish that he would dedicate himself to the goal of "forever excluding the subject of Abolition from that Body."[224] He became one of the most influential persons in the successful pursuit of this objective. By 1857, he could boast that, even though the agitation over slavery had led to division among other denominations, the General Synod was an exception, since it had eliminated all discussion of the subject "by constitutional mandate."[225]

The *Lutheran Observer*, a paper begun in 1831, reflected unofficially but accurately the majority views of the General Synod's constituency in regard to the slavery question. Its American Pietist editor, Benjamin Kurtz,

[222]*Minutes of the Hartwick Synod*, 1839.

[223]*Minutes of the Ministerium of the Evangelical Lutheran Church in the State of New York*, 1844, 7, Metropolitan-Upper New York Synod Archives.

[224]Quoted in Bost, "Rev. John Bachman," 260, from the minutes of St. John's Lutheran Church, Charleston SC, 1830–1845, 281-82.

[225]John Bachman, *Missionary* 2 (10 December 1857): 183.

attempted to adopt the hands-off policy of the synod by maintaining a careful neutrality. In response to a communication received early in 1836 signed by "A Lutheran Abolitionist" in Palatine Bridge, New York, Kurtz noted that taking sides on the "vext question of slavery" can only introduce "contention, controversy and schism" into the Lutheran church.[226] The following year "a number of readers in the North" canceled their subscriptions to the *Observer* because it had neglected to take up the cause of abolition. Kurtz replied that, after "mature and prayerful examination . . . plainly dictated by the dearest interests of our beloved Zion, to say nothing of the peace and prosperity of our country," he vowed to remain conscientiously neutral on questions "not essential and on which we know a conflict to prevail in the Lutheran Church."[227] But just one week later Kurtz had abandoned the attempt at neutrality. He now opted for complete silence. "In the future the question of abolition shall not even be mentioned in our columns in any connection whatever. Once for all then we say to our correspondents, 'Hands off.'"[228]

But the editor found to his chagrin that it was not easy to ignore the flood of letters that continued to pour into his office. Subscribers in the North and West called the *Observer* an advocate of slavery, while those in the South placed it in the abolitionist camp. "Between the two," Kurtz complained, "we might be squeezed to death."[229] The comments on slavery that on occasion continued to be expressed in the editorial columns of the *Observer*, in spite of the editor's vow to remain silent, illuminate further the majority opinion held at the time by members of the General Synod. The paper retained its allegiance to African colonization as the ultimate solution to America's peculiar problem.[230] While its pages never carried any apology for slavery and looked forward to the time when it would cease to exist, still its content was thoroughly unsympathetic to immediate abolitionism and totally opposed to its more radical purposes and methods.[231] The editorials rose to the defense of Southerners' treatment of their slaves.[232] They offered only a very reserved opposition

---

[226]*Lutheran Observer* 3 (11 March 1836): 115.

[227]Ibid. 4 (28 July 1837): 195.

[228]Ibid. 4 (4 August 1837): 199.

[229]Ibid. 12 (20 December 1844): n. p.

[230]Ibid. 18 (8 November 1850): 383.

[231]Fortenbaugh, "Representative Lutheran Periodical Press and Slavery," 153-54.

[232]*Lutheran Observer* 18 (23 August 1850): 338.

to the fugitive slave law[233] but did firmly oppose the extension of slavery to new states and territories.[234]

Lutheran leaders and educators by and large followed the pattern set by the General Synod and the *Lutheran Observer* in their refusal either to defend or to attack slavery. As a result, the largest group of Lutherans in this country, in spite of its strong liberal Pietist constituency, remained mute in regard to the key moral issue of its day. Pressure was exerted from time to time by a persistent minority to break the vow of silence. There is evidence that on two or three occasions, in 1839 and 1857 and again in 1859, "considerable discussion and extensive debate" on the subject of slavery did in fact take place during the official sessions of the synod.[235] It is highly improbable that these were the only instances when the volatile subject ignited on the synod floor. The official minutes, however, never recorded any of these outbursts. The pact of silence was kept, and the conspiracy formally and officially observed by majority action. Thus the General Synod averted outright schism until after the outbreak of civil conflict, but not without serious consequences and a cost that remains difficult to estimate.

One of the casualties was American Lutheran Pietism. Its forces were seriously weakened by the controversy over abolitionism. The large Southern wing of its party was almost totally alienated and slowly but surely turned toward a more conservative position. Northern Pietism was fragmented by its various attitudes toward the General Synod's policy of silence. In the end, only a very few leaders and groups, representing a pristine Pietist theology replete with its inherent ethical activism, held fast to the conviction that abolitionism was a moral and religious issue that the church of Christ could not ignore. This minority refused to accept the adopted policy of closing the eyes and covering the mouth. They insisted that Christians and churches were duty bound to speak out and to act on behalf

---

[233]Ibid. 18 (13 December 1850): 402.

[234]Ibid. 14 (12 February 1847): 97.

[235]Charles Willam Heathcote, *The Lutheran Church and the Civil War* (Burlington IA: Lutheran Literary Board, 1919) 60, reports "considerable discussion and debate" at the 1839 convention and cites the *Franklin Repository*, Chambersburg PA, where the convention was held, as his source. It was stated in the report of the delegate to the General Synod, W. E. Roedel, that "the questions of Slavery and Symbolism were both extensively debated at the late meeting of the Synod" [1859, in Pittsburgh] *Minutes of the Eighteenth Session of the Evangelical Lutheran Synod of Western Virginia and Adjacent Parts*, 18 August 1859, 7, Lutheran Theological Seminary Archives. Also see Wentz, *Basic History of Lutheranism in America*, 164.

of slavery's abolition. In the forefront of this small group of activists were Samuel Schmucker at Gettysburg and the Franckean Synod in upper New York. The next two chapters are devoted to a closer look at how and why Schmucker and the Franckeans resisted the prevailing strategy of silence in regard to the slavery question and the consequences of their actions. We examine each case separately, beginning with Samuel Schmucker.

An Abolitionist Leader

Samuel Schmucker thoroughly understood and empathized with the General Synod's policy of silence on the slavery question. Like the majority of its members, he did not want to see his denominational house divided. Unlike the majority, he was also a champion of inter-Protestant unity. But in addition, he was an inveterate abolitionist. His theology would not permit him to hide or alter in any essential way his deep conviction that slavery was a sin and abolition a necessity. Schmucker had always passionately pursued both ecclesiastical unity and social activism. But at this point in history the two were locked in conflict with regard to abolitionism. The advancement of one effected the curtailment of the other. Schmucker continued throughout his career to be a man deeply torn between his desire to maintain Lutheran unity and his conviction to speak out on an issue of compelling importance to his Christian conscience. The question of priority was never fully resolved, as can be seen from his dogged determination to pursue both aims in spite of their obvious incompatibility.

Schmucker's abolitionism and his ecumenism both arose from the central core of his German Pietist theological heritage. As with the Pietist fathers, Schmucker believed that real conversion to Christ inevitably expressed itself in an unrelenting war against sin in the world and in the self, thus also helping to prepare the way for the millennial reign of justice and peace on earth. Human slavery in its practical denial of fundamental Christian principles was viewed as a particularly obnoxious manifestation of both individual and corporate sin. The abolition of slavery was, in Schmucker's eyes, no mere secular or civil reform. Since slavery was a pernicious sin, holding back the dawn of the millennium, the Christian could not condone or ignore it. At the same time, ecumenical endeavor was seen as the God-directed strategy for building up the forces of the church in order to wage a successful battle against slavery and all other evils that blocked the way to the fuller emergence of God's promised kingdom. Once again for Schmucker it was not a case of either/or but of both/and. From the time he took up his teaching career at Gettysburg, he never ceased to express his opposition to slavery on theological grounds. Neither was he content to confine his abolitionist convictions to the lecture room or the pulpit. Throughout his career he involved himself in practical measures and actions designed to improve the status of an oppressed people and to implement their progress out of slavery to freedom.

An early example was Schmucker's effort to introduce legislation that would ensure industrial training for black children. In March 1839, he presented a memorial to the Pennsylvania House of Representatives that required "children of color" to learn useful trades.[1] Basically, the bill provided that Negro or mulatto females over thirteen and males over fourteen who were not in school, learning a trade, or being properly taught or employed in the home would be bound out, or indentured, while still minors, to "persons of good character . . . to serve as apprentices to some art, trade, calling or service."[2] The bill required that notice be given to parents, guardians, or friends of the minors ten days previous to their indenture and that all laws of the state of Pennsylvania for the protection of apprentices be extended to them also. The memorial passed the first and second readings.[3] Before the final vote, however, it was stigmatized by some of its opponents as an abolitionist measure, which was sufficient to cause its defeat. The next year, Schmucker again introduced the legislation, but a violent quarrel that developed in the legislature over some other matter caused so much turmoil that the bill was forgotten.[4] This particular piece of legislation, while not without patronizing aspects, had undoubted merit and potential value. It provides further evidence that Schmucker's efforts to seek equal justice for blacks was not confined to a condemnation of Southern slaveholders but dealt with the duty of Northerners to put their own house in order. It was not a popular position, but Schmucker pursued it with persistence.

---

[1] S. S. Schmucker, *Memorial of Professor S. S. Schmucker, Relative to Binding Out Minor Colored Children* (Harrisburg PA: McKinley & Lescure Printers, 1842).

[2] Ibid., 5-6.

[3] Ibid., 6-7.

[4] Anstadt, *Life and Times of Samuel Schmucker*, 295.

Schmucker's humanitarian concern never allowed him to acquiesce completely in the accepted Lutheran policy of silence on slavery in synodical affairs. In a keynote sermon that he delivered at the opening session of the General Synod Convention in 1841, he made the point that a church that tolerated human slavery could not be expected to enjoy the favor of God.[5] This particular sermon was published by his abolitionist allies in the Franckean Synod. It is likely that other comments Schmucker may have made in regard to the subject at General Synod meetings, in keeping with synodical practice, were simply not recorded.

In September 1842, at the meeting of the West Pennsylvania district Synod, of which he was a member, Schmucker arose to defend the abolitionist manifesto that had been received as correspondence from the Franckean Synod. It is the only documented testimony of any effort by a nationally known Lutheran leader to support the Franckeans' "Fraternal Appeal." Shortly after the convention had convened, the "Appeal" had been referred to a committee for study. A brief description of its subject matter was presented, and the members assembled were then asked if they wished to hear it in its entirety. At this point Schmucker made a forceful speech in favor of its full reading and discussion. He complimented the Franckean Synod for their vigorous stand against slavery and admonished his colleagues that the New York Synod had far outdistanced them in this regard. He went on to speak at some length regarding his own conviction that the American institution of slavery was sinful. He urged that the Lutheran church renounce any connection with this "outrage on humanity" and take the lead in opposing it. He then "moved that the 'Appeal' be heard, but the vote was lost, and . . . it was thrown aside."[6] Had Schmucker succeeded in his spirited attempt, the West Pennsylvania Synod might have been the only Lutheran district unit to ratify formally the "Fraternal Appeal" and the first, following the Franckeans, to speak out against slavery. The defeat of his motion was a severe personal blow to Schmucker's leadership and one of the first tangible evidences of his fall from favor.

Despite this stinging defeat, Schmucker refused to desist from his determination to prod his fellow Lutherans into some sort of antislavery action. Just three years later he was prepared for yet another attempt. Schmucker carefully revised a lecture that he had first delivered to his students at the seminary in March 1840, outlining his views on slavery and

---

[5]*Lutheran Herald* 4 (1 July 1842): 82.

[6]Rev. John Rosenberg to Rev. Philip Wieting, 19 October 1842, Franckean Papers.

abolition. He fully intended to present this document at the meeting of the district body in the fall of 1845. In addition to other minor revisions, he added to his original lecture two propositions outlining practical considerations for the implementation of emancipation. They dealt with the compensation of slaveholders and the teaching of trades to freed slaves.

Anticipating its adoption by the West Pennsylvania Synod, he also added a preamble, in which he forcefully stated why he felt it to be the duty and obligation of this church body to speak out against slavery. The preamble asserted that "it is the duty of disciples of the Savior to bear witness to the truth . . . to admonish their erring brethren, . . . and to care not only for themselves but also for the things of others." He went on to declare that the synod should issue this declaration because "the continuance of American Slavery imposes on us obligations which we have hitherto but imperfectly discharged." The resolution concluded with the hope that "the expression of our views may have some influence in favor of truth, humanity, and mercy."[7] Schmucker's resolution would have been the only attempt, outside that of the Franckean Synod, to introduce the subject of abolition at a district synodical level. Had it been adopted there, it would undoubtedly have been sent on to the General Synod, which would have been the most effective way to get the matter before the general body. If an individual had brought it there directly, it would have almost certainly been tabled or recommended by a committee for rejection. But if it had come by way of a member synodical body, it would have been difficult to ignore.

In 1845, it appears that Schmucker was ready to make the hard choice of placing the issue of slavery ahead of ecclesiastical unity. But the resolution never got presented. Sickness prevented Schmucker from attending the 1845 convention.[8] One cannot help but wonder whether this illness, probably an attack of erysipelas like that which later kept him from being present at his father's funeral, was brought on by the emotional tension generated by his desire to deal in a decisive manner with this controversial subject.[9] At any rate, there is no evidence that what Schmucker had in-

---

[7]S. S. Schmucker, "Of Slavery," 1840 version.

[8]Wentz, *Pioneer in Christian Unity*, 322.

[9]Sometimes called St. Anthony's Fire, erysipelas is a severe infection in which the skin becomes extremely swollen and inflamed. It is accompanied by chills, high fever, nausea, and vomiting. See Benjamin F. Miller, M.D., *The Complete Medical Guide*, 4th ed. (New York: Simon & Schuster, 1978). While the specific disease is apparently caused by a bacterial infection, its symptoms are all susceptible of psychosomatic origin.

tended to do in 1845 was ever pursued at a later date. Apparently he either decided that the matter was doomed to defeat or he reevaluated his decision in terms of the damage it might inflict on the peace and concord of the church. There is no question that Schmucker's thoughts were occupied at this very time with ecumenical endeavors. His efforts to effect the consummation of a Protestant union came to a climax in August 1846, when he took an active part in the organizational meeting of the World Evangelical Alliance in London.

During this convention, the British, as anticipated, introduced an amendment that excluded all slaveholders from membership in the alliance. It specifically defined them as "all individuals . . . in the unhappy position of holding their fellowmen as slaves. . . whether by their own fault or otherwise."[10] This latter phrase had the effect of technically excluding Schmucker himself, since, as we noted, he still retained at least one "servant" who had refused his offer of manumission. It was also in disagreement with the distinction that Schmucker made between voluntary and involuntary slaveholding.[11] The British amendment touched off a debate that lasted for five days and seriously threatened the Christian fellowship and spirit of goodwill that had prevailed up until that point in the meeting.[12] Not all of the American delegates to the convention opposed the British amendment, but Schmucker and thirty-three other Americans met and drew up a lengthy protest.[13] This statement, while making it clear that the Americans were definitely opposed to slavery as such, lodged vigorous objections to the proposal that made slaveholding an obstacle to membership in the alliance.[14] Three primary arguments were raised against the proposed amendment. The first contended that it was irrelevant and unnecessary, since slavery had nothing to do with the proper object of the the alliance, which was religious and not political. The other objections dealt with the fact that it singled out American slaveholders and that it was divisive in its effects.[15]

---

[10]Document among S. S. Schmucker Papers, quoted in Anstadt, *Life and Times of Samuel Schmucker*, 304.

[11]S. S. Schmucker, "Of Slavery," 1840 version, 4-5.

[12]Wentz, *Pioneer in Christian Unity*, 290.

[13]Anstadt, *Life and Times of Samuel Schmucker*, 303.

[14]Wentz, *Pioneer in Christian Unity*, 291.

[15]Document among S. S. Schmucker Papers, quoted by Anstadt, *Life and Times of Samuel Schmucker*, 304-306.

This statement is of particular interest, since Schmucker may have been its chief author and at the very least a willing subscriber. Most of the ideas expressed differed only in degree from those that he had set down in his lecture of 1840. But for the first and only time in his life, Samuel Schmucker attached his name to an affirmation he at other times resolutely opposed, one that designated the issue of slavery as wholly political and without religious significance. This action, more than any other event in his life, indicated just how far Schmucker was willing to go when the practical survival and expansion of Christian unity came into direct conflict with the controversial claims of abolitionism. Yet, this willingness to moderate immediate abolitionist goals was always based on the hope that a closer communion among Christian churches would hasten rather than delay the demise of human slavery. Furthermore, the statement that Schmucker signed at the meeting of the World Evangelical Alliance appears to be an aberrant act, the implications of which he almost immediately repudiated.

In November 1846, only two months after his return from London, Schmucker preached at Gettysburg on a special day of humiliation, thanksgiving, and prayer, designated by the governor of Pennsylvania. His sermon bore the significant title and was published as *The Christian Pulpit, the Rightful Guardian of Morals, in Political No Less than in Private Life.*[16] In clear and unambiguous language, Schmucker rejected the maxim to which he had recently (and uncharacteristically) given consent. He now reiterated his belief that political issues of clear moral import, such as abolitionism, could not be separated from the sphere of religion, the church, and the Christian pulpit. He expressed his conviction that the prophetic role of the pulpit was to proclaim God's righteous rule over the political realm. While Schmucker looked upon the United States as a land "chosen by God for the perfect development of the social compact,"[17] he was quick to condemn the "false patriotism" expressed in the motto "my country right or wrong," which he felt ought to be regarded with "contempt and abhorrence."[18] He maintained that, as soon as earthly rulers command what God prohibits, "they lose their claim to obedience and it becomes our duty to disregard their enactments."[19] While noting that nations are obviously less Christian than the individuals who compose them, Schmucker did not believe it would be the case if "the pulpit would . . . fearlessly speak out and

---

[16]S. S. Schmucker, *Christian Pulpit.*

[17]S. S. Schmucker, *Elements of a Popular Theology*, 359.

[18]S. S. Schmucker, *Christian Pulpit*, 10.

[19]Ibid., 15.

proclaim alike to rulers and private citizens the political duties enjoined in God's Word."[20]

Since the Scriptures clearly taught that God was the ruler over all nations and that the divine claims had precedence over those of Caesar,[21] it followed that there was an obligation to conform all human legislation to the ethical principles of God's Word.[22] Schmucker always remained convinced that "Christian love should be recognized by civil as well as religious rulers."[23] But in this connection he made a very careful distinction in his sermon between "party politics," which had no direct ethical implications and no place in the pulpit, and the "morals of politics . . . which are taught in Scripture and cannot rightfully be excluded from the sacred desk."[24]

These views constituted a frontal attack upon the theological premise by which conservative Lutherans defended the policy of silence in regard to abolitionism. Resistance to all moral crusades, and in particular those that were politically oriented, had always been endemic to orthodox Lutheran ethical theology. The party of strict confessionalism in nineteenth-century North America continued to follow the pattern initially introduced by Martin Luther's extreme pessimism in regard to history and formulated in the two-kingdom doctrines. Careful qualitative distinctions were made between the temporal and eternal dimensions of reality, between any realization of God's kingdom in history and in eternity. All efforts to improve external human conditions in the historical realm came under the jurisdiction of natural law and reason. It was asserted that political affairs were primarily the responsibility of civil laws and legislation, about which the Christian had no particular expertise or knowledge. Furthermore, politics by definition had little to do with the Christian life per se, since Christ's kingdom was considered not "of this world." The entire doctrinal position was epitomized in a slogan, popular in conservative circles, which declared that the church and its clergy were called to preach the gospel and stay out of politics.

---

[20]Ibid., 27.

[21]Ibid., 14, 25.

[22]Ibid., 27.

[23]S. S. Schmucker, "Address Delivered at the laying of the Cornerstone of the Shamokin Collegiate Institute," 2 August 1854, *Pohlman Collection*, vol. 433, no. 20, New York State Library, Manuscripts and Special Collections.

[24]S. S. Schmucker, *Christian Pulpit*, 28.

All of these assertions found expression in an article published by the *Evangelical Review* in January 1863, entitled "Christianity and Politics." Translated from the German of Dr. Gottlieb Harless by the Reverend G. A. Wenzel of Philadelphia, the essay contended that civil affairs are best left to human reason and decided on the basis of what is expedient, since Christian faith in no way equips its possessors to make sound political judgments. In addition, it maintained that a practical problem arises when political positions are identified with Christianity, since all who disagree are "at once unchristianized."[25] The essential bifurcation between the political and the religious is clearly defined and represents the article's primary theological assertion. "It is one thing to possess those natural gifts which God endows . . . and another to be endowed with the Holy Spirit as it fits and prepares for the kingdom of Christ . . . and eternal life. . . . The things which are to serve temporal and eternal ends spring from entirely different roots."[26] Such views were antithetical to the theological tenets of Schmucker. The ethical analysis of Pietism was diametrically opposed to this conservative diagnosis.

Two of Schmucker's close Pietist colleagues defended his position in articles also printed in the *Evangelical Review*. The Reverend Henry Ziegler, a professor at the Missionary Institute at Selinsgrove, Pennsylvania, published an essay entitled "Politics and the Pulpit." In it he asserted that, since God himself had connected politics and religion, humankind had no right to pull them apart. In a phrase reminiscent of that utilized in Schmucker's earlier sermon, he insisted that "God requires his ministers to proclaim his whole truth as faithfully when it relates to politics as to any other subject."[27] He met head-on the conservative argument based on the American concept of the separation of church and state. "When ministers of Christ yield to the clamor 'Don't meddle with politics' and thus fail to test our politics by the principles of the gospel . . . is not *this* union of Church and State? . . . not indeed [a] . . . formal union, but . . . a practical union? and therefore, so much the more dangerous because not perceived." He concludes, "Let the ministers of Christ be assured that they may as fully test political principles and conduct, as they discuss abstract doctrines."[28]

---

[25]Dr. Harless, translated by G. A. Wenzel, "Christianity and Politics," *Evangelical Review* 14 (January 1863): 245, 251.

[26]Ibid., 257-58.

[27]Henry Ziegler, "Politics and the Pulpit," *Evangelical Review* 14 (April 1865): 248, 251.

[28]Ibid., 257.

In another article, F. W. Conrad referred to ministers of the Gospel as the moral watchmen of the nation. He defined politics as a branch of ethics that dealt directly with moral distinctions. He scoffed at those who claimed the clergy had no right to preach politics and asked, "Who ever heard that the duty of communicating moral truths . . . did not belong . . . to the ministers of religion?" Conrad listed temperance, lotteries, and Sabbath observance as political issues of a moral and religious character. He then turned to the subject of abolitionism and raised questions in regard to it. "Was it the duty of the American pulpit . . . to keep silence? . . . The laity have a right to ask their ministers, 'Has slavery the sanction of God?' . . . And woe unto the watchmen of America, if, at such a time they prove dumb dogs, that will not bark. . . . And woe unto the people who love to have it so."[29]

This insistence upon the intimate and inseparable connection between religion and politics, particularly in the area of ethical and moral reform, was an intrinsic ingredient of American Lutheran Pietism. For thirty-five years, Samuel Schmucker continued to stress this truth to the seminary students at Gettysburg, while the church they went out to serve kept its silent vigil on slavery. In an 1859 baccalaureate address, as the national crisis over the "peculiar question" grew even more intense, it was undoubtedly Schmucker who implored the graduating class (among whom was his son Beale) "not merely [to] stand up against evil" but to "wield [their] tongues in the defense of whatever is good—in politics, in ethics, in religion, and in the whole range of truth."[30] From a theological perspective Schmucker never wavered from proclaiming the prophetic responsibility of the church and its leaders to speak and act forthrightly on political matters of a moral nature. When on occasion this position was moderated, it was done as a practical strategy, usually intended to preserve unity, and not on the basis of principle.

Schmucker's willingness over the years to speak out publicly and to act openly on behalf of his antislavery convictions is beyond challenge. But these pronouncements and actions were often extremely unpopular, both in the church and in the community, where he held positions of leadership. Many of the benevolent societies to which Schmucker belonged faced the problem of how to address the slavery issue and still retain their Southern constituents.

---

[29]F. W. Conrad, "Ministers of the Gospel, the Moral Watchmen of the Nations," *Evangelical Review* 16 (July 1865): 378, 382-83.

[30]"Gettysburg Seminary Baccalaureate Address," *Evangelical Review* 11 (October 1859): 287.

These groups were entirely voluntary, composed not of denominations but of interested individuals from among all the Protestant churches. Among Schmucker's papers are letters from the officers of a number of these groups, which reflect the tension of the times in regard to abolitionism and suggest various ways of dealing with it. The American Tract Society, which was always close to Schmucker's heart, had, for a number of years, published pamphlets by authors such as Wilberforce, who were radically opposed to slavery.[31] As time went on, however, the group faced severe criticism on this matter from within its own membership and for several years excluded all mention of slavery in its publications. In the early fifties, unsuccessful efforts were made to get this policy reversed. In 1856, Schmucker was appointed to a committee charged with the task of investigating the problem. The committee unanimously recommended that the society had "every right and duty to publish against the evils of slavery."[32]

Another controversial issue upon which Schmucker took a decided and unpopular stand was in regard to the so-called fugitive slave laws. As a part of the famous Compromise of 1850, these statutes had been made more stringent, and the penalties against those who in any way aided or abetted runaway slaves greatly increased. Schmucker openly counseled resistance to these laws and did not hesitate to help runaways. In later years, his youngest son, Samuel D., recalled how his father had given refuge to fugitive slaves. "Father would allow any such to sleep in his barn by day, and I am sure, assisted them, at least to the extent of supplying them with food."[33]

In this connection one must recall that Gettysburg was in close proximity to adjoining slave states and that to speak out publicly against these laws or, even more important, to violate them in practice was not only unpopular but dangerous. During his stay at the seminary in Gettysburg, Daniel Payne had observed that one professor at a nearby Methodist college was an "outspoken friend of freedom" and that he had "imperiled his life in assisting the rescue of a fugitive slave."[34] We can be sure there were not many "friends of freedom" in southern Pennsylvania, and yet Schmucker was among these few. His determination to resist what he believed to be an unjust law was based on a carefully considered rationale. After the Dred

---

[31]William A. Hallock of the American Tract Society to S. S. Schmucker, 29 June 1842, Schmucker Papers.

[32]Smith, *Revivalism and Social Reform*, 193.

[33]Anstadt, *Life and Times of Samuel Schmucker*, 293.

[34]Payne, *Recollections of Seventy Years*, 62.

Scott decision of 1857 deprived runaway slaves of all legal recourse, denying them status as a human being before the law, Schmucker's youngest son asked him what he would do if a fugitive slave were to approach him personally for aid. He replied that he would "never assist in returning a fellow [human] being into bondage, and would succor any such that were in distress, and that if he was prosecuted for it, he would admit the fact, and pay the penalty for which the law might make him liable."[35]

In a sermon entitled "Pray for the Peace of Jerusalem," Schmucker told his parishioners that they must act as well as pray. He called on them to influence their representatives in Congress to amend the present statutes so that Northern citizens would not be required to assist in the attempts by Southerners to arrest fugitive slaves. He advised them that they were duty bound to disobey any civil ordinance that directed them to do anything sinful, such as to teach or perpetuate slavery or aid in its extension.[36] Here, as always, Schmucker articulated a theology that perceived political reforms as having a moral nature, as essentially religious in character, and therefore of primary concern to the Christian life and to the Christian church. Along with a few of his close Pietist colleagues and former students such as F. W. Conrad, R. Weiser, Henry Ziegler, Benjamin Kurtz, and Samuel Sprecher, he gave leadership to the theological assertion that God's salvation encompassed society as well as the individual. This theology of ethical activism, culminating in the affirmation of a legislated abolition of slavery, constituted a major practical distinction and source of conflict between the orthodoxy of the Old Lutherans and the Pietism of the American Lutherans.

As we have noted, there were exceptions to this general rule. A few conservative leaders—William A. Passavant in particular—did actively pursue moral reforms. Passavant not only was a lifelong opponent of slavery but believed that the issue ought to have been freely discussed in the religious press. "If the church will not speak," he prophesied, "slavery will."[37] But even Passavant, who was by far the most activist leader within the conservative wing of Lutheranism, tended to confine his social concern to the role of the Good Samaritan, providing institutional care for the needs of the individual.

In contrast, Schmucker and his American Lutheran Pietist colleagues were not satisfied to circumscribe their ethical concern in this way. They

---

[35]Anstadt, *Life and Times of Samuel Schmucker,* 293.

[36]S. S. Schmucker, Sermon manuscript no. 83, Gettysburg College Archives.

[37]William A. Passavant, "Free Speech," *Missionary* 2 (10 December 1857): 182.

looked beyond the suffering and oppressed individual to the political and economic causes from which injustice arose. This willingness to carry concern for human welfare into the realm of political involvement was either slighted or rejected on theological grounds by conservatives.[38] The ensuing conflict over the validity of the church's involvement with politics generated severe hostility between Lutherans with regard to the matter of abolition. Although the nature of the issue ruled out an open debate, the covert controversy over the scope of the church's activist role was nevertheless intense and fraught with emotion. It added fuel to the fires of a confessional conflict that climaxed at the exact time the discord over abolitionism reached its apex.

We consider directly now a key question in the history of American Lutheranism: was the eventual outcome of what Vergilius Ferm has called "the crisis in American Lutheran theology" affected in some degree by Samuel Schmucker's activist ethical theology?[39] Did his abolitionism contribute to his personal loss of leadership and consequently to the demise of American Lutheran Pietism that he represented and headed? If so, to what extent?

---

[38]The experiences of J. H. W. Stuckenberg (1835–1903) illustrate the continuing conservative rejection of this aspect of liberal Pietist theology following the Civil War. Stuckenberg was a student of S. S. Schmucker's Pietist colleague and brother-in-law Samuel Sprecher at Wittenberg University and has been called "a prophet of social Christianity." He wrote several books on Christian sociology. He called on Lutherans to apply their evangelical theology to the solution of social and political problems. His fame as a scholar and his insights were ignored by a Lutheran church that was then (in the 1880s and 1890s) almost completely under conservative control. Stuckenberg had no delusions about the reasons for his rejection and wrote near the close of his life, "My isolation is due to my specialty, [the promotion of] the Christian social movement according to the teachings of the New Testament. Other denominations heartily welcome me. . . . But my own Church is closed to me because I am not doing its work." John O. Evjen, *The Life of J. H. W. Stuckenberg: Theologian, Philosopher, Sociologist* (Minneapolis: Lutheran Free Church Publishing, 1938). See the following sources for material on Stuckenberg: Wentz, *Basic History of Lutheranism in America*, 329; J. H. W. Stuckenberg, *History of the Augsburg Confession* (Philadelphia: Lutheran Publication Society, 1897); Eldon J. Underdahl, "The Social Thought of J. H. W. Stuckenberg, a Late Nineteenth Century Social Scientist" (Master's thesis, Lutheran Theological Seminary, Minneapolis, 1969) 25; J. H. W. Stuckenberg, *Christian Sociology* (London: R. D. Dickinson, 1880).

[39]Ferm, *Crisis in American Lutheran Theology.*

Few would argue that these questions are without importance. But they have scarcely, if ever, been raised. On the surface, the evidence appears to be overwhelming that the only issues of any real significance in the intra-Lutheran struggle for supremacy was that of confessional allegiance. According to this accepted analysis, Samuel Schmucker and his die-hard colleagues went down to defeat because they refused to accommodate themselves to the rising tide of confessional renewal and denominational loyalty that engulfed antebellum American Lutheranism. This basic hypothesis is in large part unassailable. Countless reams of paper were devoted to the argument over the degree of assent to the Augsburg Confession and to the Book of Concord required in order to be considered a "true" Lutheran. Hundreds of articles on the subject filled the pages of Lutheran journals, and dozens of books were devoted to the same topic. Nevertheless, when one looks closely at the context of the conflict that took place, the question arises whether the degree of doctrinal difference that separated the two sides in this dispute warranted the intensity and volume of the rhetoric. Did the vitriolic tones of the debate, the charges of heresy, and the hurling of anathemas correspond to the actual width of the confessional chasm that separated the warring parties?

THE CONFESSIONAL CONFLICT REEXAMINED

Neither German Lutheran Pietism nor its early American Lutheran expression was ever anticonfessional. Even in the first decades of the nineteenth century, when a number of synodical groups dropped any reference to the symbolic books from their constitutions, the importance of these writings was still taken for granted. It was Samuel Schmucker who, in the early 1820s, called for the renewal of a more explicit confessional allegiance as a way to ward off increasingly rationalistic interpretations of Christianity. He called on the Lutheran church to require from its ministers and teachers a pledge of conditional acceptance in regard to the Augsburg Confession. The formula he devised was utilized for nearly forty years by General Synod churches at the ordination of their clergy. It stated that "the fundamental doctrines of the Word of God are taught in a manner substantially correct in the doctrinal articles of the Augsburg Confession."[40] For two decades Schmucker's "moderate confessionalism" was well accepted. By 1840, however, it was being challenged as ambiguous and insufficient. Only a little more than ten years later, it was labeled as heretical to historical Lutheranism. How can this swift and precipitous shift be explained?

---

[40]S. S. Schmucker, "Formula for the Government and Discipline," 448.

Did Schmucker's own confessional formulation change, becoming more lax and liberal over the years? Many of his former colleagues, including members of his own family, accused him of having deserted his "conservative Lutheran stand."[41] Schmucker himself was convinced that his basic views remained constant from the time he began his teaching career until its end. Apparently anticipating some of the charges that would later be brought against him, he included a statement to this effect in his official letter of resignation submitted to the Gettysburg Seminary Board of Directors on 9 August 1864. "The textbook, my *Popular Theology* [first published in 1834] has been retained to this day as the basis of my instructions without the change of a single doctrine; and I record . . . that I this day, cordially believe every doctrine taught in the entire volume. These facts I state in justice to the institution and myself, and in view of the future history of the institution and the Church."[42]

A survey of Schmucker's writings testifies to the accuracy of this assertion, as Abdel Wentz's careful research has definitively confirmed.[43] It was not Schmucker but the overall confessional climate of American Lutheranism that swerved so swiftly to the right during the antebellum years. It became progressively more conservative in character. Under the self-designated title *Old Lutherans*, its adherents took up again much of the strict confessionalism of orthodoxy, against which Spener and Francke had reacted in seventeenth- and eighteenth-century Germany. The causes of this shift are numerous, complicated, and to some extent still unknown. A stronger confessionalism had developed in Germany as a reaction to the proclamation of union between Lutheran and Reformed churches by the king of Prussia in 1817.[44] The surge of German emigrants from mainly conservative areas in the 1840s and 1850s is the most obvious factor in the changing climate. This influx in turn resulted in a flurry of essays and books in defense of Lutheran orthodoxy, which soon became available to Lutheran clergy in the United States.

But it was clearly not the flood of German immigration or literature alone that was responsible for the shift away from Pietism to the old orthodoxy, or from a moderate to a strict confessionalism. The tide had al-

---

[41]L. Schmucker, *Schmucker Family*, 27.

[42]S. S. Schmucker, "Letter of Resignation," Schmucker Papers, 3164.0809 handwritten.

[43]Wentz, *Pioneer of Christian Unity*, chap. 4, pp. 230-42.

[44]Conrad Bergendoff, *The Church of the Lutheran Reformation* (St. Louis: Concordia Publishing House, 1967) 206.

ready begun to turn in that direction before the German influence had much significance. Already in the latter part of the 1830s, at the very time the issue of abolitionism was at its explosive height, there was a sharpening of denominational consciousness and of the sectarian spirit within nearly all groups of Christians in North America.[45] Lutherans were no exception. This drive to find a unique sense of identity, to be different from the others, led to an increasingly rigid attachment to the Augsburg Confession and the other symbolic writings. The spirit of the times during the turbulent pre-war years encouraged a combative and assertive particularism in religious circles. The national mood was far more conducive to the religious conservatism that sought to intensify individual denominational identity than to the more liberal tendency that pursued Christian union through common assent to fundamental principles.

In keeping with the ecumenical traditions of Pietism, Schmucker's concept of confessional allegiance had been formulated in broad, general terms, in the hope of finding a doctrinal consensus among not only Lutherans but all Protestant denominations. For this reason he limited the teachings of the Augsburg Confession to the *fundamental* doctrines of the Scriptures, and further qualified it as being *substantially* correct. This method of seeking an extensive area of common agreement, while still eliminating rank heresy, had been utilized by ecumenists ever since George Calixtus in the seventeenth century attempted to confine the Christian doctrinal consensus to the articles of the Apostles Creed.[46] It was a plan with great practical utility, but one that carried with it a problem difficult to solve—namely, how does one decide, on points of specific disagreement, which doctrines are of *fundamental* importance, and which are not? This uncertainty was the Achilles' heel of Schmucker's confessional approach and was the exact point at which the conservatives directed their heaviest attack.

Schmucker himself had defined a fundamental doctrine as one "regarded by the great body of evangelical Christians as essential to salvation, so that he who rejects it, cannot be saved, neither regarded as a believer."[47] The obvious flaw in this approach was that it presupposed a general agreement on the question as to precisely which doctrines are of *fundamental* importance. Even among the Lutherans associated with the General Synod, this unity proved to be illusory. Schmucker, in the tradition of Melanchthon and Spener, was convinced that the intricate theological distinctions

---

[45]Wentz, *Basic History of Lutheranism in America,* 135.

[46]Wentz, *Pioneer in Christian Unity,* 159.

[47]S. S. Schmucker, *American Lutheranism Vindicated,* 4.

regarding the mode of Christ's presence in the Eucharist were not of fundamental importance. But the majority of Lutherans in America eventually arrived at a different conclusion. To growing numbers of strict confessionalists, the doctrine of the True Presence was decidedly essential. There were other disagreements between Pietist and Old Lutherans over what was fundamental, but the eucharistic controversy was far and away the dominant one. For the orthodox party the teaching on the True Presence increasingly became the single sure source of Lutheran identity. It alone appeared capable of maintaining separation from all other Protestant groups and the sense of uniqueness that conservative Lutherans felt to be imperative. Following the Civil War, the newly emerged conservative leader and former student of Schmucker, Charles Porterfield Krauth, provided a comprehensive and scholarly presentation of eucharistic theology. In his book *The Conservative Reformation*, Krauth called this doctrine "the most fundamental of all fundamentals."[48]

During the last decades of the antebellum period, the opposition to Schmucker expressed itself through increasing pressure to define in detail his position in regard to the Augsburg Confession. It was no longer sufficient to maintain that it contained, in a manner substantially correct, the fundamental doctrines of God's Word. The Old Lutherans demanded to know what "substantially correct" meant in concrete terms and which items in the confession were considered as nonfundamental. In plain words, the question put to Schmucker was, If the Augsburg Confession is not in full agreement with Scripture at every point, then at what precise points and to what extent, is it in disagreement? Schmucker had addressed this question before, but always in a diffuse manner. Now the call to clarify the doctrinal position of American Lutheran Pietism in a concise summary statement gained momentum. Attempts to do so were made by the Maryland Synod in 1844 and by the General Synod itself in 1845. The fact that both of these formulations failed to be adopted was a clear signal of growing conservative strength.[49]

A further indication of this development was evidenced in the establishment of two new Lutheran journals geared toward the presentation of conservative views. In 1848, the *Missionary* began its existence under the direction of William Passavant, and in 1849, the *Evangelical Review* was first published at Gettysburg. In the beginning the *Review* was edited by Wil-

---

[48]Charles Porterfield Krauth, *The Conservative Reformation and Its Theology* (1871; reprint, Minneapolis: Augsburg Publishing House, 1963) 655.

[49]Wentz, *Pioneer in Christian Unity*, 204.

liam M. Reynolds, an antagonist of Schmucker who later moved to Capital University in Columbus, Ohio. The following year Reynolds was joined by Charles Philip Krauth, father of Charles Porterfield and Schmucker's colleague at the seminary, who had moved to a more rigid confessionalism than he had previously held. In the opening editorial statement Reynolds vowed that the new journal would be open to all points of view and not hostile toward any other denomination, even though it would be "Lutheran in the broadest and strictest sense of the term."[50] It very quickly became apparent, however, that the *Evangelical Review* would promote primarily the strict confessional position of conservative Lutherans. The very next issue contained a lengthy article by Krauth entitled "The Relation of Our Confessions to the Reformation and the Importance of Their Study, with an Outline of the Early History of the Augsburg Confession."[51] The article was indicative of what was to follow.

One of Schmucker's brothers-in-law, Charles F. Schaeffer, contributed numerous articles to the *Review* on the importance of the confessions. He soon revealed himself as Schmucker's most abrasive foe. Schaeffer was expressing gratification in the *Review*'s first year that it was an "appropriate channel" through which the real facts regarding the confessions could be made known to its English readers.[52]

In the opening sermon at the 1850 Convention of the General Synod, Charles Philip Krauth issued a pointed and portentous plea for the doctrinal position of the synod in regard to the Augsburg Confession to be made more firm.[53] He noted that to receive the confession as *substantially* correct meant that not all of its doctrines were in accord with the Word of God. "But which are these?" he asked. "As it stands it could be related to all. They must be specific."[54] During that same convention a committee was appointed, with Schmucker as chairman, to frame "a clear and concise view of the doctrines and practices of the American Lutheran Church." The

---

[50]"Introductory: The Objects and Position of the *Evangelical Review*," "*Evangelical Review* 1 (July 1849): 16-18.

[51]Charles Philip Krauth, "The Relation of Our Confessions to the Reformation and the Importance of Their Study, with an Outline of the Early History of the Augsburg Confession," *Evangelical Review* 1 (October 1849): 234-63.

[52]Charles F. Schaeffer, "Symbolic Theology," *Evangelical Review* 1 (April 1850): 458.

[53]Wentz, *Pioneer in Christian Unity*, 205-206.

[54]Charles Philip Krauth "The Lutheran Church in the United States," *Evangelical Review* 2 (July 1850): 12.

committee report, which accurately reflected the views of Schmucker and his American Lutheran party, was decisively rejected.[55] Schmucker was quick to realize both the significance of Krauth's penetrating questions and the decreasing popularity of his own position. He swiftly penned a direct and carefully constructed answer to Krauth's challenge, entitled "Church Development on Apostolic Principles." He dealt first with the question of what constitutes fundamental doctrines. He asserted that the basic principle of Protestantism lay in the conviction that the Word of God was a sufficient rule of faith and practice. He reiterated his conviction that the essential doctrines contained in that Word are "agreed upon" by all major denominations. He believed them to be those adopted by the Evangelical Alliance in 1846. Among the nine basic doctrines that he listed, he designated the one concerning Christ's person and work as the "corner-stone" by which all others are to be tested.[56]

Next Schmucker turned to the question of how to interpret the phrase *substantially correct* with regard to the Augsburg Confession. He admitted the validity of Krauth's assertion that there was a need to make the subscription to this creed more specific. He then suggested two possibilities: (1) to give normative authority to the whole Augsburg Confession, allowing "those who can conscientiously do so" to subscribe to it "unconditionally," while others could specify "any points to which they could not assent," as long as they were not "essential" ones; or (2) to "enumerate the doctrines . . . which we regard as fundamental," as he had just done and as the Maryland Synod had attempted to do, and to make the "confession absolutely binding on all these enumerated points." Schmucker considered the second suggestion "clear, definite and positive" and by far the best procedure to follow. He concluded his article with a strong plea for tolerance and for a willingness to compromise on minor points in order to maintain unity on essentials. He begged his fellow Lutherans "not to turn their weapons against one another" or to "interpose Luther between ourselves and Christ or his Word." Finally, he issued a warning against the prevailing mood of the church. "The disposition to magnify . . . points of difference, though it may confirm the work of sectarianism . . ., glorify a particular denomination, and minister to sectarian pride, is . . . hostile to the unity of the

---

[55]A. R. Wentz, "The Work of Samuel Simon Schmucker," *Lutheran Quarterly* 57 (January 1927): 85.

[56]S. S. Schmucker, "Church Development on Apostolic Principles," *Evangelical Review* 2 (October 1850): 156-57.

spirit and the bond of peace . . . and cannot fail to be displeasing to our common Lord and Savior."[57]

Some of the more moderate conservatives, like Charles Philip Krauth, were still willing to listen to Schmucker, but for the most part his proposals for compromise and pleas for unity fell on deaf ears. Already the attacks on Schmucker were assuming a personal and abusive nature. One writer caustically implied that he was driven by an "ambition to become distinguished."[58] Another stated with heavy sarcasm that he had substituted the S.S.S. (Samuel Simon Schmucker) as the "only rule of faith" in place of the A.C. (Augsburg Confession).[59] The backlash against Schmucker's compromise proposals reached its ultimate fury in an article by his inveterate family foe, Charles F. Schaeffer, which appeared in the July 1851 issue of the *Evangelical Review*. He labeled Schmucker's call for an agreement on fundamentals an impossible dream. Schaeffer carried his opposition to the extreme. He claimed that "every doctrine taught in the Scripture was a fundamental doctrine" and also that all the articles of all of the confessional books (not just the Augsburg Confession but the entire Book of Concord) were fundamental.[60] Here was expressed the doctrinal ultraconservatism toward which Lutheran orthodoxy naturally gravitated. The position left no room whatever for compromise with Schmucker's more moderate confessionalism. In 1853, Schaeffer brought a resolution to the convention of the Pennsylvania Ministerium containing the essence of this extreme conservatism. It called for the synod to make full allegiance to all the confessional books a binding rule for its clergy and member churches. During this same convention the ministerium voted to rejoin the General Synod, after a separation of thirty years. Up until the middle of the century the constitution of the Pennsylvanians had made no mention of the Augsburg Confession. By 1853, they were moving rapidly into the conservative camp. But they were not yet ready to accept all of Schaeffer's proposals. His report failed to pass and was replaced by a somewhat less rigid stance that centered confessional allegiance in the Augsburg Confession.[61]

---

[57]Ibid., 179-81.

[58]"Church Feeling in the Lutheran Church," editorial signed "Y.S.R.," *Evangelical Review* 2 (January 1851): 401.

[59]J. N. Hoffman, "The Symbols," *Evangelical Review* 2 (January 1851): 406.

[60]Charles F. Schaeffer, "The Nature of the Fundamental Articles," *Evangelical Review* 3 (July 1851): 65, 75, 86.

[61]"The Confession of the Evangelical Lutheran Church," *Evangelical Review* 5 (October 1853): 189-213.

The Pennsylvania Ministerium was not only the oldest but by far the largest of all the district groups. In 1853, it constituted about one-third of all the clergy and nearly one-half of the membership of the entire General Synod. Its return into the ranks of the General Synod ensured that the conservative opposition to Schmucker's continued leadership would intensify. For a number of years the ministerium had contemplated the organization of a new seminary in opposition to the one Schmucker headed on behalf of the General Synod at Gettysburg. This project proved not to be feasible at the time. However, soon after rejoining the General Synod, the ministerium began efforts to place a "German" professor at Gettysburg. The man they finally appointed was none other than Schmucker's determined conservative foe, Charles F. Schaeffer.[62] Obviously feeling the pressure of the mounting antagonism and the moves to subvert his leadership, Schmucker once again attempted a positive defense of his position.

In the spring of 1855, Schmucker published his *Lutheran Manual on Scriptural Principles.*[63] This book contained 200 pages of comment on the articles of the Augsburg Confession, defending the basic positions he had taken all along. The work was irenic in spirit and obviously another effort to appease the growing severity of his critics. He once again expressed a substantial agreement with the Augsburg Confession, limited only by a primary allegiance to Scripture. He defended this thesis with copious references to the history of Lutheranism and its most illustrious leaders.

The treatise expressed nothing new, yet it was met with a greatly increased barrage of adverse and even violent criticism. Schmucker had for a long time attempted to reconcile himself to the burgeoning opposition. A few years earlier, in a letter to his son Beale, he commented on how Spener had been bitterly opposed, although he "adhered to all features of true Lutheranism, because he preferred the Bible to the Symbolic Books."[64] But now many of Schmucker's critics went as far as to cast aspersions on his personal ability and integrity. An editorial in the *Evangelical Review* called Schmucker's *Manual* "ridiculous [and] utterly inexcusable." It deplored its

---

[62]F. A. Muhlenberg, "Educational Efforts of the Pennsylvania Synod," *Evangelical Review* 10 (April 1859): 530-63.

[63]S. S. Schmucker, *Lutheran Manual on Scriptural Principles, or, The Augsburg Confession Illustrated and Sustained, Chiefly by Scripture Proofs and Extracts from Standard Lutheran Theologians of Europe and America: Together with the Formula of Government and Discipline, Adopted by the General Synod of the Evangelical Lutheran Church in the United States* (Philadelphia: Lindsay & Blakiston, 1855).

[64]S. S. Schmucker to his son Beale, 17 March 1850, Schmucker Papers.

"gratuitous assertions . . . [and] amazing misconception or misrepresentation."[65] Schmucker's biographer, A. R. Wentz, was hard pressed to understand the reason for the vitriolic language and bitter invective directed toward him at this time. It seemed to Wentz that it was borrowed "from the political controversy which was . . . rapidly reaching the boiling point." Wentz even questioned whether his critics were afflicted with an "ecclesiastical form of contemporary war neuroses."[66] In spite of this insight regarding the inadequacy of confessional differences to account for this bitter animosity and the intuitive instinct that it was somehow related to the current political controversy, Wentz never made any concrete connection between the spiraling invective and Schmucker's abolitionism.

Although Schmucker refused to reply in kind to the vituperative censure with which he was bombarded, the intensity of the attack undoubtedly helped to elicit a response that he lived to regret. In the summer of 1855, urged on by friends and assisted by Samuel Sprecher and Benjamin Kurtz, he hastily constructed a short document, later known as the *Definite Synodical Platform*.[67] Throwing caution to the winds, Schmucker, probably in conjunction with Kurtz and Sprecher, composed a forty-two-page pamphlet, the first part of which was entitled "The American Recension of the Augsburg Confession." Here the twenty-one articles of the confession were all listed, omitting those sections that Schmucker felt contained errors. These errors were designated as:

1. The Approval of the ceremonies of the mass
2. Private confession and absolution
3. Denial of the Divine Obligation of the Sabbath

---

[65]Editorial, *Evangelical Review* 7 (October 1855): 234-44.

[66]Wentz, *Pioneer in Christian Unity*, 203.

[67]*Definite Platform Doctrinal and Disciplinarian for Evangelical Lutheran Synods: Constructed in Accordance with the Principles of the General Synod* (Philadelphia: Miller & Burlock, 1855). The state of Schmucker's physical health and mental tranquillity at this time is an interesting question and may possibly have also contributed to the precipitous action, which was not in keeping with his usual careful and deliberate way of expressing his ideas. His father, to whom he was very close, had died the previous fall (on 7 October 1854), and Schmucker became so violently ill at the time that, when he attempted to attend the funeral in nearby York PA. he had to turn back home. He termed his illness 'erysipelas' and described it as a "swelling of the face and other parts of the body" which "threatened to fix upon the brain" (letter to his son, 14 October 1854, Schmucker Papers). This particular episode was quite prolonged. In other letters, Schmucker frequently referred to this illness, which appears to have afflicted him at times of emotional crisis.

4. Baptismal Regeneration

5. The Real Presence of the Body and Blood of the Saviour in the Eucharist.[68]

In addition, a second and longer section, under the title "Symbolic Errors Rejected," noted nine items in all, including the five above, that occurred in one or more of the "former symbolical books of the Lutheran Church in Europe, but which have no scriptural basis and are rejected by the great body of the American Lutheran Church."[69]

Early in September 1855, the *Definite Synodical Platform* was mailed, without signature, to most of the pastors of the General Synod. It called for each district synod to adopt its "Doctrinal Platform" as a more definite expression of the pledge prescribed by the General Synod and suggested that no minister who refused to subscribe to it be received into synodical membership.[70] That a proposal advocating an official American revision of the Augsburg Confession elicited strong negative response could have come as no surprise to Schmucker, especially after the recent reaction to his *Lutheran Manual*. But the opposition to the *Platform* was further increased by its somewhat imperious request that clergy who failed to accept its doctrinal platform be denied membership in the synod and by its distribution without a signature. As a result, of the twenty district groups affiliated with the General Synod, only three of the smallest, located in Ohio and Indiana, actually adopted the *Platform*. A number of other synods reaffirmed their allegiance to the old doctrinal position of the General Synod, a stand with which Schmucker expressed satisfaction, since he regarded his *Platform* as simply a more specific formulation of the statement that he had previously authored. But a majority of the synodical judicatories rejected the *Platform* outright.

The East Pennsylvania Synod acted first, expressing "unqualified disapprobation of this most dangerous attempt to change the doctrinal basis . . . of the General Synod."[71] The most humiliating blow to Schmucker came when the West Pennsylvania District, to which he had belonged for more than thirty years, turned a deaf ear to his personal pleas and voted to "deprecate and most solemnly protest against bringing in any new issues or tests of church mem-

---

[68]*Definite Platform*, preface.

[69]Ibid., 13-42.

[70]Ibid., preface.

[71]*Proceedings of the Fourteenth Annual Convention of the Evangelical Lutheran Synod of Eastern Pennsylvania, Sept. 21-26, 1855* (Gettysburg: C. Neinstadt, 1855) 13-14.

bership."[72] The widespread and ferocious debate evoked by the *Definite Synodical Platform*, along with its emphatic rejection by a large majority of Lutheran groups connected with the General Synod, makes it one of the most important documents in the history of the Lutheran church in America. It marked the "crest of the crisis" in American Lutheran theology and, for all practical purposes, the end of Schmucker's leadership.[73]

Schmucker, however, was not one to acknowledge defeat. He struggled on in the vain attempt to explain and defend his views. The intensity of his efforts was evidenced in the productivity of his pen. But the tide was not to be reversed. The opposition only increased. In 1857, formal allegations were presented to the Board of Directors of the Lutheran Theological Seminary at Gettysburg, charging Schmucker with teaching false doctrines and with violation of the oath of office (which he himself had composed). But this attack was going too far, and in compliance with the urgent request of Schmucker's most capable conservative opponent and former student, Charles Porterfield Krauth, the charges were quietly dropped, and no impeachment trial was ever held.[74] Even though the actions of considerate conservative leaders like Krauth had spared Schmucker the indignity of being driven from office, the hostility directed at him from other quarters did not lessen. He remained at his professorial post for seven more years, but his health was in decline, and pleading the desire to spend more time in writing, he tendered his resignation in 1864. J. S. Brown, the man who had brought the charge of heresy against Schmucker, was later elected as his successor. The choice of Brown over Charles Porterfield Krauth appears to have been determined by the fact that he had made a more aggressive attack upon Schmucker than Krauth had been ready to support.[75] Schmucker lived on for nine years in retirement, writing and working for the cause of Protestant unity, until his death in 1873.

Even to this day, the term *American Lutheranism* remains under a cloud, and the diatribe *Schmuckerism* still smacks of heresy among the ranks of conservative and confessional Lutherans in America. There can be little question that the fate of the *Definite Synodical Platform* was a turning point of momentous consequence for the Lutheran church in the United States. It

---

[72]*Proceedings of the Thirty-First Annual Convention of the Evangelical Lutheran Synod of Western Pennsylvania, Sept. 27-Oct. 1, 1855* (Gettysburg: C. Neinstadt, 1855) 19.

[73]Wentz, *Pioneer in Christian Unity*, 212.

[74]Ibid., 228.

[75]Henry E. Jacobs, "The Confessional Reaction in the General Synod in the Nineteenth Century," *Lutheran Church Review* 31 (1912): 155.

signaled the rejection not only of Schmucker's personal theological convictions but of that entire segment of American Lutheran Pietism for which he had been the acknowledged leader and spokesman for over three decades. But the *Platform* was by no means the cause of Schmucker's rejection. It was only the means by which it was effected. Its hasty composition, authoritarian tone, and poorly conceived strategy of distribution, so out of keeping with Schmucker's usual approach, gave his opponents the opportunity for which they had been searching, to apply the coup de grace. But the opposition to Schmucker and his American Lutheran Pietism had been building steadily for nearly two decades and had reached its climax before the publication of the ill-fated *Definite Platform*.

Is it reasonable to conclude that this violent opposition can be attributed only to doctrinal differences? Schmucker's published views on the sacraments, especially in regard to the Lord's Supper, did become increasingly disturbing to conservative Lutheran theologians, but this controversy did not reach its zenith until after he had resigned. Furthermore, Schmucker was universally acknowledged among Lutheran leaders as having earlier rescued the church from the spirit of rationalism and anticonfessionalism. One would expect that this record alone would have somewhat softened the criticism coming from conservative circles. In addition, he had held consistently to the doctrinal stand of the General Synod, which implied toleration for, although not full agreement with, an unconditional subscription to the Augsburg Confession.

Six months after the *Platform* was issued, he, along with Charles Philip Krauth, his former colleague turned opponent, and thirty-six other Lutheran leaders of both liberal and conservative persuasion, signed a highly significant and much-overlooked document called the *Pacific Overture*. In it, they agreed to "unite on the doctrinal basis of the General Synod,"[76] the same formula that Schmucker had authored, supported, and defended for thirty years and to which he had proposed alterations only because of the insistent pressures to do so! Up to the very time of Schmucker's resignation in 1864, Charles Porterfield Krauth, Schmucker's most articulate orthodox adversary, stated that he was entirely satisfied with the formula of the General Synod in regard to the Augsburg Confession, a position with which Schmucker was in the fullest accord![77] These facts testify to the tenuous character of the historical assessment, which has insisted that the contro-

---

[76]Ferm, *Crisis in American Lutheran Theology*, 296.

[77]J. W. Richard, "The Confessional History of the General Synod," *Lutheran Quarterly* 25 (October 1895): 467-69.

versy between Old Lutherans and American Lutherans was strictly motivated by disagreement over the degree of allegiance to the Lutheran confessions.

ABOLITIONISM: A CAUSE FOR REJECTION?

If one proceeds on the assumption that the opposition to Samuel Schmucker and his American Lutheran Pietism was not solely due to confessional considerations, then another question may be legitimately posed. Did Schmucker's abolitionism contribute to his personal loss of leadership and consequently to that of the American Lutheran Pietism that he represented, and, if so, to what extent? Hard evidence or documented proof is lacking for an affirmative answer to this question. This lack is not really surprising, however, because Schmucker's opponents felt free to attack him on matters of dogma or the confessions, while they were under strong constraints to refrain from discussion or debate on the issue of slavery. Schmucker's views on slavery clearly met with opposition from within his church body. The antagonism toward his ethical activism in general and his participation in the major moral crusades of his day is a matter of record. For the most part, this antipathy was simply expressed by apathy and lack of support. Lutherans and Episcopalians were the only major Protestant groups that did not adopt strong endorsements on Sabbath observance, temperance, and abolition.[78] Lutheran opposition was more widespread to the slavery issue than to the others, and even more overt, because of its added controversial and political nature.

At least to some degree the opposition to Schmucker's abolitionism from within his church can be documented. His first biographer, Paul Anstadt, who was also his student, tells how in the lecture room the professor "frequently expressed his aversion to slavery as it existed in the Southern States, and not infrequently to the ill-suppressed opposition of students from the South."[79] Schmucker's classroom was the scene of some spirited debates on slavery. At these times he was far from being a neutral observer. Anstadt describes one of these incidents. "It was my duty to write and read an essay on 'African Slavery' in the South. This was long before the war, while slavery was yet in full force in the Southern states. I gave expression to some very strong anti-slavery sentiments, and a Southern brother took offense. But the Doctor [Schmucker] sustained me in my position."[80]

---

[78]Bodo, *Protestant Clergy and Public Issues*, 184.

[79]Anstadt, *Life and Times of Samuel Schmucker*, 293.

[80]Ibid., 272.

At least one out of every five Gettsyburg students came from the Southern synods.[81] Even though the open condemnation of slavery was bound to cause resentment, Schmucker persisted in his attack. It was obviously not the route of political expediency, in terms of maintaining his leadership within the General Synod and in holding together the Pietist constituency that formed the backbone of his support. The South, as was already noted, constituted one of the chief strongholds of Lutheran Pietism. Southern Pietists were in full accord with those in the North in their commitment to revivalism, millennialism, ecumenism, and social activism. Both John Bachman, its acknowledged leader, and Ernest Hazelius, the head of its only seminary, held to theological and confessional views that were nearly identical with Schmucker's. Had it not been for the Gettysburg professor's decided stand on behalf of abolitionism, these leaders and their constituents might have remained Schmucker's defenders during the 1840s and 1850s, when his confessional views were challenged and overthrown.

As it was, the Southern synods began a very slow but measured march in the direction of a more conservative position. This turn was due in part to their coalition with Old Lutherans in the North on the policy of silence regarding slavery. Their support on this issue was a considerable factor in its success. By the time of the Civil War, Southern groups composed about one-fifth of the General Synod's districts and approximately one-seventh of its clergy and communicant members.[82] The assertion by A. R. Wentz regarding the eventual secession of the Southern district groups from the General Synod after the outbreak of war, that it "further diminished the strength of the conservative party in the General Synod," is puzzling.[83] If by "conservative" Wentz referred to strict confessionalism, as is the case throughout his book, then the statement is in error. It makes sense only if he meant that it diminished those forces within the General Synod that had opposed action on the slavery question. At any rate, Schmucker's abolitionism was the one and only factor that alienated the Southern Pietists who would otherwise have been his allies.

Schmucker's popular theological textbook, replete with its strong anti-slavery statements, had been widely circulated throughout the South. As

[81]Hugh George Anderson, "A Social History of Lutheranism in the Southeastern States, 1860-1886" (Ph.D. diss., University of Pennsylvania, 1962) 18-19.

[82]A. R. Wentz, *History of the Gettysburg Theological Seminary, 1826–1926,* vol. 1 (rpt., Harrisburg PA: Evangelical Press, 1965) 148.

[83]Wentz, *Basic History of Lutheranism in America,* 148.

a result he became the object of much bitterness among the people of the Southern states. Wentz notes that, "by the influence of war psychology, he was . . . branded as an abolitionist . . . without any modifying terms whatever."[84] As an influential molder of thought in the North, he was even held to be partly responsible for the war. Accordingly, during the Civil War, when Lee's army advanced toward Gettysburg, Schmucker was warned that some Confederate soldiers intended to arrest him. He fled the city in time, but the seminary and its campus received "a terrible baptism of fire and blood."[85]

The Southern soldiers took special pains to wreak vengeance on Schmucker's personal property, subjecting it to a devastating desecration. In a report to the seminary directors following the battle, Schmucker described the damage to his home. "Thirteen canon balls or shells pierced the walls, . . . window frames were shattered to pieces . . . everything . . . in my house . . . broken open . . . and the contents scattered promiscuously with my books, papers, letters, etc., over the floor."[86] Much of his furniture was also plundered and rendered useless, his books thrown from shelves, torn and defiled, and his personal papers tossed out the windows and trampled in the mud. Yet, Krauth's home, situated less than a block away, was not ransacked at all. When the Confederates left the area and Mrs. Krauth discovered that a silver set was missing, she complained to the Southern army, and an officer obligingly ordered its return.[87] Schmucker's grief over the severe strain and loss incurred during the battle undoubtedly contributed to his decision to retire the following year. In spite of all that he suffered personally and his passionate hatred of war, Schmucker was able to justify the awful conflict. He believed it had been fought and its terrible sacrifices offered, at least in part, for the abolition of human slavery.

Schmucker's position as a leader had been successfully challenged before the war, while the hostilities over abolitionism were at their height. Considering the degree of animosity openly directed at him because of his abolitionism and not by any means limited to the South, it is almost certain that this stance considerably increased the opposition to his doctrinal views regarding the Lutheran confessions. At one point in his excellent biography of Schmucker, Wentz acknowledged this connection. "It seems probable that the resentment on the part of some students to the profes-

---

[84]Wentz, *Pioneer in Christian Unity*, 320.

[85]Wentz, *Gettysburg Theological Seminary*, 201-27.

[86]Wentz, *Pioneer in Christian Unity*, 328.

[87]Ibid., 329-30.

sor's views on . . . . slavery later contributed to their alienation from his doctrinal views."[88] Wentz never elaborated on this point at all, apparently considering it to have little significance. This insight, however, is of major importance to a full understanding of the rejection that Schmucker experienced. The fact that opposition to Schmucker reached a peak at the exact time that the issue over slavery approached its climax, expressing itself in a shrill hostility and personal abusiveness that Schmucker's biographer found difficult to comprehend, can hardly be dismissed as mere coincidence.

There is every indication that Schmucker's abolitionist views served as a focus for conservative fears that there was a definite danger in "American Lutheran" thought.[89] It is certainly not demonstrable, nor is it suggested, that Schmucker's abolitionism was the chief factor in his rejection. But there is evidence that it may have played a significant role, as a catalytic agent created by the chemistry of emotional and largely suppressed hostilities and racial antipathies, sufficient to tip the scales against him. In the case of William Passavant, his conversion to rising tides of strict confessionalism and his hesitancy to promote a political activism may have saved him from a similar fate. Had it not been for Schmucker's politically oriented abolitionism, he might have survived the onslaught of opposition that was based on purely doctrinal grounds, or at the very least might have not been so categorically and summarily deposed.

Behind the acerbity of the confessional debate lurked the conservative Lutheran aversion to Schmucker's activism and to his involvement in moral reform through political action. It was Schmucker's unwillingness to curb this involvement with regard to the sensitive political issue of abolition that was the source of greatest irritation. His conservative opponents viewed his efforts not only as heretical to historic Lutheran ethical theology but as a distinct menace to denominational harmony and cohesion. This threat to internal unity was in turn tied to a pervasive and consuming fear, namely, the loss of Lutheran identity. The resulting division of Pietist forces together with the invigoration of conservative opposition led to Schmucker's complete repudiation.

---

[88]Ibid., 320.

[89]David T. Bailey, *Shadow on the Church*, (Ithaca NY: Cornell University Press, 1985) 231. Bailey documents this factor in the Presbyterian schism.

C·H·A·P·T·E·R 6

An Abolitionist Synod

The Franckean Synod was the only group of Lutherans in the United States to challenge aggressively its denomination's policy of silence and neutrality on the question of slavery. A few weeks following the Franckeans' organization in 1837, the editor of the *Lutheran Observer* referred to the resolutions opposing American slavery in the new synod's constitution as "calculated, under existing circumstances to be productive of more evil than good."[1]

Early in 1839, the Franckeans began to publish a paper of their own called the *Lutheran Herald*. It was specifically designed to combat the strategy of neutrality pursued by the *Lutheran Observer*. The *Herald's* policy was proudly proclaimed as "anti slavery." It was designed as an "efficient instrument for the final overthrow and complete death of the indescribable sin of slavery."[2] The Franckeans regularly mailed copies of this paper to most of the synods of the Lutheran church in the United States, including those in the South. Throughout the church it met with opposition, because of its radical antislavery spirit.[3] Although a few wealthy abolitionist leaders, such as Gerrit Smith, were listed among its contributors,[4] the *Herald* was in constant financial trouble. The paper's first series ran from early in 1839 until the end of 1842.

---

[1]Fortenbaugh, "Representative Lutheran Periodical Press and Slavery," 155.

[2]*JFS*, 1840, 28; *Lutheran Herald* 4 (1 February 1842): 21.

[3]Archibald Wieting to his uncle, Philip Wieting, 18 August 1841, Middletown PA: Franckean Papers.

[4]*Lutheran Herald* 1 (16 June 1839): 96.

After discontinuing publication for over a year and a half, a second series began in August 1844 with the name of its new editor, the Reverend
H. L. Dox, listed for the first time on the masthead.[5] Possibly out of pecuniary concern, Dox attempted at first to make the paper more palatable
to the general public, noting in his first issue that his highest aim would be
to "give no one just reason to complain." He also promised not to "deviate
attention chiefly or exclusively to any one or all of the moral enterprises."[6]
The initial issue contained not a single mention of slavery, probably a first
for the *Herald*. It was also a last, for the very next issue contained a particularly passionate antislavery article. The change in tone was noticed by a
liberal reader, who wrote to encourage the new editor to treat the antislavery question as a part of the gospel. This reader had known Dox as a
"worthy abolitionist," but he admonished him to "come out strong at the
start . . . and let the people know where you stand. . . . Remember," he
counseled, "no conservatism where humanity is concerned!"[7] Dox replied
that he had always treated slavery as a part of the gospel and that the subject would be given its "proper place, . . . though our columns cannot be
exclusively devoted to it."[8] It was not long before it once again assumed
that "proper place" of priority. But the paper designed to "reflect the light
of God's truth . . . upon the darkness of slavery"[9] once again encountered
monetary difficulties, and within a year it ceased to be published.
    The effort of the Franckean Synod to nudge their Lutheran colleagues
in the direction of a pronounced abolitionist stand was an uphill battle
marked with meager success. We have already noted the slim response to
the stirring invitation to action issued in the Franckeans' "Fraternal Appeal"
of 1842. This manifesto, urgently requesting their fellow Lutherans to take
direct actions against the continuation of slavery in America, had been received with an emphatic silence. But the Franckeans remained character-
istically undaunted by this massive lack of support. They were still
determined that Lutherans should be in the forefront of what they referred
to as the new reformation. At their convention in 1846, further efforts were
made to solicit the involvement of ministers from the various Lutheran syn-

---

[5]Ibid., 1 (13 August 1844).

[6]Ibid., 1.

[7]*Lutheran Herald*, n.s. 1 (16 October 1844): n.p. The writer signs the note "G."
It might well have been the Reverend Beriah Green, a good friend of the Franckeans.

[8]Ibid.

[9]Ibid. 4 (1 February 1842): 21.

ods in the abolitionist cause. A special committee was appointed to correspond with these groups "in order to induce them to appoint a committee to draft a protest, . . . against slavery, and secure the signatures of as many clergy as possible." The petitions were sent only to those synods who had already "taken action on the subject."[10] It apparently received few, if any, signatures outside of the Franckeans themselves.

In spite of these rebuffs the Franckeans would not acquiesce. They were determined to be heard as the voice of conscience within their church body. Precisely against the policies of muteness and of neutrality on slavery the Franckeans concentrated their most devastating attack. They repeatedly called silence a sin[11] and condemned those who supported slavery by "their masterful inactivity."[12] They looked upon the studied neutrality of the General Synod and of the *Lutheran Observer* as a "mode of conniving at sin . . . a source of vacillation unworthy a Christian."[13] For its part the *Observer* continued to ask abolitionists to consider whether the possible good they might accomplish could "counter balance the inevitable evil."[14] The Franckeans answered that abolitionism was far more beneficial than harmful. Yet they were not unsympathetic to the quest for unity. They lamented the "hostility existing between the different synods of the Lutheran denomination . . . as a cause of destruction and inefficiency in . . . benevolent operations."[15] They looked forward to the day when concord would prevail and all parts of the church could work in harmony to build up the Redeemer's kingdom. But they refused, whatever the cost, to desist from raising a protest against "that system by which millions of our creatures are despoiled of all their social, civil, and religious rights."[16]

As far as the Franckeans were concerned, the church that refused to advocate actively the rights of the enslaved had become fundamentally corrupt in doctrine and practice. As a result they resolved that they could not hold fellowship with any synod or ecclesiastical body that "tolerates, apologizes for, or is silent on the sin of American slavery."[17] The cause of

---

[10]*JFS*, 1846, 16.

[11]Ibid., 1857, 17.

[12]Ibid., 1846, 16.

[13]Ibid., 1840, 27.

[14]*Lutheran Observer* 4 (28 July 1837): 179.

[15]*JFS*, 1850, 14.

[16]Ibid., 15.

[17]Ibid., 1845, 10, 18.

church unity they admitted to be one of grave concern. But if that unity could be maintained only at the terrible cost of ignoring the clear needs of suffering humanity and the plain commandments of God, then the Franckeans conjectured that perhaps it ought not be preserved. They declared, "We dislike strife and agitation, nevertheless, hoping and believing that the result will be purification from slavery's corruption, we cheerfully endure the process." Quoting Christ's words "I came not to send peace . . . but a sword [Matt. 10:34]," the Franckeans noted that there is "a *necessary* commotion when Gospel truth comes in conflict with sin."[18] In connection with this fundamental affirmation, they had adopted as their motto "First purity, and then peace."[19] They were convinced that those who pursued this policy could expect, like Jesus himself, to be persecuted. They anticipated and even welcomed opposition and rejection. In an article entitled "Pure, Then Peaceable," editor Henry Dox wrote, "The zealous Christian . . . must live and die, a hated man. Let us make our minds to it." Those who contended earnestly for the faith had to dispense with "the smiles, and applause, the friendship of the world."[20]

The decision to place Christian conscience ahead of church unity was demonstrated by the Franckeans in a practical way with regard to the actions of the Evangelical Alliance. Their strong endorsement of the organization was based in part on its decision to exclude slaveholders from its membership.[21] Yet it was the adoption of this clause that led to internal dissension and postponement of the group's primary ecumenical goal. As noted in chapter 5, Samuel Schmucker, in spite of his abolitionist ideals, opposed the measure for its restrictiveness. As far as the Franckeans were concerned, the unity of the church was not as important as the liberation of the enslaved. In their eyes only one question in regard to slavery had any validity: was it right? If slavery was wrong, then, they insisted, it is not only wrong to practice it or apologize for it, but "it is wrong to pass over it in silence, to treat it with indifference, to neglect any proper means of showing opposition to it."[22]

This frontal attack upon the central strategy that Lutherans had adopted and carefully defended in regard to slavery was persistently pursued. Si-

---

[18]Ibid., 1859, 11.

[19]Ibid., 1858, 29.

[20]*Lutheran Herald* 1 (30 April 1845): n.p.

[21]*JFS*, 1846, 27.

[22]Ibid., 1857, 15.

lence and neutrality were often described as more evil than an open defense of slavery because of the hypocrisy involved. A Franckean author, writing in the synod paper under the name "Consistency," declared that the minister who claims that "he is opposed to slavery as much as any man and believes it to be a sin, and opens not his mouth for the oppressed poor and downtrodden dumb, should be hurled from the pulpit."[23]

By far the most persuasive arguments launched against Lutheran neutrality were those of Nicholas Van Alstine. He labeled his target "Pro-slavery theology." It was, he pointed out, the exact advice that the South gave to the North in regard to slavery. "Let it alone. . . . So the demons cried out to the son of God, 'Let us alone.' Shall we leave it alone? Nay verily, we have drawn the sword of truth, and kissed its keen blade, and it shall not be sheathed until slavery is dead."[24]

In an earlier article, Van Alstine quoted a resolution adopted by a Lutheran synod in Ohio that stated, "Slavery, either pro or con, shall not be a subject of discussion or action in this body." The statement neatly summarized the position of nearly the entire Lutheran church, and Van Alstine proceeded to assail it with the persuasive passion of a deeply felt religious conviction. He asked the Ohio Lutherans to consider carefully the solemn position they had taken up in regard to slavery. "Look at it and turn it to the crushed and wailing slave and then read it before the judgment bar of Almighty God. . . . Can you say that you . . . administered to the distressed, or have you shut up your bowels of compassion to the groaning slave and composed your nervous arm on the lazy lap of neutrality and dead faith?" Then Van Alstine comes to the heart of the matter.

I . . . allow that you wished to take the stand of neutrality without favoring slavery in the least,—that you abhor it, . . . yet your position will not prevent you from being construed as pro-slavery. . . . Indeed . . . [it] will give all your ecclesiastical influence to the vile monster slavery and against its abolition. You have sought for neutral ground where God never created any,—between right and wrong, . . . humanity and brutality, truth and error.[25]

REACTION AND OPPOSITION

The overt reaction on the part of those who received these stern admonitions was remarkably mild. They did not engage in any bombastic de-

[23]*Lutheran Herald* 2 (16 February 1840): 14.

[24]Ibid., n.s. 1 (2 April 1845): 1; (30 April): 1.

[25]Ibid. 4 (1 January 1842): 4.

bate or return in kind the salvo of dreadful diatribes that had been hurled at them. They rejected the accusations with a polite but quiet rebuff, presented primarily in the form of silence. We might say they resorted to a variation of the Fifth Amendment. They refused to answer their accusers not on the grounds that they might incriminate themselves (although the Franckeans would have argued that point) but that, by so doing, they would embroil themselves in the very debate they had chosen to avoid in order to maintain the peace and unity of the church.

According to psychologists, anger that cannot for some reason be directly expressed is apt to find release in a disguised or indirect manner. In such a case the suppressed hostility may seek a substitute object against which to vent its ire, which may in turn appear to be irrational in nature. This psychological fact might provide a possible clue regarding the cause of the concerted and abusive attack launched against the Franckeans' alleged lack of confessional orthodoxy. It becomes more understandable if behind it lay an emotional rejection of Franckean abolitionism, combined with a hostile reaction to the moral challenge that the Franckeans persisted in pressing upon their fellow Lutherans.

Among Lutherans in the South, where there was a large Pietist constituency, there was less of a disposition to attack the Franckeans on theological grounds or to write them out of the church because of their confessional stance.[26] Here the most open opposition to Franckean abolitionism was expressed. On occasion, Southerners had directly denounced or challenged the Franckeans' stand on practical and biblical grounds. It was primarily in the North, where the issue of abolitionism remained hidden behind a more rigid ecclesiastical taboo and where the charges regarding the "sin of neutrality" touched the raw nerve of a troubled and sensitive conscience, that the hostility toward the Franckeans took on the characteristics of an obsession. Here the official and public charge was always directed at the Franckeans' alleged denial of the historic Lutheran symbols, in particular, of the Augsburg Confession. It was further claimed that the rejection of the Augsburg Confession was tantamount to an outright denial of historic Lutheranism and constituted a forfeiture of any right to the name *Lutheran*. Shortly before the Civil War, a critic concluded, "The Franckean Synod . . . has cut itself off from the rest of the Lutheran Church by tacitly, if not formally abandoning the Augsburg Confession. It has published a sort of confession of faith. . . . They may

---

[26]The single exception was the Tennessee Synod, which was the only ultra-conservative group in the South.

properly be ranked as one of the few sects to which Lutheranism has given birth."²⁷ This accusation of having deserted the Lutheran Church was leveled against the Franckeans by the majority of their fellow Lutherans up until the conclusion of the Civil War.

CONFESSIONAL CONTROVERSY

Did the Franckeans in fact either reject or abandon the Augsburg Confession and substitute for it one that was inconsistent with the historic faith of the Lutheran church? According to the testimony of their own leaders and representatives, they did not. They categorically denied that the desire to shed their confessional heritage had played any part in the organization of their synod or that it was reflected in the Franckean constitution. This specific charge was in fact denied by the Reverend Philip Wieting under oath in a court of law.²⁸ Of course, these self-assertions of confessional allegiance do not constitute sufficient proof of one's orthodoxy. But they must be taken seriously. The very fact that the Franckeans continued to appeal to their Lutheran heritage and to their respect for the Lutheran symbols indicated a commitment to Lutheranism that cannot be ignored.

More important, the records available appear to support the Franckeans' claim that they had no intention of rejecting the Augsburg Confession or the historic faith of Lutheranism. The first president of the Franckean Synod, John D. Lawyer, devoted a considerable portion of his inaugural address to a refutation of what he called this "high charge"²⁹ and maintained that it was "entirely destitute of truth . . . where in all our proceedings is there one word found about or against the Augsburg Confession? Let the place be marked. We have waged no war against that instrument. We have left it where it is and just as it is."³⁰ Two years later he wrote, "The

---

²⁷"The Present Position of the Lutheran Church," *Evangelical Review* 11 (July 1859): 35.

²⁸"Kniskern and others vs. the Lutheran Churches of St. John's and St. Peter's, Philip Wieting, and others," in *Report of cases argued and determined in the Court of Chancery of the State of New York (1843–1847)*, 2d ed., vol. 1, p. 461 (New York: Gould, Banks, 1846), New York State Library, Manuscripts and Special Collections.

²⁹The "high charge" referred to by Lawyer was, he claimed, stated at an official meeting of a Lutheran synod (undoubtedly the Hartwick Synod) by its presiding officer. It accused the Franckeans of having "denounced all connection with the Lutheran Church, by renouncing the Lutheran Confession of faith" and forming a new one in its place (*JFS*, October 1837) 24-25, 28-29).

³⁰*JFS*, October 1837, 29.

Franckean synod has never formally received nor rejected the Augsburg . . . Confession. . . . We believe it nearly as much now as we did before the formation of the Franckean Synod, and so do our people."[31]

The record upholds Lawyer's assertions. The minutes of the Hartwick Synod in the six years prior to the Franckean secession in 1837 fail to register any argument whatever against the Augsburg Confession or any attempt to modify or reject it. On the contrary, they certify that, in 1831, when the Hartwick Synod by a unanimous vote united with the General Synod and accepted its *Formula of Discipline*, which involved a tacit acceptance of the Augsburg Confession, three of the four future founders of the Franckean Synod were present and therefore voted in the affirmative.[32] To contend that these three might have gone along with the majority or quietly abstained, even though they were opposed to the action, does not fit well with their character and habitual pattern of behavior. But this contention is further weakened by the official minutes, which state that, following the adoption of the resolution, none other than the Reverend Philip Wieting, one of the most influential founders of the Franckean Synod, moved that the General Synod's *Formula of Discipline* be published and 1000 copies distributed.[33]

The circular letter mailed early in 1837 to those who were invited to the organizational meeting of the Franckean Synod outlined in some detail the reasons for the synod's formation, but it contained not a syllable of grievance against the Augsburg Confession.[34] None of the Franckean records refer to the Augsburg Confession as a cause for severing connections with the Hartwick Synod, and neither do they include at any time an outright rejection or renunciation of that historic symbol. In his history of the synod, Nicholas Van Alstine testified that there was no desire at the time of its formation "to wage war against doctrinal errors [of] any creed, ancient or modern, of . . . our own denomination."[35] And Henry L. Dox insisted that the charge that the Franckean synod had "assailed the Augsburg Confession" was carried on by misapprehension and misrepresentation. In reality, Dox wrote, "the confessional matter amounted to nearly nothing."

---

[31]*Lutheran Herald* 1 (1 June 1839): 85.

[32]*Minutes of the Hartwick Synod*, 1831, 10.

[33]Ibid.

[34]Circular letters, signed Philip Wieting, 26 April 1837, Franckean Papers Metropolitan-Upper New York Synod Archives.

[35]N. Van Alstine, *Historical Review*, 8.

The only real question, he maintained, was whether the Augsburg Confession was to be accepted "as a whole or only in part."[36]

The Franckeans' assertion that they never formally rejected or renounced the Augsburg Confession was unassailable. The record spoke for itself. The argument raised against them was therefore based upon the sin of omission—they had failed to mention the confession in their constitution. In the eyes of their opponents, this constituted a tacit abandonment of the Lutheran church. Furthermore, the Franckeans' adoption of a "Declaration of Faith" was arbitrarily designated by detractors as a substitute for the venerable confession.

Soon after the Franckeans organized, attempts were made by officials of the Hartwick Synod to induce individual members from the congregations that had seceded to remain in fellowship with their synod. The appeal was based primarily on the assertion that remaining in the Hartwick fold would assure connection with the true doctrines of the Lutheran Church. Later the Hartwick Synod printed large numbers of copies of the Augsburg Confession for distribution among the members of these parishes.[37] The Hartwick president, J. Z. Senderling, conducted meetings with members of parishes located in Sharon and West Sand Lake, then under the pastorates of Philip Wieting and John Lawyer, apparently without their knowledge. At these meetings motions to remain with the Hartwick Synod were introduced but lost by large majorities.[38] However, in West Sand Lake, J. Z. Senderling, who himself was a former pastor of that parish, made personal visitations and wrote letters to the members of the congregation, in addition to holding private meetings. This interference resulted in considerable division.[39] The argument over which group would retain possession of the church building was finally taken into the courts, where it was later adjudicated in favor of the Hartwick minority. In most cases this kind of split did not occur, and, with the exception of Richmondville, where a compromise was finally reached and both factions used the same building,[40] the overwhelming majority of parishioners in the contested congregations supported the Franckean organizers.

---

[36]H. L. Dox, ed., "Historical Fidelity," in *A Reunion of Ministers and Churches, Held at Gardnersville, May 14-17, 1881* (Philadelphia: Lutheran Publication Society, 1881) 12.

[37]Kreider, *History of the United Lutheran Synod*, 128.

[38]Ibid., 103.

[39]History, Trinity Lutheran Church, West Sand Lake NY, Franckean Papers.

[40]History of St. Paul's Lutheran Church, Richmondville NY, Franckean Papers.

A CIVIL COURT DECISION

The trustees, elders, and deacons of the two parishes served by Rev. Philip Wieting solidly supported affiliation with the Franckean Synod. They were located in Sharon and New Rheinbeck. Only two leaders in the New Rheinbeck parish remained loyal to the Hartwick Synod, and none in the Sharon parish.[41] The congregational vote to join the Franckean Synod was nearly unanimous. The Franckeans contended that it was only afterward, when Hartwick leaders alleged that the new synod had renounced the Augsburg Confession and declared that those adhering to it could no longer be considered Lutheran, that a division was created by a small minority who then professed loyalty to the Hartwick Synod.[42] Perhaps encouraged by the judicial decision handed down at West Sand Lake, the small group of Hartwick loyalists in the New Rheinbeck and Sharon parishes filed a civil suit in the court of chancery on 23 March 1839. They sought jurisdiction over the church properties, claiming that they belonged legally only to those who were committed to the doctrines of the Lutheran church as taught in the Augsburg Confession.

The action was bitterly contested. Scores of witnesses were called. The proceedings were long and costly. Not until five years later, on 17 July 1844, was a decision rendered by the Honorable Lewis H. Sanford, assistant vice-chancellor of the state of New York, in favor of the complainants.[43] Judge Sanford ruled that the Hartwick minority had proven that, at the time the congregations in question were organized, their founders had publicly proclaimed the standard of faith to be the Augsburg Confession. He further agreed that they had established that the Franckeans' "Declaration of Faith" differed from the Augsburg Confession on essential points of doctrine. He concluded that, since the Franckean doctrines deviated from the original purposes for which the congregations were founded, they were no longer entitled to its properties. Philip Wieting was forced to vacate his living quarters and the farm on which it was situated, and nearly the entire membership of his two parishes had to retire from the premises they used for worship. In addition they were assessed the costs of the lengthy court battle.

It was a bitter pill to swallow, but the Franckeans took it in stride. They admitted it was "an important decision for the complainants as regards

---

[41]"Kniskern vs. Wieting," 448.

[42]*Lutheran Herald*, n.s. 1 (13 November 1844).

[43]"Kniskern vs. Wieting," 439-40, 499-568.

property" but insisted that it was "a glorious triumph for the defendants, in respect to principle."[44] They consoled themselves with the thought that both Jesus Christ and Martin Luther were condemned by the highest civil authority and that "modern courts are capable of equal outrages upon right and justice."[45] Finally, they noted with bitter irony that, during the five years the suit was in process, there had been in their parishes "no less than three revivals of religion by the preaching of the doctrines of the Bible, and upwards of one hundred fifty members received . . . while during the same time, three persons were confirmed by the preaching of the doctrines of the Augsburg Confession."[46]

Judge Sanford's judicial decision, which runs to over 125 printed pages, was based upon two main points at issue. The first was whether or not the founders had officially dedicated the churches involved in the suit to promulgate the doctrines of the Augsburg Confession. On the surface, this was extremely unlikely, since these parishes at the time of their dedication, prior to 1800, belonged to the New York Ministerium, which made no reference to the Augsburg Confession in its official documents until fifty years later. The ministerium was in fact known for its opposition to that confession, a reason that had led to the formation of the Hartwick Synod in 1830. There was no written record of the ceremonies. A single witness, present at the dedication some forty-five years earlier and belonging to a different denomination, testified with surprising certainty that the ceremony had specifically referred to the Augsburg Confession. Four other eyewitnesses, who were all Lutherans, said they heard nothing about the Augsburg Confession. Incredibly, the chancellor accepted the testimony of the single witness because he considered his recollection to be more precise. The judge also felt that the fact this lone witness was a non-Lutheran made it more certain that "he would remember the use of the term, 'Augsburg Confession.' "[47]

Once this first point was established, it remained only for the complainants to prove that the Franckeans' "Declaration of Faith" differed in essential ways from fundamental doctrines of the Augsburg Confession. It was inferred that such differences would constitute a departure from it, tantamount to its rejection. The Hartwick loyalists based their case on three allegations against the "Declaration of Faith": (1) the article on the Holy Trinity declared the ex-

---

[44]*Lutheran Herald,* n.s. 1 (13 November 1844).

[45]Dox, *Reunion at Gardnersville,* 19.

[46]*Lutheran Herald,* n.s. 1 (13 November 1844).

[47]"Kniskern vs. Wieting," 472, 479-80, 523-24.

istence not of three persons in the Godhead but of only one divine Being, revealed under three different names; (2) the article on belief in Jesus Christ did not declare his equality with God but only his attributes as Redeemer; and (3) the article on original sin failed specifically to condemn to eternal punishment all who did not repent and receive baptism.

The first two assertions were denied by the Franckeans, and with substantial cause, as can be ascertained by a quick reading of the relevant sections.[48] The historic Lutheran doctrines of the Trinity and divinity of Christ were in essence upheld. The argument against the Franckeans' Trinitarian and Christological formulations was based almost entirely on their failure to use the word *person* in regard to the manifestations of the triune God, and the word *equal* in regard to the relation of the Son to the Father, even though both of these attributes were clearly implied.

The third charge, asserting that the Franckeans failed to teach universal punishment for original sin, they frankly admitted. However, they insisted that this concept, along with several other teachings of a nonessential nature contained in the Augsburg Confession, had in practice been rejected by large numbers of Lutherans in this country. They quoted from Schmucker's *Elements of a Popular Theology* and other authorities to prove their point.[49] There was an obvious contradiction involved on the complainants' part in this particular point, for the Hartwick Synod had always been highly complimentary of Schmucker's analysis of the Augsburg Confession. The Hartwickians later officially agreed with Schmucker's *Definite Platform* and in practice also rejected the concept of baptismal regeneration, a point very similar if not synonymous to their final allegation against the Franckeans.[50]

The heart of the Franckeans' defense consisted in the contention that their "Declaration of Faith" was a faithful condensation and summation of the doc-

---

[48]*Constitution of the Franckean Synod*, Art. 12, Secs. 2 and 4, p. 17. Sect. 2, *Of God and Creation*, reads as follows: "That there is only one true living God, and that in this one God there is a distinction of three, revealed in the scriptures, as the Father, the Son, and the Holy Ghost; inseparably connected with one another, possessing the same essence, and equal and alike infinite and immutable, in all natural and moral perfections; the Almighty Maker of heaven and earth, and of all things visible and invisible." Section 4, *Jesus Christ and Redemption*, reads as follows: "That Jesus Christ, the only begotten son of God, in the fullness of time, was manifested in the flesh, and is the only Redeemer, that he was crucified, dead and buried, that he arose from the dead, ascended into heaven, and is now exalted at God's right hand, to make intercession for the whole human race."

[49]"Kniskern vs. Wieting," 490-91.

[50]Strobel, *Memorial Volume*, 37.

trines of the Bible and of the Augsburg Confession, in keeping with the manner in which that confession had been interpreted by large numbers of Lutheran Pietists in this country. The Franckeans testified that their "Declaration of Faith" was intended to set forth the essential doctrines of the Augsburg Confession without enumerating those few minor points with which they disagreed.[51] This defense, while mainly accurate, was clouded and encumbered with the intricacies of intra-Lutheran theological debate. In the end, Judge Sanford ruled that the Franckeans had departed from fundamental doctrines of the Augsburg Confession in all three of the alleged instances and had, in his words, sought to "attack and destroy" those doctrines.[52]

The judge made an assiduous effort to render a fair evaluation of a highly technical and denominational theological debate, but as a non-Lutheran layman, in spite of his intelligence and diligence, it was not within his competence to do so. During the trial the defendants declared that the question of Lutheran orthodoxy could be decided only by the proper ecclesiastical tribunal and not a civil court.[53] This assertion was, without question, correct. The vice-chancellor was legally and constitutionally in error. He exceeded the limits of his office by rendering a decision concerning church doctrine, which clearly constituted a violation of the separation of church and state. But he did not view it in this light. He made every effort to educate himself on the theological issues. He read volumes of church history and doctrine, which undoubtedly led to the long delay in rendering a decision. He frankly confessed that he approached the examination of the questions "with great diffidence and profound reluctance [and] . . . with an oppressive sense of the inherent difficulties," but it was a duty from which he "could not shrink." It was a satisfaction to know, he said, that, "if I err in [the] performance, the parties can readily review and redress my judgment."[54] Following the decision in 1844, the Franckeans did indicate their intention to appeal to a higher court,[55] and obviously should have done so. No mention was made of any such action, however, and no record of it has been discovered. Its abandonment was undoubtedly due to lack of energy and funds.

An objective reading of the transcripts of the trial, apart from the question of constitutionality, leaves the distinct impression that the grounds upon which

---

[51]"Kniskern vs. Wieting," 459, 494.

[52]Ibid., 561.

[53]Ibid., 492.

[54]Ibid., 540.

[55]*Lutheran Herald*, n.s. 1 (13 November 1844): n.p.

the Franckeans were convicted of having deserted the Augsburg Confession and the Lutheran church, were extremely tenuous, if not entirely untenable. It was not so much the Franckeans' omission of reference to the Augsburg Confession but their including in their constitution a "Declaration of Faith," different from the Augsburg Confession, that was the most telling point raised against them in the courtroom. They were the only Lutheran Synod in this country to summarize their specific doctrinal convictions in their constitution. Thus their concern for biblical doctrine, a hallmark of historic Lutheranism, was turned against their claim to retain its name. They were accused of being the only synod claiming to be Lutheran that had adopted a new declaration of faith.[56] The accusation, while technically true, became damaging to the Franckeans' claim to Lutheran orthodoxy only if it could be demonstrated that this new declaration set forth beliefs essentially different from those in the Augsburg Confession. Judge Sanford decided that in fact the beliefs were different. It is doubtful if this crucial point would have carried in any Lutheran ecclesiastical court of appeal, where the Franckeans rightly claimed it should have been decided.

A few years after the publication of this legal decision, the editor of the *Lutheran Observer*, Benjamin Kurtz, a former seminary teacher and keen student of Lutheran theology, and no friend of the Franckeans, acknowledged that, on the basis of their authorized writings, he "considered the Franckeans sound in all their fundamental doctrines." Making specific reference to the very doctrines on which the courts had convicted them of a departure from the Augsburg Confession, Kurtz stated, "On the Trinity and inherent depravity," the Franckeans had "expressed themselves somewhat differently . . . but not heretically."[57] Hard evidence in support of the Hartwick Synod's charge that the Franckeans had abandoned the Augsburg Confession was almost totally absent. The accusation itself may have been more strategic than sincere. It may have been utilized as the only practical way to demonstrate a rejection of historic Lutheranism and thus to accomplish the goal of retaining possession of church properties. But the concern for real estate alone could hardly have motivated a small minority to engage in such an extenuated and costly legal battle, whose outcome was far from certain. The transcript of the trial reveals an undertone of bitterness that belies the contention that the entire argument was only about the rejection of the Augsburg Confession. A noted American historian has indicated that 1839, the very year in which the civil proceedings

---

[56]"Kniskern vs. Wieting," 469.

[57]*Lutheran Observer* 3 (17 September 1847): 10.

against the Franckeans took place, marked the "climax of excitement" on the subject of American slavery.[58] The Franckeans had unceremoniously pricked the consciences of their fellow Lutherans. Least of all did they spare the synod from which they had seceded. One of the chief causes of that rupture had been the unwillingness of the Hartwick Synod to stand up for the abolitionist cause.

Resentment against the Franckeans' abolitionism was given clear, albeit guarded, expression during the course of the trial. In the original charges brought against them, the lawyers for the complainants referred to the antislavery clause in the Franckean constitution. They stated that the exclusion of ministers who were slaveholders or who advocated the system of American slavery and of lay persons in this category from serving as representatives of their church was something unknown to the Augsburg Confession and the Lutheran church.[59] In their rebuttal the Franckean lawyers did not deny that this was an innovation. They claimed there was nothing in the Franckean constitution or practices contrary to the Augsburg Confession or established usages of the Lutheran church except perhaps their opposition to "intemperance and the traffic in human flesh."[60] But they also contended there was no evidence that "total abstinence and anti-slavery tenets are a departure from *ancient usages.*"[61]

The Hartwick attorney, Samuel Stevens, did not follow up on these charges, nor did he reply to their rebuttal. He was apparently aware that a concentrated attack on Franckean abolitionism could lead into deep waters. More important, it could be an embarrassing and unfruitful way of attempting to document a departure from Lutheran doctrine. And yet, an occasional thrust in that direction could not be suppressed. At one point in his summary remarks, Stevens suddenly switched from his line of thought and said, "There are other new doctrines, which the defendants support. . . . They are abolitionists. . . . What right have the defendants to interpolate these notions as a part of the creed or government of these Churches? If they had remained in the Hartwick Synod, could they expel or excommunicate a member for omitting to join the fanatics against the South?"[62] Here for a fleeting moment the intense hostility against the Franckeans' ab-

---

[58]Barnes, *Antislavery Impulse,* 161.

[59]"Kniskern vs. Wieting," 445-46.

[60]Ibid., 459.

[61]Ibid., 489.

[62]Ibid., 487-88.

olitionism was exposed and recorded for history upon official court records. But it happened rarely, and the vice-chancellor, in his lengthy summary and decision, did not once refer to this subject.

On the basis of the available records, there is no way of determining with certainty the exact motives of the bitter battle conducted by the Hartwick leaders against the Franckean insurgents. Granted the desire to retain property was of paramount concern, still other divisions among Lutheran synods, including the one in 1830 between Hartwick and the New York Ministerium, did not result in this kind of protracted estrangement. It did not, even though a major part of that dispute centered on the ministerium's repudiation of the Augsburg Confession. Only three years after that separation occurred, the respective parties had again established amicable relations and were exchanging official delegates at their annual conventions. In the case of the Franckean cleavage, there was no reconciliation whatever for over a decade. No official relationships were established until the time of the Civil War.[63] When a merger was finally effected with Hartwick in 1908, strong evidences of ill will still existed.[64]

These facts add plausibility to the theory that resentment toward the Franckean Synod's aggressive and missionary stand on abolitionism was an important motivating factor in the Hartwick Synod's decision to attack them for an alleged doctrinal deviation and to move against them in the courts. This conclusion may appear tenuous and based in large degree upon conjecture and circumstantial evidence. But it is considerably strengthened by the fact that another historical phenomenon seems to require its assumption.

CONFESSIONAL STANCE OF OTHER LUTHERAN SYNODS

A number of Lutheran synods who allied themselves with the Hartwick attack on Franckean orthodoxy, and whose assistance was not only accepted but solicited, had taken almost exactly the same stand in regard to the Augsburg Confession as had the Franckeans. The constitution of the General Synod contained not a single reference to the Augsburg Confession until after the Civil War.[65] The General Synod did approve, as early

---

[63]Kreider, *History of the United Lutheran Synod*, 128-33.

[64]*JFS*, 1908.

[65]Many district groups who affiliated with the General Synod as late as the 1840s and 1850s also did not mention the Augsburg Confession in their constitutions, including the Allegheny and the East Pennsylvania synods, organized in 1842; the Pittsburgh Synod, in 1845; and the Northern Indiana Synod, in 1855. This information is found in the official minutes of these synods for the years of their organization, Lutheran Theological Seminary Archives.

as 1823, the *Formula of Discipline* authored by Samuel Schmucker. It included an oath for licensure and ordination in which candidates were asked to confess their belief that the "fundamental doctrines of the Word of God are taught in a manner substantially correct in the doctrinal articles of the Augsburg Confession."[66] But it was only recommended that district groups uniting with the General Synod adopt the *Formula*. There was no requirement to do so. Most affiliating synods did accept it, but not all. The extreme leniency with which this matter was viewed by the General Synod is indicated in a "Pastoral Address" written on its behalf by Samuel Schmucker in 1829. Although adoption of the *Formula* was preferred, district groups who had reservations about it could affiliate by adopting only the constitution, without reference to the Augsburg Confession. And if even this requirement posed a problem, they could join by merely indicating their desire to do so.[67] The single doctrinal requirement for membership in the General Synod at the time of the Franckean organization was a subscription to "the fundamental doctrines of the Bible as taught by our Church." Only much later, as Lutherans moved toward a more conservative stance in the years leading up to the Civil War, did the enigmatic phrase "as taught by our Church" come to be interpreted as having a definite implied reference to a strict interpretation of the Augsburg Confession.

Both the Pennsylvania and the New York ministeriums, two of the oldest, largest, and most influential district synodical bodies of Lutherans in the United States, omitted any mention of the Augsburg Confession, either in the body of their constitutions or in their oath of licensure and ordination, until after the middle of the century.[68] As noted above, the Pennsylvania Synod remained apart from the General Synod until 1853, by which time it had shifted to a definite conservative position. The New York Ministerium, however, united with the general body in 1836. But the action was taken over the strenuous objections of those members who were opposed to numerous aspects of the General Synod, including its moderate approval of the Augsburg Confession. As a result, the ministerium's application for membership was coupled with the stipulation that their action not be interpreted as an acceptance of all the principles contained in the *Formula of Discipline* and that the General Synod be recognized as an "advi-

---

[66]Schmucker, "Formula for the Government and Discipline," 447-48.

[67]Wentz, *Pioneer in Christian Unity*, 91.

[68]From this point on, however, they moved rapidly in a conservative direction and became leaders of the confessional position.

sory body only."[69] The General Synod accepted these reservations without question and voted to "hail with peculiar gratification our brethren of the New York Synod." The resolution expressed the fond hope that "the good example of that revered body will soon be imitated by all the district synods of our Church in the United States, who are as yet not connected with our body."[70] At this same convention of 1837, the General Synod took steps to further alleviate the fears of the New York Ministerium, along with other groups who might be considering affiliation, by amending their constitution. These amendments were designed to make it even more clear than before that they would require no doctrinal statement from their constituent groups that "might in any way tend to burden their consciences."[71]

The New York Ministerium took full advantage of this tolerant policy in regard to doctrinal commitment. It was not until 1858, twenty-two years after their entry into the General Synod, that the ministerium finally required persons whom they licensed or ordained to receive the Augsburg Confession and Luther's *Small Catechism* as a "satisfactory exhibit of the doctrines of our holy religion, as taught in the Word of God."[72] Yet, in 1838, the New York Ministerium joined hands with former dissidents from their own ranks who had attacked the Franckean Synod for its alleged lack of allegiance to the Augsburg Confession. It was a strange partnership, ostensibly created by their common opposition to a doctrinal stance over which these "partners" themselves had only recently quarreled and were still in fact divided! Naturally, the New York Ministerium could not directly press the matter of confessional opposition against the Franckeans. That criticism would have been too obviously hypocritical. Their opposition was couched in the form of vague allegations against certain Franckean practices and their disrupting effect on Lutheran unity. The resolution adopted by the New York Ministerium in September 1838 read as follows: "That we entirely disapprove of the test of Christian fellowship adopted by the Franckean Synod, and of their disorganizing proceedings."[73]

Later, the Franckeans, commenting on this action in the *Lutheran Herald*, pondered over its intention, since it contained no commentary or "pream-

---

[69]*Lutheran Herald* 1 (16 November 1839): 175.

[70]Kreider, *History of the United Lutheran Synod*, 125.

[71]*Constitution of the General Synod*, as amended, 1837; contained in the *Minutes of the General Synod*, 1839, 48.

[72]Kreider, *History of the United Lutheran Synod*, 128.

[73]*Lutheran Herald* 1 (16 March 1839): 44, quoting from the *Minutes of the Hartwick Synod*, 1838.

ble, by which we can be guided to find out what the resolution means." They declared that they had a perfect right to determine "who shall be admitted to the membership of our association" and further maintained that these restrictions pertained only to the clergy. After conjecturing on possible reasons for the disapproval expressed by the ministerium, the Franckeans concluded, "Perhaps they dislike the exclusion of the advocate and apologist for slavery," in which case the ministerium would have to be considered upholders of a system of "inequity, oppression, and injustice."[74]

Earlier in 1837, and only a few weeks after the New York Ministerium had been received with "peculiar gratitude" into the ranks of the General Synod, the *Lutheran Observer*, which so often expressed the majority views of the General Synod, took official notice of the Franckeans. The editor, Benjamin Kurtz, first registered his regret that the Hartwick Synod, for whom he expressed "unqualified respect and admiration," had experienced division within its ranks for "reasons not all evident." He then went on to challenge the Franckeans on precisely the same grounds that were later reflected in the 1838 resolution of the New York Ministerium. The test for admission of ministers into their synod struck him as being most objectionable. He referred specifically to the requirement of total abstinence and the restriction against slaveholders and advocates of slavery. "Can this test be found in the Bible?" he inquired. The editor had no desire to engage in controversy with these "beloved brethren" of the Franckean Synod, but he wondered whether their zeal had not gotten the better of their knowledge. He considered it "presumptuous . . . to set up a test that is not scriptural." While expressing fraternal regard, he warned the Franckeans against "ultraism . . . a blighting epidemic . . . the prevailing error of the age. Extravagance and excess . . . are a fatal mistake . . . the work of the devil, [the Franckeans] are rapidly moving in that direction, if they had not already fallen into it."[75]

Several years later, in 1847, Kurtz, while affirming that he considered the Franckeans sound in all their fundamental doctrines, reminded his readers that he had judged them from the beginning as ultra and wrong, in regard to the slavery question. As a "true moderate," the editor of the *Lutheran Observer* was convinced that, if the North had been more cautious and prudent in its strategy and had permitted the South to proceed at its own pace, more progress would have been made toward a "gradual but

[74]Ibid.

[75]Editorial by Benjamin Kurtz, *Lutheran Observer* 4 (30 June 1837) (no page).

speedy abolition. The middle way is the best way," he concluded.[76] This editorial contained one of the few, if not the only, open and public condemnations of Franckean abolitionism made by the *Observer*, or by any Lutheran publication that served Northern constituents. The General Synod never specifically condemned the Franckeans for their abolitionist stand, although the majority of its members undoubtedly held views similar to those expressed in the editorial.

THE GENERAL SYNOD

The story of the stormy relationship of the Franckean Synod with the General Synod over a period of thirty years contains the most conclusive evidence that the major cause for the rejection of the Franckeans by their fellow Lutherans was their abolitionism. It also strongly supports the contention that opposition to the Franckeans' antislavery sentiments was often expressed under the guise of an objection to their lack of a "confessional standard" and their right to a place within the Lutheran Church. It is therefore important to present the story of that relationship in considerable detail.

APPLICATION FOR MEMBERSHIP

The Franckeans discussed the matter of affiliation with the General Synod at their organizing meeting in May 1837. The result of this discussion was the appointment of a select committee, including three of the founding clergy, to draft a *Discipline of Government* for recommendation to the churches of the new synod.[77] The resulting code, presented at a special meeting of the synod held in October 1837, was based upon the *Formula of Discipline* recommended by the General Synod. Certain articles contained in the *Formula* were excluded, including the reference to the Augsburg Confession in the oath of licensure and ordination. The Franckeans' right to do so was justified by noting that the General Synod was not a "judicatory, but only an advisory body."[78] On the whole, these disclaimers were very similar to those that had been made a year earlier by the New York Ministerium when it united with the General Synod and was received with a sense of "peculiar gratitude," along with the hope that all other district synods not yet affiliated would follow its example. At their first meeting in June 1838, the Franckeans, after some debate, voted

---

[76]Ibid. 15 (17 September 1847): 10.

[77]*JFS*, 1837, 18.

[78]*JFS*, Special Meeting, 5 October 1837, 11. See also letter from the committee on file, 1 October 1837, Franckean Papers.

to unite with the General Synod and to adopt its constitution.[79] Later in the same meeting, delegates were elected to attend the next assembly of the General Synod, to be held at Chambersburg, Pennsylvania, on 31 May 1839, at which time the Franckeans fully expected to be received into membership. The synod also designated that its own next convention would be held beginning 6 June 1839, immediately following the meeting of the General Synod.[80]

For reasons unknown, the General Synod's convention was at a late date rescheduled to begin on 4 June. This action made it impossible for the Franckean delegates to attend, since their own meeting was scheduled on overlapping days. When the Franckeans gathered on the sixth in their chapel at Fordsbush, those who the previous year had been elected delegates to the General Synod reported that, in "consequence of the unconstitutional alterations of the meeting of the General Synod to a different time from its original appointment, they could not attend."[81] In spite of this unavoidable absence of their delegates from the General Synod convention, the Franckeans appeared to expect a favorable reply to their request for membership, since later in the convention they unanimously adopted the *Discipline of Government*, based in large part upon the *Formula* recommended by the General Synod.[82]

REJECTION

There was ample reason for the Franckeans' optimism regarding their application for membership in the General Synod. Up until this time, no district group had ever been refused. In fact, synods had been actively recruited, cajoled, and practically begged to affiliate for the sake of a larger Lutheran unity. Yet on 5 June 1839, just one day before the Franckeans gathered for their own annual meeting, the General Synod passed a resolution of an unprecedented character that rudely rejected the Franckean overture. The action led to a violent antagonism between the two groups that remained unhealed for nearly two decades. The bizarre nature of the resolution was amplified by the fact that the condemnation of the Franckeans was coupled with that of the ultraconservative Tennessee Synod. The complete resolution along with its preamble and brief preliminary remarks

[79] *JFS*, 1838, 8.

[80] Ibid., 25.

[81] *JFS*, 1839, 10-11.

[82] Ibid., 23.

was printed in the official minutes of the General Synod under the heading "Franckean Synod and Tennessee Conference."

> Some statements having been made respecting the bodies known by the above names, and the opinion of the Synod having been asked, various resolutions and substitutes were offered without success, when the Synod finally adopted the following:

> Whereas certain persons, claiming to be ministers and members of our Church, have formed themselves into ecclesiastical bodies, called "The Tennessee Synod," and also "The Franckean Synod of the Evangelical Lutheran Church;" and whereas, said persons are introducing practices which we consider contrary to the Word of God, thereby causing disturbances and divisions in our Churches: Therefore

> VII. Resolved, that we deem it our sacred duty to give a public expression of our disapprobation of these proceedings, and to exhort the Churches in our connection, and all Evangelical Lutheran Churches in the United States, to beware of the efforts of these men to cause divisions and offenses contrary to the Spirit of the Gospel. [83]

The whole tenor of this resolution was shockingly out of character with both the nature and purpose of the General Synod and with its previous actions. Its own constitution clearly denied it the right to judge or condemn other synodical bodies. Its stated goal was to gather as many district synods as possible under the umbrella of its union. Over the years it had developed a highly politic and sophisticated method of deleting from its official minutes all discussions of a controversial nature. Yet, in this case, there had apparently been no alternative. Those who pushed the issue had been determined to pass a resolution of condemnation and to have it officially recorded. The vagueness of its phrasing is understandable. But why was it worded in such a harsh and almost insulting manner, referring to those "claiming to be ministers and members of our Church?"

Even more puzzling, why was the Franckean Synod condemned in the same resolution and with the identical wording as the Tennessee Synod? No two Lutheran groups in the country were more widely separated in theology and practice. The founders of the Tennessee Synod had objected vigorously to what they considered laxity in doctrine and practice on the part of those groups who formed the General Synod. [84] Its members looked

---

[83]*Proceedings of the General Synod,* 1839, 23.

[84]Wentz, *Basic History of Lutheranism in America,* 71.

upon most "Pietistic practices" as fanaticism and insisted upon a strict and complete adherence to the "unadulterated" Augsburg Confession and the other symbolic books of the Lutheran church. They opposed Schmucker's appeal for Christian union as "unpracticable and inexpedient" and condemned the " 'New Measures' being introduced into the Lutheran church by modern enthusiasts, . . . as contrary to the Word of God and the doctrines of the Augsburg Confession."[85] This blast at the New Measures was directed not only at Schmucker and the General Synod but at the Franckean Synod in particular.[86] The history of the Tennessee Synod differed drastically from that of the Franckean Synod. In 1839, the Tennessee group had already existed for nearly twenty years, and during all this time they had never expressed any desire whatever to affiliate with the General Synod. The Tennessee group was similar to the Franckeans in only one respect. It did not hesitate to rebuke its synodical neighbors directly and repeatedly.[87]

It is little wonder that this resolution labeling two such diametrically different groups with the same offense was considered by many as an amazing and even ludicrous action. In its report on the convention, which was hosted by their city, the Chambersburg, Pennsylvania, *Weekly Messenger*, commenting on the resolution in question, wrote:

> It appears that the [Tennessee] Synod adheres strictly to the Augsburg Confession . . . and finds fault with its brethren, who have departed from the ancient doctrines of the Church . . . as . . . taught by Luther. . . . The Franckean Synod on the other hand seems to go to the opposite extreme, by casting off . . . the 'land marks' of the Church, and setting up new tests of Church membership. . . . The members of this Synod are all for activity—the others for passivity; or as it was aptly expressed . . . 'the one has all the sediment, the other has all the froth.'[88]

---

[85]*Proceedings of the Twenty-First Session of the Evangelical Lutheran Tennessee Synod,* September 1841, 10-11, Lutheran Theological Seminary Archives.

[86]The Franckeans had taken notice of these remarks and replied that the so-called New Measures of revivals, prayer meetings, and family worship were really old, having been instituted by Luther, Arndt, Spener, and Francke (*Lutheran Herald* 4 [15 March 1842]: 4).

[87]*Proceedings of the Nineteenth Session of the Evangelical Lutheran Tennessee Synod,* September 1839, 14-15.

[88]*Lutheran Herald* 1 (16 August 1839): 124, quoting an article from the *Albany Argus* originally carried in the *Chambersburg Weekly Messenger*.

The Franckeans added their own postscript to these comments, noting that the "Tennessee Synod is denounced for holding fast literally to the Augsburg Confession and we for casting it off; thus, whether we adhere or remove this 'landmark' we must be denounced. What a dilemma!"[89]

The more serious reaction of the Franckeans was akin to the furious anger of a rejected suitor. They were bitterly resentful over what was considered an unwarranted, unjust, and uncharitable judgment. They labeled the resolution a "high-handed measure," both "ridiculous and unaccountable," and called on the members of the General Synod to read and pray over the words of Scripture, " 'judge not, that ye may not be judged,' in order that they might see their error."[90] The primary objection of the Franckeans was not just that they had been judged but that this judgment had been rendered without constitutional authority, that it was imprecise and ambiguous, and that their representatives had not been present to defend themselves. In an article signed "Francke," a contributor to the *Herald* compared the General Synod's assumption of ecclesiastical jurisdiction and power to that of the Old School Presbyterian General Assembly, which had condemned and excommunicated four of its synodical groups. However, in that case, "Francke" complained,

> These synods were represented and a constituent part of the Assembly. But . . . we are condemned and denounced for . . . 'practices which are causing disturbances and divisions in our Churches,' without being cited, heard or even being united with the General Synod. . . . The practices are 'contrary to the Word of God' but in vain do we ask what are those practices? They lie concealed among the Archives of the secret conclave.[91]

The Franckeans protested that there were few courts in the world where persons could be condemned without being informed of their offense and without being heard, "unless it be the bloody Inquisition," and called for the cry of "Condemned Unheard" to be sounded abroad and proclaimed throughout the churches. In their eyes it was "rank Popery," and throughout their history they referred to the Resolution of 1839 as the "Bull of Denunciation."[92]

---

[89]Ibid.

[90]Ibid.

[91]*Lutheran Herald* 1 (16 October 1839): 158.

[92]Ibid. 4 (15 December 1842): n.p.

REASONS FOR REJECTION
SOUGHT AND DISCOVERED

The Franckeans were determined to discover the real meaning of the General Synod's resolution and the reasons for their rejection. Early in September 1839, the members of their Central Conference addressed an official letter to the secretary of the General Synod, John G. Morris, requesting information. They asked to be instructed concerning the nature and content of those "practices and proceedings" of which they were charged in the resolution as being "contrary to the Word of God." They further requested the names of those who had made the statements referred to in the preamble of the resolution and what evidence was produced to show that their synod had engaged in the practices of which it was accused.

The letter was designated by the writer as friendly, and its aim simply to become "acquainted with the charges, so that we may judge of their correctness, and the public mind be disabused."[93] The reply received from the secretary of the General Synod provided few answers. Morris replied that it was impossible for him to furnish the information requested. He "took no notes of the debate" and had only "a vague recollection . . . at this remote period." He did remember that the "alleged irregular proceedings of your synod and those of the Tennessee Conference were indiscriminately spoken of," but he did not recall the specific charges brought against the Franckeans. He did, however, have a distinct recollection that "something was said in relation to theological error and irregularity in the formation of your synod" and that "your printed proceedings or other publications were adduced as proof of the charge." However, he was not certain these charges were sustained and suggested that someone else who "paid more attention" might furnish the Franckeans with "more definite information." As for the request to identify the persons involved, Morris considered it improper and declined to answer. The General Synod would sustain its own actions and could not allow its members "to be drawn into unpleasant and unprofitable controversies, and held accountable for the doings of the whole body." Morris considered the matter closed. The synod had expressed a "deliberate opinion," and he declared that it would not be discussed any further.[94] Far from contributing to a peaceful settlement of the controversy, this curt reply added fuel to the fire.

The Franckeans rejected the secretary's appeal to a lack of recollection, noting that "some men have very treacherous memories, especially when . . . they wish to *evade* a plain, honest and just question." As to Morris's

---

[93]Ibid. 1 (16 November 1839): 169.

[94]Ibid.

assertion that the General Synod would sustain its actions, the Franckeans wanted to know if the method of doing so was by *"silence* and *evasion?"* And as for the refusal to discuss the matter further, they labeled it "usurpation" and prayed God would "forgive the erring acts of our brethren." The Franckeans took special notice of the fact that their alleged "anti-Biblical practices" referred to in the original resolution had been reduced by Morris to "irregularities." They were curious as to whether this modification was due to the secretary's "vague recollections" at such a "remote period?" At any rate they were interested in the precise nature of these irregularities. Then for the first time they openly voiced their suspicions as to what they were. "Perhaps it is deemed 'irregular' in us that we do not admit drunkards and slave-holders as ministers into our synod. . . . This we presume is departing from the regular course pursued by some synods and Churches."[95]

By the time of their next convention, held in June 1840, the Franckeans were prepared to react forcefully and officially to the infamous Bull of Denunciation. They first accused the General Synod of proceeding against them "without any shadow of authority." They rescinded the action taken the previous year to unite with the General Synod, declaring that action null and void and ordering it to be "forever obliterated and erased from our Journals." They further resolved that they never had and never would join the General Synod. Finally, they once again raised the question concerning the meaning of both the preamble and the resolution. They maintained that none of their practices had been shown to be contrary to the Word of God. Their conviction about the specific reasons for which they had been condemned appear by this time to have been strengthened. "Although our sentiments and efforts, on the subjects of *American Slavery—Total Abstinence—Temperance*—and the 'Bible our only standard,' does meet the 'disapprobation' of the [General Synod] . . . yet we have assurance that they meet the complete and unqualified approbation of the Holy God of Israel."[96] A Baptist newspaper reported that the Franckeans believed they had been censured especially for their views on abolition and temperance.[97]

The suspicion that the ostracism by their fellow Lutherans stemmed from their moral activism rather than from doctrinal differences continued to grow with the passing of time. After the unsatisfactory reply to their request for information regarding the reasons for their condemnation by the General Synod, the Franckeans continued to seek for answers in other

---

[95]Ibid., 170.

[96]*JFS*, 1840, 20-21.

[97]*Lutheran Herald* 2 (2 November 1840): 81.

areas. By November 1839, it was reported in the *Herald* that information had been received indicating that, in its "original form . . . the mover of the sweeping resolution" had wished to denounce the Franckeans alone "as anti-Lutheran, because we have not adopted the Augsburg Confession as our standard of faith."[98] This source further indicated that, when there was seen to be insufficient support for this charge, the resolution was finally modified to its "present form," which included the Tennessee Synod. It is evident from this report that the Franckeans had at last ascertained that the reason the accusation had been formulated in such an amorphous fashion had been to gain the necessary additional support for its passage. The minutes of the General Synod had indicated that "various resolutions and substitutes were offered without success" until a compromise motion was "finally adopted."[99] The primary reason for yoking the Tennessee Synod with the Franckeans had apparently been to secure the support of Southern Pietists, who, while deploring the Franckean's abolitionism, were much more deeply opposed to the Tennessee Synod's strict confessionalism, which directly threatened to divide some of their own congregations. This concern existed primarily in the Virginia Synod and the synods of North and South Carolina.[100]

This analysis of the Southern viewpoint was confirmed by letters written to the *Lutheran Observer* by the Reverend P. A. Strobel, pastor of a parish in Columbia, South Carolina, an author and historian of considerable repute,[101] and by the Reverend Ernest Hazelius, the professor of theology at the South Carolina Seminary. Hazelius wrote that he would never consider having fellowship with the Tennessee Synod ministers until they "sincerely repent of their sins." Among that synod's most objectionable features, he listed (1) their opposition to "all the benevolent operations of the day" and (2) their literal adherence to the Augsburg Confession.[102] Strobel's letter was written when efforts were being made within the General Synod to rescind the 1839 resolution. The delegates from South Carolina had been instructed by their synod to vote against the proposal to rescind, which was due primarily because of opposition to the Tennessee and not to the

---

[98]Ibid. 1 (16 November 1839): 170.

[99]*Proceedings of the General Synod*, 1839, 17.

[100]*Proceedings of the Nineteenth Session of the Evangelical Lutheran Tennessee Synod*, September 1839, 14-15.

[101]Jones, *Saltzburger Saga*, ix.

[102]Ernest L. Hazelius, *Lutheran Observer* 4 (31 May 1839).

Franckean Synod. Strobel, who had also been in attendance at the 1839 meeting and who was a delegate from his synod, wrote:

> We have no very great objections to the rescinding of that *part* of the resolution which relates to the Franckean Synod. We know that the brethren composing that synod are 'abolitionists' of the ultra school, but we do not and cannot object to them on that ground, for we are fully aware, that some very prominent and highly useful ministers in our Church are 'abolitionists' and yet we honor and love them. I was opposed to classing the Franckeans with the Tennessee Synod from the very outset, and every day's experience confirms me in the correctness of this opinion. We of the South will never consent however to acknowledge the Tennessee synod. [103]

The "prominent and highly useful" abolitionist ministers Strobel referred to are without doubt Samuel Schmucker and some of his colleagues. Here is concrete evidence that the most intense opposition to the abolitionism of Schmucker as well as the Franckeans came not from Southern Pietists but from strict confessionalists in the North. Even more important, the letter offers direct testimony by a reliable witness that the action taken against the Franckeans was due primarily to their abolitionism and strongly implies that the creation of a motion ambiguous enough to apply also to the Tennessee Synod's ultraconfessionalism was a strategy designed to secure its passage.

The Franckeans had earlier received a letter dated 27 December 1839 from a brother minister "who had been in attendance at the meeting of the General Synod when the resolution against them had been passed," which confirmed their suspicions. This letter may have also come from P. A. Strobel, who on numerous other occasions corresponded with them. We cannot know for certain, since the author was not disclosed by the Franckeans. It read as follows:

> Dr. L. [George Lintner of the Hartwick Synod] introduced a paper containing various charges against the Franckean Synod. These consisted of two classes, 1st *doctrinal* and 2nd *practical* errors. The first consisted of your departure from the Augsburg Confession(!!!!) and unsoundness upon the subject of the Trinity, the establishment of unwarranted tests, etc. But these charges met with little sympathy from the great body of the delegates in the synod, to say nothing of other brethren in attendance. Your *Orthodoxy* was strenuously de-

---

[103]*Lutheran Herald* 4 (15 December 1842): n. p., quoted from the *Lutheran Observer*, n. d.

fended by several of us, and generally admitted (!!!). It was the set of charges relative to your irregularity, the admission of unqualified persons into the ministry . . . wild fire fanaticism . . . etc., but especially perhaps your anti-slavery movements that effected your condemnation.[104]

To use the Franckeans' own words of reaction to this letter, "Here then we have it."[105] Lintner had presented the charges accusing the Franckeans of both doctrinal and practical errors. The doctrinal errors were nearly identical to those raised in the civil suit that had been initiated by his synod only a few weeks earlier. The Hartwickians were supported by others who wished to act against the Franckeans so that they could "adversely affect" this "chancery suit."[106] The Hartwick representatives and their allies had obviously wanted a direct accusation from the General Synod asserting that the Franckeans were doctrinally unsound and had abandoned the Augsburg Confession. But it had not been possible. There were too many defenders of Franckean orthodoxy. The final wording of the resolution and its passage relied primarily on a more widespread reaction against the alleged "practical errors," that is, the involvement of the Franckeans in the abolitionist movement, an opposition that few, if any, were prepared to express openly.

According to still other information they received, the Franckeans did indeed have a number of friends who vigorously defended their cause during the debate over the resolution. A letter from a former Franckean clergyman, who at the time was serving under a district synod in Pennsylvania, mentions some of these persons by name. In addition to Strobel there was the Rev. R. Weiser, a representative of the West Pennsylvania Synod, whom the writer describes as a "fearless preacher . . . and a most decided friend of our Franckean Synod."

The author of this letter, who appears to be giving an eyewitness account of the 1839 Convention of the General Synod, says that Weiser "was restrained from acting in your defense, in open Synod, by his friends, because he was agitated and would have made dreadful havoc." However, other representatives from Maryland and Pennsylvania did the speaking,

---

[104]Ibid.

[105]Ibid.

[106]J. Rosenberg to Philip Wieting, Middleburg PA, 2 March 1841, Franckean Papers. During the trial, a copy of the resolution of the General Synod condemning the Franckeans for practices contrary to the Word of God was presented as evidence of their lack of Lutheran orthodoxy. See "Kniskern vs. Wieting," 471.

while Weiser prompted them. The letter identified a Rev. Sahm, also from the West Pennsylvania Synod, as a "man of sterling worth . . . and a devoted friend" of the Franckeans. Samuel Schmucker's brother-in-law, Samuel Sprecher, was portrayed as "a warm friend of our synod [who] considers the conduct of the General Synod an unconstitutional and unparalleled outrage." Apparently there had been conflicting reports circulating concerning the position Samuel Schmucker had taken on the matter, for the writer assures his Franckean colleagues that "Professor Schmucker is not your enemy, nor is Dr. Schmucker his father against you, for I have had personal conversation with him on that subject." All of the persons named in this letter were close colleagues of Samuel Schmucker. The writer further noted that the representations made against the Franckeans had no effect on the minds of the "pious revived ministers" in attendance. Finally, the letter threw further suspicion on the fact that the last-minute change in the date of the meeting may have been part of a conspiracy to keep the Franckean delegates from attending, for its author added, "Had [the resolution] not been so unexpected it could never have happened, and had any of you been there they would have been blown up entirely."[107]

One further item of correspondence provides additional evidence that the primary issue at stake in the resolution directed against the Franckeans was abolitionism. In a letter to Philip Wieting from his nephew Archibald Wieting, written in the early spring of 1843, the younger Wieting protested his uncle's attack on his personal decision to unite with the East Pennsylvania Synod. Philip Wieting had been critical of the synod for not speaking out publicly against the General Synod's 1839 attack on the Franckeans. Archibald defended the East Pennsylvanians. He felt sure that they would vote to rescind the resolution because he was convinced that its members were "all abolitionists."[108] This letter clearly implied that the question of voting for or against the resolution rested upon the presence or absence of abolitionist convictions.

The cumulative evidence suggesting that the rejection of the Franckean Synod in 1839 by the largest body of Lutherans in the United States was based primarily upon an opposition to the Franckeans' abolitionism is formidable and nearly irrefutable. A number of Lutheran historians have in fact agreed with this conclusion. Douglas Stange, Robert Fortenbaugh, and Abdel Ross Wentz all comment to the effect that the General Synod's Res-

---

[107]J. Rosenberg to Philip Wieting, 2 March 1841, Franckean Papers.

[108]Archibald Wieting to Philip Wieting, Hummulstown, 2 March 1843, Franckean Papers.

olution of 1839 was directed at the Franckeans' antislavery activities.[109] Strangely enough, not one of these writers produced a single item of evidence to support this contention. Either it seemed so obvious as not to require documentation or they had none in hand.

It is far more surprising that these historians see little if any significance in this conclusion. They simply relate, in passing, that the action of the General Synod was directed at the antislavery sentiments of the Franckeans and then appear to blot it from memory. They fail, for the most part, ever to mention it again.[110] They continue to accept at face value the Franckeans' alleged lack of Lutheran orthodoxy and allegiance to the Augsburg Confession as the real reason for their rejection, without making any reference whatever to the antiabolitionism that, according to their own earlier admission, lurked behind these allegations.[111] Not a single Lutheran history interprets the ongoing relationship of the General Synod and the Franckeans up until the end of the Civil War with any reference whatever to the slavery question, even though the tension between these two groups continued throughout all those years and at the time of the Civil War erupted dramatically, with grave and lasting consequences for the unity of the Lutheranism in this country. This represents a serious and significant historical omission.

REJECTION RETRACTED

Once the Franckeans had a more accurate knowledge of what had actually transpired and of the motivating factors behind the passage of the infamous Bull of Denunciation, they made it known that the General Synod could make amends in only one way. They would have to rescind the resolution at their next session.[112] In response to this demand, efforts were

---

[109]Stange, *Radicalism for Humanity* (St. Louis: Oliver Slave Limited, 1970) 42; Fortenbaugh, "American Lutheran Synods and Slavery," 78; Wentz, *Basic History of Lutheranism in America*, 164.

[110]Wentz does comment that the action taken by the General Synod in 1857 to rescind the Resolution of 1839 also had a relationship to the abolitionist controversy (*Basic History of Lutheranism in America*, 164).

[111]For instance, Wentz, *Basic History of Lutheranism in America*, 149, in explaining the severe negative reaction to the Franckeans' tentative acceptance by the General Synod in 1864, simply says, "Now the Franckean Synod had never accepted the Augsburg Confession. It had its own 'declaration of faith' in which the distinctive doctrines of Lutheranism were not contained."

[112]*Lutheran Herald* 3 (15 February 1841): 29.

immediately set in motion by the friends of the Franckeans to do so. During the next convention of the General Synod, in 1841, a motion to rescind was made by the Reverend John B. Davis, the president of the Virginia Synod and a delegate from that body.[113] It was presented in the following form: "*Resolved* That the eighth Resolution of the . . . [1839] convention of this synod, with its preamble, is not in accordance with the spirit of this constitution, and is not the sentiment of this Synod."

Immediately upon the introduction of this motion, another member rose and moved that the consideration of the resolution be indefinitely postponed. The vote was called for, and the result was a tie—twelve persons in favor of indefinite postponement (in reality a vote against the motion to rescind), and twelve opposed. As fate would have it, the president and presiding officer of the General Synod for that year was none other than George Lintner, of the Hartwick Synod, inveterate foe of the Franckeans, who had introduced the original resolution against them. Lintner then cast the deciding vote, which squelched the effort to rescind.[114] It was requested that the names of those voting for and against the measure be recorded in the minutes. The Franckeans, who for some inexplicable reason received a copy of these minutes in German, even though the General Synod sessions were conducted in English, protested their limited knowledge of that language and their inability to decipher most of it. However, they carefully translated the motion to rescind.

Referring to its language, which characterized the 1839 resolution as out of harmony with the spirit of the General Synod's constitution, the Franckeans added that it was even less in harmony with "the spirit of the Gospel of God." They believed the action was not just unconstitutional but "unChristian," a "spot on all their proceedings and a dark . . . transaction . . . until it is repealed and restoration made." They noted with an almost grim satisfaction that "the vote of the President, G. S. Lintner, was the responsible one" and that "by it, the righteous deed was postponed." They presumed that "the vote . . . will pretty correctly declare, who are our friends, or enemies." Among the enemies in addition to Lintner they noted the name of John G. Morris, the secretary of the 1839 convention from whom they had unsuccessfully sought information, and Benjamin Kurtz, editor of the *Lutheran Observer*, whom they characterized as having "stabbed them under the fifth rib." Among their friends the Franckeans singled out the principal of the theological seminary at Gettysburg, S. S. Schmucker,

---

[113]Ibid. (15 September 1842): 102.

[114]*Proceedings of the General Synod*, 1841, 20.

and added with a solemnity reminiscent of Hamlet's dedication to the spirit of his father, "We will remember you."[115]

The Franckeans fully expected that the motion to rescind would again be presented at the 1843 Convention of the General Synod in Baltimore and even reported that Virginia Synod delegates had once again been instructed to do so.[116] But there is no record that the motion was ever made, and during the coming years it remained unchallenged. As the tension over the slavery issue continued to build and as abolitionism became more politicized than ever, the movement to repeal the action appears to have been temporarily discontinued. Then suddenly in 1857, eighteen years after its original passage, the offending resolution was finally annulled by "a large majority." The vote was not recorded. It appears that the action as well as its outcome had been anticipated, for representatives from the Franckean Synod had been invited to attend the General Synod Convention in Reading, Pennsylvania. Rev. Philip Wieting and Nicholas Van Alstine were cordially received as "advisory members" and sat in on all sessions.[117] A few weeks later they reported to their fellow members that they were gratified with what they had seen and heard and that much good feeling had been expressed toward them.

What had brought about this change within the membership of the General Synod? Why, in 1857, could an action that had remained on the record for nearly twenty years, in spite of repeated efforts to remove it, be retracted by "a large majority?" Why at this point was there a greater willingness to show leniency toward the Franckean Synod? There is little evidence to provide any conclusive answer. However, it is important to look carefully at possible reasons for shifts in attitudes that might account for the timing of this rescinding action. The change could certainly not be traced to any tendency on the part of the General Synod to look with more moderation upon any lack of confessionalism exhibited by the Franckeans. On the contrary, a stricter confessionalism had increased immeasurably within the ranks of the General Synod, and its exponents had only just fought and won a decisive battle against Schmucker's *Definite Platform.* Could it, on the other hand, have arisen from a lessening of hostility toward the Franckeans' abolitionism?

Although the tension over the abolition of slavery had increased dramatically by 1857, it was primarily in terms of a North-South division. In

---

[115]*Lutheran Herald* 3 (1 September 1841): 132.

[116]Ibid. 4 (15 September 1842): 102.

[117]*Proceedings of the General Synod,* 1857, 1.

the North itself, it had rather decreased, as Northerners became more united in the conviction that the slavery issue was not to be solved through compromise. By 1857, the mood in the North had become much more militant against slavery. *Uncle Tom's Cabin* was published in 1852, arousing millions of otherwise complacent persons against the evils of slavery. The hopes and dreams of a compromise solution were shattered by the Kansas-Nebraska Act of 1854. The Whig party quickly dissolved, and the Democrats divided into warring factions, while the intensely ideological Republican party was born. The rapidity of these changes continues to amaze historians. Previous to 1854, Lincoln was a comfortable Whig opposed to abolitionism. After 1854, he, like many other politicians, became a different person.[118] John Brown's holy crusade against slavery, in the form of a paramilitary action in Kansas, was a direct result of the Kansas-Nebraska Act. The savage beating in May 1856 of Senator Charles Sumner of Massachusetts by a Southern congressman as Sumner sat in the United States Senate chamber stirred militant emotions even more. Finally the Dred Scott decision, rendered by the Supreme Court in March 1857, proved to be the final nail pounded into the coffin of compromise.

By the early summer of 1857, the inevitability of open conflict to resolve the slavery issue was more thoroughly accepted than ever before. Many of those who had been moderates on the issue of slavery had come to look upon the call for immediate abolition with newfound insight and more sympathetic understanding. The original hostility to Franckean abolitionism, as was noted before, had come more from the conservative neutrality of Lutherans in the North than from the more open opposition of Pietists in the South. If abolitionism was indeed the key issue, then it follows that a diminution in the belligerency of Northerners toward abolitionism could at least in part account for the fact that in 1857 a majority was at last secured to pass legislation opening the door to Franckean membership in the General Synod.

CONTINUING CONFLICT

In spite of the "large majority" who finally voted to rescind the 1839 resolution, a minority remained unconvinced of its rectitude, and their resentment toward the Franckeans continued unabated. The Hartwick Synod, at their convention later in 1857, took action to "reject the repeal of the Resolution" on the grounds that "it was a dangerous precedent for future

---

[118]Charles B. Strozier, *Lincoln's Quest for Union: Public and Private Meanings* (New York: Basic Books, 1982) 198.

action in the General Synod."[119] The Franckeans themselves were for the most part delighted by the action they had called for so long. Their delegates reported that the detested resolutions of 1839 had been repealed and "prefaced by many cordial expressions." Wieting also noted that "strong desires were expressed from various sources, that our body might at no distant period be connected with the General Synod." In his president's report he recommended the immediate consideration of this subject by the members of the synod.[120] Years later, Nicholas Van Alstine recalled that "the mind of our Synod was changed, and feelings reconciled by the fraternal action of the General Synod."[121] Still, many of the Franckean members were not so ready to rush into the waiting arms of the General Synod as their president had hoped. When a resolution was introduced at their convention in 1857 simply noting the propriety of forming a union with the General Synod, it "elicited a protracted discussion" before it was finally adopted. "The position occupied by the General Synod in regard to symbolism and slavery were the principal reasons urged against such a union."[122]

In 1859, President Wieting reminded the Franckeans that they still had taken no decisive steps to unite with the General Synod. He believed the time had come and that it was in the best interests of all concerned to do so. His appeal was couched in the rhetoric of the day. "We all know that in Union lies strength . . . we are almost the only synod that sympathizes with the General Synod, that stands aloof from it. . . . Brethren, let us act wisely and prudently, for our benefit and the benefit of the whole Church."[123] But in spite of the influence of this respected founder, the majority of the Franckean delegates were not yet ready to request membership in a synod that had made no official proclamation against slavery.

Following the outbreak of the Civil War, as more and more groups rallied around the antislavery cause, the Franckeans issued their own call for unity. They entreated "all the members of the Churches to lay aside . . . every feeling of animosity and discord, which may have arisen among them, in view of our national trials, as well as other causes . . . and to come by the help of the Lord against the foes of Christ."[124] Putting this sentiment

---

[119]*Missionary* 2 (1 October 1857): 141, Lutheran Theological Seminary Archives.

[120]*JFS*, 1857, 7.

[121]N. Van Alstine, *Historical Review*, 18.

[122]*Lutheran Observer* 25 (10 July 1857): n. p.

[123]*JFS*, 1859, 6.

[124]Ibid., 1862, 20.

into action, they engaged in an exchange of official delegates and fraternal greetings with the New York Ministerium and appointed a committee to confer with representatives from both the ministerium and the Hartwick Synod on the status of Hartwick Seminary.[125]

The General Synod postponed their regular meeting in 1861, still vainly hoping, even as armed conflict raged between the states, that they could avoid a break with the Southern synods. Finally rejecting this illusory hope, they met at Lancaster, Pennsylvania, in 1862, with no delegates present from the synods in the South. Here for the first time the General Synod belatedly spoke out against the evils of human slavery, ascribing the cause of the war to the "spread of domestic slavery." They endorsed President Lincoln's plans for emancipation and condemned the military action of the South as "rebellion . . . most wicked in its inception . . . and destructive to the highest interests of morality and religion."[126] The Franckeans now could agree fully with the General Synod. At their next convention, in 1863, a quarter of a century after their first overture was rejected, the Franckeans voted again to unite with the larger body. They adopted its constitution and appointed a committee to select delegates to its next convention, to be held at York, Pennsylvania, in 1864.

TENTATIVE ACCEPTANCE AND REACTIONS

But the wounds and resentments of the past were not yet fully healed, and a vocal minority of General Synod delegates were still determined to deny the Franckeans' request for membership. An official protest was lodged on the grounds that the admittance of the Franckeans violated the constitution of the General Synod, which stated that only Lutheran synods were to be received into union. Once again it was claimed that the Franckean Synod was not Lutheran because it had never officially adopted the Augsburg Confession as a doctrinal basis.[127] Yet, at its previous conventions in 1862, the General Synod had issued a plea to all of its district synods to adopt its *Formula of Government and Discipline*,[128] clearly indicating that a number of synods were in the same position as the Franckeans.

During the heated debate that followed the protest over the Franckean admission, the legal decision of the civil courts rendered in 1844 by Vice-

---

[125]Ibid., 23, 29.

[126]Wentz, *Basic History of Lutheranism in America*, 167.

[127]Heathcote, *Lutheran Church and the Civil War*, 133.

[128]*Proceedings of the General Synod*, 1862.

Chancellor Sanford was quoted as proof that the Franckeans had renounced the Augsburg Confession.[129] At this point in the debate, the
Franckean delegation, headed by Philip Wieting and Nicholas Van Alstine, submitted a report stating that they had been misunderstood. They
testified that they never had any problems with the doctrinal position of
the General Synod, namely, "that the fundamental truths of the Word of
God are taught in a manner substantially correct in the Augsburg Confession." They assured the delegates that, when their members officially
adopted the constitution of the General Synod at its meeting in 1863, they
had understood they were also affirming that confessional concept.[130] A
conciliatory attempt was then made to satisfy the objections being raised
to the Franckean reception. Stating that it was desirable for the Franckeans
to express in "a more formal manner, its adherence to said doctrinal basis,"
the following resolution was presented for adoption: "That the Franckean
Synod is hereby received into connection with the General Synod with the
understanding that said synod at its next meeting, declare, in an official
manner, its adoption of the doctrinal articles of the Augsburg Confession,
as a substantially correct exhibition of the fundamental doctrines of the
Word of God."[131] This resolution was passed by a vote of 97 to 40, with
all votes being recorded by name in the minutes.

Even this tentative reception, contingent on further formal action, did
not assuage the strong feelings of the minority group. The next day, a formal protest against the Franckeans' admission to the General Synod on the
aforementioned alleged constitutional grounds was presented. It was signed
by twenty-eight delegates, including those from ten of the approximately
twenty-five district synods affiliated with the General Synod.[132] Ten of the
signatories were members of the Pennsylvania Ministerium, the oldest and
largest of the affiliated groups. Immediately following the filing of this
general protest, the delegation from the Pennsylvania Ministerium presented their own. They then withdrew from the sessions of the General
Synod in order to report the synod's "unconstitutional" actions to their own

---

[129]N. Van Alstine, *Historical Review,* 19. Van Alstine contended that, according
to this ruling of the vice-chancellor, which held that one must hold to the Augsburg Confession in its entirety to be Lutheran, the whole General Synod would
be excommunicated from the Lutheran church.

[130]*Proceedings of the General Synod,* 1864, 17.

[131]Ibid., 18-19.

[132]Ibid., 24-25.

approaching convention.[133] Following this walkout, an official reply to the Pennsylvanians' protest was presented by a committee of the General Synod. It expressed confidence that in reality the Franckeans had done everything required by the constitution for their admission. By requesting that further formal actions be taken, they felt they had "yielded to the consciences of some of the brethren, . . . in order to harmonize the whole synod."[134] There the matter was left, and the Franckean delegates returned home to their own convention, upset by the proceedings but satisfied by the majority vote for their tentative acceptance. They were pleased that their representative, Philip Wieting, had been able to attach his name to a resolution of the General Synod denouncing all attempts to prove the divine institution of American slavery from the Scriptures and condemning it as "a system of human oppression which exists only by violence, under cover of iniquitous laws."[135]

But before the convention of the General Synod had ended, a portentous amendment to its constitution had been proposed. Its intention was to change its doctrinal basis from the traditional qualified acceptance of the Augsburg Confession to a complete approval of that confession in all of its parts.[136] This action appears to have been, at least in part, an attempt to conciliate further those offended by the Franckean reception and especially the large Pennsylvania Ministerium, whose delegates had left the convention.[137] Some of those who voted for it undoubtedly viewed it as a final attempt to keep the Franckeans out. It did indeed pose a problem for that beleaguered synod. The Franckeans' reception by the General Synod had been left contingent on their formally adopting a doctrinal standard with which they fully agreed, but one that they had been accused for two decades of rejecting. Now, they were faced with the possibility of having to accept a position that had been drastically altered.

During their convention a few weeks later, the Franckean delegates to the General Synod related what had transpired. They reported that their "application was met by a small minority . . . with strong opposition; one that indicated that our case was prejudged . . . it seemed to us . . . on issues that were not expressed in the Constitution of the General Synod."

---

[133]Ibid., 25-26.

[134]Ibid., 41-42.

[135]Ibid., 35.

[136]*JFS*, 1864, 8, 20-21.

[137]Wentz, *Basic History of Lutheranism in America*, 150.

They proceeded to recommend that the request to adopt formally the historical doctrinal basis of the General Synod be taken, which was done.[138] However, the proposed amendment to the Constitution of the General Synod, radically altering its confessional stance, was spoken of in most disparaging terms. The Franckeans would have none of it and vigorously protested. "There are those in our Church who assume to Lord it over Lutheranism in America. . . . Let us . . . remember that Lutheranism is only . . . a schoolmaster to bring us to Christ. . . . These symbolists are putting up partition walls in the house of Lutherans . . . they contend for denominational distinction."[139] After having spoken, the Franckeans proceeded to act. They rejected the proposed amendment, with only one vote cast in the affirmative.[140]

SCHISM AND ITS CAUSES

The 1866 Convention of the General Synod was held at Fort Wayne, Indiana. It was the first attended by the Franckean delegates after their tentative reception as members and was destined to be one of the most disruptive meetings in the history of the Lutheran church in this country. After five days of wrangling over procedural matters, the delegation of the Pennsylvania Ministerium, which had walked out of the 1864 convention over the question of the Franckeans' acceptance, declared their connection with the General Synod dissolved. By the following year the Pennsylvania insurgents, under the leadership of Charles Porterfield Krauth, had organized the "General Council of the Evangelical Church of North America," united on the basis of an "unqualified allegiance to the unaltered Augsburg Confession."[141] The more conservative elements of the General Synod withdrew to join with this newly formed body. Those who continued in union with the General Synod remained the most receptive of all Lutheran groups to an involvement in social and political concerns, which began to

---

[138]*JFS*, 1864, 18-19.

[139]Ibid., 1865, 8-9.

[140]Ibid., 39. At the next convention of the General Synod, in 1866, the Franckean delegation accordingly voted against the proposed amendment, but it was nevertheless adopted.

[141]*The Synod of Pennsylvania and the Late Convention at Fort Wayne, Indiana, 1866* (Philadelphia: Jas B. Rodgers, 1866) 25.

manifest itself in what became known as the Social Gospel movement.[142] The Franckeans retained their separate existence, including affiliation with the General Synod, until the time they united with other New York district groups in 1908. However, they faced several other challenges to their authenticity as Lutherans from within the General Synod, in the years immediately following their admission.[143]

While the reasons that led up to "the Great Schism of 1866" were complex in nature and multiple in number, opposition to the acceptance of the Franckeans into the membership of the General Synod was a primary precipitating cause. Most Lutheran historians, including Abdel Wentz, have accepted on face value the contention of the Franckean opponents that this opposition was based solely upon the Franckeans' lack of confessional orthodoxy.[144] Yet this conclusion ignores the fact of the intense opposition that had earlier been exhibited toward the Franckean's abolitionism. Credulity is stretched to the breaking point when one is asked to assume that the main reason for which the Franckeans were barred from membership in the General Synod from 1839 until 1857 was no longer in evidence in 1864, and that residual resentments had entirely ceased to exist. Years later, when Nicholas Van Alstine wrote a historical account of the Franckean Synod, he flatly stated that their application for membership in the Gen-

---

[142]Lloyd Svendsbye, "The History of a Developing Social Responsibility among Lutherans in America from 1930 to 1960, with Reference to the American Lutheran Church, the Augustana Lutheran Church, the Evangelical Lutheran Church, and the United Lutheran Church in America" (Th.D. diss., Union Theological Seminary, 1966) 32-110, 544. The continuing unique concern among Lutherans for social concerns on the part of the General Synod is fully documented by Harold Lentz, "History of the Social Gospel in the General Synod of the Lutheran Church in America" (Ph.D. diss., Yale University, 1943). (The continued social activism of the General Synod is reflected by the fact that it alone among all Lutheran bodies affiliated with the Federal Council of Churches at its organizational meeting in 1907.) The schism of 1866 went unhealed for over a half a century, until the General Synod and the General Council, along with the United Synod of the South, in 1918 merged into the United Lutheran Church in America. As a condition of this merger the General Synod agreed to give up membership in the Federal Council of Churches and, in general, to moderate its activist approach. However, the U.L.C.A. developed the highest degree of social responsibility among Lutheran bodies in the United States.

[143]Proceedings, General Synod, 1866, 23; 1868, 26.

[144]Wentz, Basic History of Lutheranism in America, 149.

eral Synod in 1864 was opposed, among other reasons, because of "our stand on the slavery question."[145]

Looking back on the Franckean saga, we can have little doubt that abolitionism was the most distinguishing and controversial characteristic of its synodical life. Yet, while the charge that the Franckeans were heretics to the Lutheran cause was widely maintained, it was only connected to their abolitionism in an oblique manner, if at all. The indictment was never made concrete or direct. The general allegation was usually to the effect that the Franckeans deviated dangerously from historic or fundamental Lutheran doctrines and confessions and that one result of this error was an especially radical stand on abolition. The reason for this hesitance to relate Lutheran heresy directly to Franckean abolitionism was obviously a reticence to deal with the resulting historical embarrassment.[146]

Lutheran historians who have categorized the Franckeans as an aberration from genuine and historical forms of Lutheranism leave the obvious implication that Lutheran abolitionism was in some way connected with doctrinal delinquency. To argue that Lutherans failed to plead the cause of the slave or to deal directly with the most critical moral problem of their day because to do so was opposed to bona fide Lutheran doctrine or, conversely, that the Franckeans did these things because they were somehow un-Lutheran leads to a disconcerting if not defamatory conclusion. Such a conclusion, however, will continue to be drawn as long as historians insist that the only abolitionist Lutheran synodical group in this country held to a doctrinal position that was antithetical to authentic Lutheranism. The historical facts do not warrant such a conclusion, even though it has been asserted for a century and a half. Rather, the Franckean Synod, like Samuel Schmucker and other Lutheran Pietists in America, held to a tradition that remained within the framework of German Lutheran Pietism and that was, only in a moderate and reformist sense, anticonfessional. The charges of false doctrine brought against the Franckean Synod by their Lutheran contemporaries was in many cases, a cloak, behind which was disguised a determined opposition to the Franckeans' insistence that Lutherans speak out against slavery. It was not primarily false doctrine but the moral activism of the Franckean Synod, expressed so passionately in the cause of abolitionism, that was the main reason for its rejection.

---

[145]N. Van Alstine, *Historical Review*, 18.

[146]Sernett, "Lutheran Abolitionism in New York State," 1-2.

Samuel Schmucker
and the Franckean Synod

Samuel Schmucker as an individual leader and the Franckean Synod as a corporate body were the most vigorous exponents of abolitionism in the Lutheran church. It appears that this concern issued directly from the theological traditions that they had mutually imbibed from the classical Lutheran Pietism of the Spener-Francke school in Germany. We turn now to the nature of the relationship that existed between Schmucker and the Franckean Synod. Did they ever join hands, publicly or privately or both, to achieve common goals or to pursue in conjunction their activist and abolitionist convictions? And what were the causes of the obvious restraints exhibited in this relationship?

Both Schmucker and the Franckean Synod did on a few public occasions give expression to their admiration and respect for each other, and to their agreement on basic theological concepts, including the subject of abolition. In 1834, the Hartwick Synod recorded its sentiments in regard to the first edition of Schmucker's *Popular Theology*, describing it as a book filled with "great talent . . . good judgment . . . a penetrating mind . . . sound doctrine, and clear and scriptural illustrations of the subjects discussed, [and one that] . . . ought to be next in rank to the Bible in the library of each Lutheran."[1] The Franckean founder, the Reverend Philip Wieting, had presented the resolution. Sentiments of a similar positive nature were later expressed by the Franckean Synod in regard both to

---

[1] *Minutes of the Hartwick Synod*, 1834, 12-13.

Schmucker's *Popular Theology* and to his proposal for Protestant union, in *Fraternal Appeal to the American Churches*.[2] A few years after the publication of this book, the Franckeans, in their fruitless attempt to unite the forces of Lutheranism around an abolitionist banner, chose Schmucker's title "Fraternal Appeal" as the heading of their antislavery manifesto. Throughout their history the Franckean Synod alluded more often to Schmucker as an authority for the theological and practical matters that it advocated than to any other contemporary. In a special meeting held only a few months after their organization in 1837, the Franckeans referred to the opinions of the "eminent and respected Professor Schmucker" relative to their concern to provide an adequate supply of missionaries and ministers to meet the pressing needs of the church, even if it meant moderating some accepted educational standards. They stated that Schmucker's views on this subject "perfectly agree with the principles advocated and method pursued by the Frankean Synod," and they quoted Schmucker's words that "unless [we] make . . . far greater exertions to seek out suitable young men [for] the work of the Lord, it must still remain undone."[3]

It was normal procedure for the Franckeans to defend their theology and practice on the basis of quotations from Schmucker's *Popular Theology*.[4] During the course of the litigation with the Hartwick Synod loyalists, the Franckeans defended the authentic quality of their Lutheranism by again stating that "Dr. Schmucker's view and ours agree exactly." They quoted his *Popular Theology* to the effect that no minister is bound to believe everything in the Augsburg Confession but only its fundamental doctrines.[5] On the basis of testimony given during this trial, probably submitted as early as 1840, it is clear that the Franckeans' reservations concerning some of the doctrinal statements of the Augsburg Confession were nearly identical to those of Schmucker and to the "five errors" he later articulated in his *Definite Platform*.[6] Through the years the Franckeans continually expressed their agreement with the Schmuckerian concept that the Augsburg Confession exhibited a summary of the fundamental doctrines of the Word of God contained in the canonical books of the Bible. They never had any argument with this view. They remained advocates

---

[2]These references have been documented in chapter 6. As this is the case with many of the events referred to in this chapter, specific documentation provided in the earlier chapters is not repeated.

[3]*JFS*, October 1837.

[4]See, for example, *Lutheran Herald* 4 (1 July 1842): 82.

[5]"Kniskern vs. Wieting," 490.

[6]Ibid., 477, 483.

of Schmucker's interpretation and of the viewpoint expressed in his *Definite Platform*, even after the General Synod moved to a more conservative position following the Civil War.

Although there apparently exists no record of a personal statement from Schmucker in regard to the overall doctrinal views of the Franckean Synod, he did, as was indicated, support their efforts to unite with the General Synod, over the protests of some delegates that they were unorthodox in regard to the Augsburg Confession.[7] In this respect the comment of the editor of the *Lutheran Observer* that, in matters of fundamental doctrine, the Franckeans were orthodox,[8] likely reflected Schmucker's own convictions. We are assured, however, that, unlike editor Kurtz, who voted that the General Synod not accept the Franckeans, Schmucker voted for their admission, thus indicating that he did not reject their abolitionism as being either "ultra" or "fanatical."

One of the most significant aspects of agreement between Schmucker and the Franckeans lay precisely in the area of their social and political activism. Both agreed that the dictates of the Christian religion applied as much to civil and political affairs as they did to private life. The intensity of their common dedication to this principle resulted in what, for Lutherans, was an exceptional commitment to the abolitionist cause. This basic commitment was fully shared in principle and publicly acknowledged on both sides. In 1841, the Franckeans gleefully quoted a sermon that Schmucker had delivered earlier that year at the opening of the General Synod's convention. The Gettysburg professor had implied that a church that tolerated slavery could not expect to enjoy the favor of God. With tongue in cheek, the Franckeans inquired whether the General Synod should not have considered such opinions as a "defamation of patriarchial and domestic institutions" and whether Schmucker should not have been charged as guilty of "spiritual censorship?"[9] At that same convention of the General Synod in 1841, Schmucker's name appeared in the minutes as voting on the Franckean side of the narrowly unsuccessful effort to rescind the infamous resolution that had accused them of introducing "practices contrary to the Word of God" and of fomenting division within the church. The Franckeans took special note of his name, called him a friend, and vowed that they would remember.[10]

---

[7]See letter from J. Rosenberg to Philip Wieting, 12 March 1841, Franckean Papers.

[8]*Lutheran Observer* 3 (17 September 1847): 10.

[9]*Lutheran Herald* 3 (1 July 1841): 101.

[10]Ibid. (1 September 1841): 132.

Just a year later, in September 1842, Schmucker, as noted in chapter 5, placed his still well-accepted leadership at risk by speaking at the district meeting of the West Pennsylvania Synod in favor of the Franckeans' abolitionist manifesto, the "Fraternal Appeal." During that speech he not only paid the Franckeans a high compliment for their antislavery stand but intimated that it put the rest of the Lutheran church to shame. Immediately after his unsuccessful effort on behalf of the Franckeans, Schmucker was characterized as a defender of "those despised disorganizers and radical rabble rousers, whom the General Synod had twice over rejected by official vote."[11] In spite of the obvious jeopardy to his leadership role, it appears that Schmucker never moderated his unqualified support of the Franckeans' stand on abolition. We know, for instance, that in 1845 Schmucker had every intention of presenting to the same West Pennsylvania Synod a paper that sharply opposed slavery and called for resolutions denouncing it. This statement, even though it approved the use of some practical and moderate means of implementation, such as financial compensation for slaveholders, was, in its opposition to the sin of slavery, fully as radical as the Franckean manifesto. But illness intervened, and Schmucker's intention was never fulfilled.

In spite of the evidence that Schmucker and the Franckeans remained on friendly terms, supported each other publicly on a number of occasions, and were in basic agreement on theological as well as abolitionist principles, the fact remains that the professor and synod did not maintain a close relationship with each other. The apparent absence of any direct correspondence between them does not paint a picture of "Pietist partners" battling together against the sin of slavery. Their efforts to promote the cause of abolition were never, to any extent, coordinated. There are a number of explanations for this seeming enigma. A part of the reason was geographic. Because Hartwick Seminary was located near the center of their activity, the Franckean clergy received their training there rather than at Gettysburg. As a result they had no direct contact with Schmucker and had to base their judgments of him almost entirely upon what they read and heard. The one notable exception was, of course, Daniel Payne. But Payne remained with the Franckeans for only a short time, and to that extent his influence on behalf of Schmucker was limited. It should not, however, be underestimated. It would appear that Payne was directed to the Franckean Synod for ordination by Samuel Schmucker. There is no proof for this, but as Schmucker was his closest confidant and counselor, it is the most

----

[11]John Rosenberg to Philip Wieting, from Dickinson PA, 19 October 1842, Franckean Papers.

obvious explanation, especially since Payne went to the Franckeans directly from Gettysburg. Payne's close association with and admiration for Schmucker may well have increased the goodwill that existed between the Pietist leader and the embattled abolitionists in New York.

The Franckeans and Schmucker were also separated by virtue of the Franckeans' exclusion from the General Synod. The synod was a public forum, not only where those allied in their advocacy of abolition might have become better acquainted with each other's views, but where they might have encouraged one another and coordinated their efforts to move the Lutheran church in the direction of the antislavery crusade. One can imagine that Schmucker would have exerted himself more forcefully to bring the cause of abolitionism to the attention of the synod, had he been surrounded and supported by Franckean constituents.

There is evidence that Schmucker not only lent his official prestige to the effort to bring the Franckeans into the General Synod but that he kept himself fully informed on all their activities and worked behind the scenes to effect the desired reconciliation. The archives of the seminary at Gettysburg contain today the most complete record of the Franckean Synod journals and newspapers to be found anywhere because Samuel Schmucker personally subscribed to these papers. It would thus appear that he was an astute and careful observer of Franckean affairs. There is also evidence that Schmucker's colleagues from Gettysburg attended meetings of the Franckean Synod during the years following 1857, when strong efforts were being made to bring the Franckeans into the General Synod. A personal note, attached to the cover page of Schmucker's copy of the *Journal of the Franckean Synod* for 1859 and signed by P. A. Barnitz, whose family had close associations with Gettysburg and with Schmucker, notes with satisfaction that a resolution has been passed indicating "that the necessary steps are being taken to unite into the General Synod." However, by the time the Franckeans were at last united with the General Synod in 1864, the slavery issue was for the most part decided, while Schmucker had already tendered his resignation from Gettysburg Seminary and his leadership in the church was at an end.

The distance that separated Schmucker and the Franckeans, however, cannot be attributed wholly to a lack of proximity, personal relationship, or mutual synodical affiliation. A definite aspect of that distance was due to differences of a deeper kind. These differences have been described at some length in previous chapters. They need only to be recapitulated and summarized. Schmucker was a Southerner by birth and experience. He understood and had empathy with the slave owner through close personal relations with family and parishioners. He was optimistic about the Southern capacity to reform itself. His close associations with the South led him to assess the future of race relations with a seemingly unrealistic sanguineness.

The Franckeans, on the other hand, were Northerners without close personal ties to the South or identification with its mores. Their acquaintance with slavery both past and present was, for the most part, negative. Their association with Daniel Payne reinforced these views. They were deeply pessimistic about the ability of Southerners to move toward abolition. In their approach to race relations they relied far more on a prophetic stance than on a pastoral appeal. As a result of this different experience and outlook, the Franckeans rejected the distinction, often made by Schmucker, between voluntary and involuntary slaveholding. They refused to believe that there were any slaveholders sincerely dedicated to the eradication of the evil in which they participated. They wrote, "The time has come, and now is, when pious and honest slaveholding is as manifest an absurdity as *pious polygamy, or honest robbery.*"[12]

This disparity of background also accounted for the divergent opinions of colonization held by Schmucker and the Franckeans. Schmucker continued to cling to the conviction that colonization was one way to help solve the problem of slavery and that it was not in essence opposed to the call for immediate abolition. The Franckeans, on the other hand, considered colonization as a Southern strategy to rid the country of free blacks and to "fatten up the enormous system of slavery by removing free labor." They called colonization "humbugism" originating in sheer selfishness, the opponent of universal emancipation.[13]

But the most profound difference separating these two Pietist allies arose from the intensity of Schmucker's dedication to the goal of church union. Schmucker's consuming desire was to unite the churches so that together they might evangelize the world, effect moral reform, oppose slavery, and bring in the millennium. He had given his entire life to the creation and expansion of the General Synod in order to unify the Lutheran Church in the United States. He was, if anything, even more fully committed to the goal of interdenominational Protestant union, outlined in his famous *Fraternal Appeal*. Abolition was a vital concern of Schmucker's life, but if forced to choose, he was ready to postpone temporarily its pursuit out of regard for the goal of ecumenism.

The Franckeans saw things differently. Their commitment to abolitionism was supreme. Slavery was the primal sin, the blasphemy against

---

[12]*JFS*, 1845, 18.

[13]Ibid., 1843, 20; *Lutheran Herald* 3 (1 July 1841): 101.

God that had to be removed before there could be any reason for bringing the churches together or any hope of evangelizing the world and ushering in the millennium. They believed in church union, but they were willing to sacrifice or postpone ecumenism while they concentrated their efforts on the eradication of human slavery. This fundamental difference was most clearly illustrated at the World Convention of the Evangelical Alliance held in London in 1846. Here Schmucker, for the only time in his life, was willing to label abolitionism a political matter that by its nature ought to remain outside the realm of ecclesiastical concern. It was a direct denial of the theological position he had affirmed all his life. It was based on a pragmatic, but futile, attempt to keep the ecumenical boat from capsizing over the issue of slavery. The Franckeans, on the other hand, were elated over the decisions to refuse any slaveholder a seat in the Evangelical Alliance.[14] They were for Christian union on that basis alone.

The relationship between Samuel Schmucker and the Franckean Synod, while restrained, is nevertheless revealing. We behold here the classic example of the pragmatic churchman and the radical reformer, pursuing the common goal of abolitionism. On the basis of their fundamental theology and concept of Christian ethics and moral reform, they were in almost total agreement. In Schmucker's absolute condemnation of slavery as a sin against God, he was as clear, courageous, and radical as were his Franckean brethren. In this common commitment lay the unyielding manifestation of their activist Pietist heritage and their basic unity. But when it came to strategy and to methods of procedure, Schmucker was a moderate, ready to compromise, willing to delay, always concerned with practical considerations, with pragmatic political realities, and above all with the unity of the church. With these things the Franckeans would have little to do. They were idealists. They understood themselves to be radical reformers; they reveled in the role and proudly bore its banner. Since slavery was wrong, they believed the only strategy open to the Christian was unrelenting opposition. All neutrality, hesitation, silence, and moderation was a sin. On this ground they took their stand, and from this position they vowed never to waver.

The fact that those closely united in principle could be sharply divided in practice should not be surprising. We see it illustrated throughout history and in contemporary events. What is surprising is the almost complete absence of any expression of personal animosity between the Gettysburg professor and the Franckean pastors. In spite of their differ-

---

[14]*JFS*, 1846, 27.

ences they remained keenly aware of their essential affinity and unity of purpose in their opposition to slavery. Each attacked methods that the other firmly upheld. But they never associated these differences with each other. The differences, where they occurred, were never made personal. And this toleration is significant, because the tendency of the day, particularly insofar as radicals such as the Franckeans were concerned, was to call the opposition by name. But as early as 1841, the Franckeans had observed and solemnly declared that Samuel Schmucker was their abolitionist ally and friend and vowed to remember him as such. It was a pledge they kept, a promise that neither distance nor difference could deter. In the final analysis it was their abolitionist convictions that welded these two representatives of a common Lutheran Pietist tradition in irrevocable union. This same abolitionism helped to trigger and facilitate their rejection, along with their particular activist brand of Lutheranism. So Schmucker and the Franckeans together became catalysts in a decided and critical shift of the American Lutheran Church to a more conservative and strictly confessional theology, a position that has never since been successfully challenged.

CONCLUSION

The attempt to clarify and comprehend the course of past events is sufficient cause in itself for historical research. There is, however, additional value to be found in examining the possible relevance of history to current events. I am convinced that this study on American Lutheran Pietism contains insights germane to critical issues that currently confront American Lutheranism and, to a lesser extent, the whole of Christendom.

First, a renewal and reacceptance of the positive elements in the Pietist legacy could immeasurably enhance the inherent richness and diversity of Lutheran theology and practice. Since the time of the Civil War, Lutheran identity has been defined in rather rigid terms. It has centered in a search for a distinctiveness that has too often taken on the characteristics of a self-serving sectarianism. It has been closely associated with a strict and literal allegiance to its confessional books, in particular, with a sacramental theology that has stressed the importance of a realistic interpretation regarding the mode of Christ's presence in the Lord's Supper. None of these concerns were of primary importance to American Lutheran Pietism. It accentuated what Lutherans held in common with other churches, rather than their differences. The emphasis was placed more upon the practical expression of faith in the life of the believer rather than upon doctrinal formulation. In keeping with this approach Pietism stressed the benefits of Christ's presence in the sacrament rather than its precise mode. It gave prominence to an ethical rather than a sacramental theology.

The differences between Lutheran orthodoxy and Pietism are real and will continue to arouse tensions that must be addressed. But this debate needs to be carried on in the spirit of kindred souls who belong to the same family of faith rather than in the hurling of anathemas. The divergent theological strands of orthodoxy and Pietism are not contradictory. Neither approach is inimical to the fundamental insight of historical Lutheranism regarding the nature of justification by faith alone through grace. The positive insights of the Pietist heritage, its fervent spirituality, and in particular its ethical activism have played an important role in the historical development of the Lutheran church. While the warmth of Pietism's spiritual emphasis has been recognized in some degree, its unprecedented stress on moral reform and political activism resulting from a definite shift in theological priorities has been strangely neglected and nearly totally ignored. The future vitality of Lutheranism in the United States will be stimulated to the extent that it not only allows but encourages the diversity of theological viewpoints that has characterized its past.

Second, American Lutheran Pietism can provide its entire denomination with a more accurate understanding of Protestant evangelicalism, which could result in more fruitful dialogue and cooperative endeavor with this fast-growing segment of the Christian church. The distinguished American historian Timothy L. Smith has described nineteenth-century Protestant evangelicalism as a revivalistic, Bible-centered, missionary-minded movement, strongly motivated in the direction of social and moral reform.[1] Lutheran Pietism had much in common with the theology and spirit of this evangelicalism, which it both helped to shape and by which it in turn was influenced. Twentieth-century Protestant evangelicalism retains some of the basic characteristics noted by Smith. But this historical understanding of evangelicalism has in our time become, in large degree, distorted and neglected. Today, Lutherans as well as other mainline Protestants and Roman Catholics regularly fail to distinguish adequately the widening gulf between evangelicals and fundamentalists. While some fundamentalists have recently become much more concerned and involved with issues of a political nature, they do not share the historical commitment of evangelicalism and of Lutheran Pietism to ecumenism, peace, and social justice, a commitment that still characterizes many evangelicals today.[2]

One of the primary reasons that Lutherans do not feel more comfortable with evangelicals and find it difficult to communicate and cooperate with them may lie in a lack of basic understanding related to the rejection of their own Pietist heritage. Both Lutheran Pietism and Protestant evangelicalism, at their best, contained an inherent ethical activism that manifested itself in a primary commitment to moral reform and to the improvement of the human situation in general. This activism was generated by a spirituality that insisted upon tangible evidence of religious commitment and that defined faith itself as activist in essence. This vital aspect

---

[1]Smith, *Revivalism and Social Reform*.

[2]Karl H. Hertz, *Lutheran*, 19 September 1984, 33, Letter to the Editor.

of the Pietist heritage contains the key to the future development of a closer working relationship between Lutherans and evangelicals in general. In particular it has importance for building a closer communion with that large segment of evangelicalism represented in the black churches of North America. These churches have remained relatively untouched by the liberal-conservative debate[3] that characterized the first half of this century and that contributed so heavily to the rise of fundamentalism following World War I.[4] It was not by accident that Pietism attracted the first potential black leaders to Lutheranism during the antebellum period. Its primary appeal to Daniel Payne and others lay both in its advocacy of abolitionist sentiments and in its biblical emphasis, linked closely to a deep moral concern. Pietism's failure to retain the outstanding talents of Payne or even to channel his unique abilities in a ministry to persons of his own race was, from the Lutheran perspective, tragic. But it ought to be instructive.

Today the Lutheran church finds itself not only cut off from any meaningful communion with the black churches but still unable to utilize fully the outstanding abilities of the few black leaders and clergy within its ranks. It also finds itself ill equipped to attract potential black leaders into its schools and seminaries. Even when it has done so, the theologies taught there have tended to denigrate some of the most creative and innovative gifts that these persons bring with them. While a large part of this failure lies in the stubborn persistence of racist attitudes, which erects subtle barriers to any real cultural and theological exchange, another part of it resides in the loss of Lutheran appreciation for its own revivalistic, activist, and politically oriented Pietist traditions. A reevaluation of these traditions and of their rightful place within historic Lutheranism could provide a bridge to better communication with black churches and allow a fuller acceptance of the valuable cultural and individual gifts that people of color have to offer modern-day Lutheranism.

Third, the American Pietist heritage can furnish Lutheranism with valuable insights for the development of a new, or at least alternative, ethical theology. With its present monolithic approach to ethics, especially

---

[3]William H. Bentley, "Bible Believers in the Black Community," in *The Evangelicals: What They Believe, Who They Are, Where They Are Changing,* ed. David F. Wells and John D. Woodbridge (Nashville: Abingdon Press, 1975) 120.

[4]For the best studies on fundamentalism, see George C. Marsden, *Fundamentalism and American Culture: The Shaping of Twentieth-Century Evangelicalism, 1870-1925* (New York: Oxford University Press, 1980); and Ernest R. Sandeen, *The Roots of Fundamentalism: British and American Millenarianism, 1800-1930* (Chicago: University of Chicago Press, 1970).

as related to political matters, the Lutheran church is poorly equipped to respond adequately to the increasing moral challenges of the times. Its ethical theology remains tied to complicated and unwieldy two-kingdom doctrines, which in practice provides a basis for passive acceptance of the status quo and a convenient rationalization for opposing any direct application of gospel principles to the political arena. This analysis was uniquely equipped to meet the purposes of Luther's sixteenth-century Reformation, aimed at the abuse of churchly power. Today it is much more of a hindrance than a help. As a result, Lutherans have been unable to develop a strong tradition of social and political action in this century, and to the extent that it has done so, it has not sprung from the heart of Lutheran theology but has grown up beside it, or developed in spite of it. At its best, the two-kingdom theology tends to apply one standard of conduct to the individual and another to the corporate realm. Since the Christian lives and acts in both realms simultaneously, the effect is to split up the person of the believer in a confusing and unrealistic manner. At its worst it degenerates into a dualism that confines the Christian gospel almost completely to the personal arena.

In addition to this rigid two-kingdom confinement, Lutheran ethical theology has been hampered by its insistence on a radical dichotomy between justification and sanctification, between the act of being made righteous and the tangible manifestation of righteous activity. The tendency is to emphasize the importance of the former to the neglect of the latter, thereby creating a separation between faith and good works contradicted by the testimony of the Bible as well as the Lutheran confessions. The result is that American Lutheranism has been hobbled with a truncated doctrine of sanctification related almost exclusively to private and personal expressions. Lutheran Pietism sought to restore the indivisible relationship between faith and good works. It maintained that the obedience of faith expressed in holiness of life and the quest for human justice was intimately and inseparably connected with the justifying act of God's grace through faith. It insisted that to tear the two apart, to treat them as separate experiences, or to make a qualitative spiritual distinction between them was to undermine the proper Christian understanding of both and the meaning of faith itself. As a result, Lutheran Pietists were enabled to view both the spiritual and the ethical, the personal and the political, as interrelated aspects of a single whole. For this reason Samuel Schmucker and the Franckean Synod had no problem in confronting the American system of slavery as sinful and unjust, on both the personal and the political levels.

This ethical approach involves certain dangers of its own. It can degenerate into a self-righteous legalism. It also contains a theocratic tendency. Yet, the great problem of our modern world is not so much, as in Luther's day, the political power of the church but the military and totalitarian power of the state. The danger for the church lies not in the direction of its unwarranted assumption of worldly or secular power but in its capitulation to and absorption by the state. It lies in the withdrawal of its prophetic proclamation and the humanistic concerns of its gospel from the realm of the political.

Liberation theology, like Lutheran Pietism, has understood that the experience of the love of God in Christ results inevitably and simultaneously in works and deeds that fly directly in the face of all oppression, undue privilege, and narrow nationalism. It insists that justification and human justice can never be separated. It has perceived, as did Samuel Schmucker and the Franckeans, that this truth leads inevitably to a direct and prophetic application of the gospel to the political realm. Like Pietism, it has intuitively grasped the rationalizing shallowness and inconsistency in advocating that this responsibility belongs only to Christian individuals on a personal level and not to the church as a corporate body. Furthermore, liberation theology has noted how it becomes increasingly true in our modern world that the gospel cannot even reach the personal lives of individuals until the historical conditions of economic and political enslavement, oppression, and injustice have been modified by the redeeming power of that gospel. The liberationists have accurately contended that the key to this theology lies in the elimination of every dualism.[5] The key to a Lutheran theology come of age lies in a similar direction, a course already charted in its own Pietist traditions. A new ethical and political theology, unhampered by the more drastic two-kingdom distinctions and steadfastly refusing to separate justification from sanctification, would also allow Lutherans to work more closely with major segments of evangelicals and other Protestants, as well as Roman Catholics, who are moving rapidly in the direction of a more radical involvement with crucial moral and political problems such as hunger, poverty, racism, economic oppression, the environment, nuclear disarmament, and world peace.

A fourth potential contribution of the American Pietist heritage to modern-day Lutheranism is its valuable insight into a positive strategy for ecumenical endeavor. The resolute opposition of American Lutheran Pietists to slavery was indicative of their conviction that the true unity of the church could not be realized apart from a quest for justice and the service

---

[5]Gustavo Gutierrez, *A Theology of Liberation* (Maryknoll NY: Orbis Books, 1973) 231-39.

of a suffering humanity. This practical ecumenicity was grounded in a theological agreement with Spener and Francke, who were convinced that the deepest confession of faith lay in the loving service of humankind. Ecclesiastical unity is pursued today primarily in the search for doctrinal consensus. Lutherans continue to insist that all ecumenism must be grounded in a strict confessional commitment. Yet, true ecumenicity is realized less in theological dialogues on justification, biblical inerrancy, the Lord's Supper, or apostolic succession than in the community established among all Christians engaged in efforts to realize peace and social justice. Doctrinal concord, even if realized, might represent an empty accomplishment if not accompanied by agreement on critical issues of social and political ethics. The latter is no more and no less divisive than the former, no more and no less important.

Lutheran and Catholic theologians who have reached some degree of consensus on the sacraments, the creeds, and justification still find their churches taking widely divergent positions in regard to birth control and the place of women in the church. Differences in regard to ethical concerns such as world peace, racism, and apartheid exist as much within the various denominations as between them. As this study has indicated, social and political practices often have far greater impact upon churches and their people than do the esoteric doctrinal formulations of their theologians. The search for real ecumenicity must place the focus on ethical as well as doctrinal agreement. Liberation theology once again comes closest to the ecumenical insights of Lutheran Pietism in the insistence that the unity of the church will be forged not by those who only say "Lord, Lord" but among those who seek to "do the will of the Father."[6] By basing its ecumenism on the practice of a faith active in love and justice, the church is able to contribute not just to its own unity but to the unity of the world it is called to love and redeem. As long as it fails to deal with the unity of the whole world, the church's perception of ecumenism is limited, deceptive, and, in the end, altogether artificial.

Fifth, and finally, the American Pietist tradition offers to its Lutheran communion the theological gift of an optimistic eschatology. German Lutheran Pietism bequeathed to its North American successors a moderate form of postmillennialism that expected Christ's reign on earth to be realized apart from catastrophic events, by the power of the gospel and its resulting moral reform. Grounded in the views projected by Philipp Spener in his "hope for better times,"[7] it was basically the millennial concept

---

[6]Ibid., 278.

[7]See Stein, "Philipp Jakob Spener's Hope."

of a gradual and progressive, albeit partial, realization of the kingdom of God on earth, as a prelude to its fulfillment in eternity. This eschatological hope led Pietism, both in Germany and in North America, to a depth of humanitarian concern and commitment to moral reform unparalleled in the history of Lutheranism. Apart from this contribution of Pietism, the Lutheran church, from Luther's day to the present, has labored within the framework of an eschatology deeply pessimistic in its view of this earth and this life and, as a result, decidedly otherworldly in its emphasis and its hope.

As a result of its captivity to a literal and complete acceptance of the Augsburg Confession, Lutheran theology has continued to renounce all forms of chiliastic thought as "Jewish opinions."[8] The hermeneutical difficulties connected with the interpretation of the millennium in Revelation 20 are indeed manifold. Is the passage to be understood symbolically and spiritually or in a more literal and realistic fashion? Does its message apply, then, to a future world or to this one? Has the millennium already arrived, or is it still to come? Will historical conditions worsen until the time of its sudden arrival, or will these conditions gradually improve until the reign of peace is realized? These questions have never received definitive answers and probably never will. There will be a continuing difference in interpretation and lack of certainty. But this prospect in itself does not argue for the dogmatic assertion of the traditional Lutheran view in regard to chiliasm. The motive behind the acceptance of an interpretation of Revelation 20 that views the millennium as a future hope is, without doubt, the recognition that "the gospel of Jesus Christ is meaningful not only for a future, other worldly reality, but also . . . for our current historical development, for earthly reality."[9]

Both Althaus and Bonhoeffer commented that the most compelling argument for a theology that encompasses some form of millennialism lies in the necessary "this worldliness" of the Christian hope.[10] How can the triumph of Christ and the glory of the Lord be fully expressed in the abdication of God's creation to the forces of sin and evil, or in the acquiescence to a despair that believes the world can only become worse in its sure race to destruction? The American Lutheran Pietism of Samuel Schmucker

---

[8]*The Book of Concord*, ed. and trans. Theodore Tappert, "The Augsburg Confession," Article 17, p. 38.

[9]Berkouwer, *Return of Christ*, 294.

[10]Paul Althaus, *Die letzten Dinge*, cited by Berkouwer in *Return of Christ*, 299-300. See also Dietrich Bonhoeffer, *Letters and Papers from Prison*, ed. Eberhard Bethge (New York: Macmillan, 1972) 336-37.

and the Franckean Synod adopted the more optimistic and hopeful eschatology provided by Spener and German Lutheran Pietism. They believed that God works in history to redeem people from oppression and death.[11] They believed that Christ's victory would be realized on this earth and in human life and that Christians were called to be instruments in building God's kingdom on earth, "as in heaven." Conversion to the Lord resulted in service to one's neighbor. To be converted was to commit oneself concretely to the building of God's kingdom on earth. Once more, liberation theology offers the most apt contemporary commentary on this basic understanding of Lutheran Pietist eschatology. It asserts that "a Christianity which has given up the mediation of work and the world, as a constituent core of faith, can only lead to reducing redemption to a parody lived out in the realm of ideas [doctrine] instead of the real world of creation."[12] These words capture the essence of the Lutheran Pietist eschatology and reveal its present potential motivating power. Only the future will determine whether this "explosive eschatological force" can provide a new impulse for the whole of Lutheranism.[13]

It is a regrettable fact of history that both Samuel Schmucker and the Franckean Synod were renounced by the Lutheran majority for an alleged "doctrinal deviation," never adequately defined and motivated in part by an animosity directed toward their abolitionism. Even more regrettable, in the process, many positive contributions of their Pietist tradition and theology, particuarly their moral activism and humanitarianism, have been ignored and forgotten. It is my hope that this history may in some small way contribute to a process of recovering these precious lost treasures.

---

[11]One of the foremost exponents of this viewpoint among twentieth-century Lutheran theologians was A. D. Mattson, a professor at Augustana Lutheran Seminary and author of *The Social Responsibility of Christians* (Philadelphia: Muhlenberg Press, 1960). See the recent biography of Mattson by Gregory Lee Jackson (Chicago: Augustana Historical Society, 1986).

[12]José Miquéz Bonino, *Doing Theology in a Revolutionary Way* (Philadelphia: Fortress Press, 1975).

[13]Martin Greschat, "Die 'Hoffnung besserer Zeiten' für die Kirche," in *Zur neueren Pietismusforschung*, vol. 440 (Darmstadt: Wissenschaftliche Buchgesellschaft, 1977) 239.

BIBLIOGRAPHY

————————■ ■ ■————————

ARCHIVAL DEPOSITS

Lutheran Theological Seminary Archives
Abdel Ross Wentz Memorial Library
Gettysburg, Pennsylvania

Constitution and Minutes of the Evangelical Lutheran Synod of East Pennsylvania. 1842–1860.

Constitution and Minutes of the Evangelical Lutheran Synod of Maryland and Virginia. 1820–1860.

Constitution and Minutes of the Evangelical Lutheran Synod of Northern Indiana. 1855–1860.

Constitution and Minutes of the Evangelical Lutheran Synod of Western Virginia and Adjacent Parts. 1842–1860.

Constitution and Minutes of the Wittenberg Synod of the Evangelical Lutheran Church. 1850–1865.

Constitution and Proceedings of the Allegheny Evangelical Lutheran Synod of Pennsylvania. 1842–1865.

Constitution and Proceedings of the Evangelical Lutheran Synod of Western Pennsylvania. 1842–1856.

Constitution and Proceedings of the Evangelical Lutheran Tennessee Synod. 1838–1860.

Constitution and Proceedings of the Pittsburgh Synod. 1845–1860.

Constitution and Standing Ordinances of the Franckean Evangelic Lutheran Synod, together with *A Discipline Recommended as a Guide for the Churches,* originally adopted 25 May 1837; revised and adopted 7 October 1837; printed August 1839, Hartwick NY; revised and adopted June 1847, printed June 1849, Norwich NY.

Definite Platform Doctrinal and Disciplinarian for Evangelical Lutheran Synods: Constructed in Accordance with the Principles of the General Synod. Philadelphia: Miller & Burlock, 1855.

Journal of the Franckean Synod. 1837–1908.

Proceedings of the Fourteenth Annual Convention of the Evangelical Lutheran Synod of Eastern Pennsylvania, Sept. 21-26, 1855. Gettysburg: C. Neinstadt, 1855.

Proceedings of the General Synod. 1820–1868.

Schmucker, Samuel Simon. Collected Papers; Letters, Sermons, Lectures, Church and Synodical Documents, and Miscellaneous. All materials catalogued, numbered 3000 through 3780.

The Synod of Pennsylvania and the Late Convention at Fort Wayne, Indiana, 1866. Philadelphia: Jas. B. Rodgers, 1866.

Wentz, Abdel Ross. "Church History Pure and Applied." Gettysburg: Lutheran Theological Seminary, 1916.

Gettysburg College Archives
Musselmann Library
Gettysburg, Pennsylvania

Schmucker, Samuel Simon. Collected Sermons and Addresses.

Metropolitan-Upper New York Synod Archives
Hormann Library, Wagner College
Staten Island, New York.

Burgess, Ellis B. "Survey of Trinity Lutheran Church," West Sand Lake NY.

The Doctrine and Formula for the Government and Discipline of the Evangelical Lutheran Church. Troy NY: N. Tuttle, 1832.

Franckean Evangelic Lutheran Synod. Collected Papers and Correspondence.

Gruver, C. B. "History of the Second Lutheran Church, West Sand Lake, N.Y.: Seventieth Anniversary, 1909."

"Historical Sketch of the Poestenkill Evangelical Lutheran Church, Poestenkill, N.Y."

"A History of the Evangelical Lutheran Church. Raymertown, New York. 1840–1940."

Minutes of the Hartwick Synod and Ministerium of the Evangelical Lutheran Church in the State of New York. 1830–1865.

Minutes of the Ministerium of the Evangelical Lutheran Church in the State of New York. 1786–1865.

Oberholtzer, H. M. "An Address on the History and Work of the Franckean Synod." Delivered in St. John's Lutheran Church, Albany NY, 4 June 1929.

Simmons, George M. "History of St. Paul's Lutheran Church, Richmondville."

"Survey of the Evangelical Lutheran Church of Fordsbush, Minden." Montgomery County NY, 1937.

Van Alstine, Robert W. "Steadfast. A Biography of Nicholas Van Alstine, 1814–1900." Ballston Spa NY, 1979.

New York State Library, Manuscripts and Special Collections
Albany, New York

Articles, Addresses, Essays, and Sermons by H. L. Dox, John D. Lawyer, Sefferenas Ottman, Samuel S. Schmucker, and Nicholas Van Alstine. In *Pohlman Collection,* vols. 23, 36, 161, 206, 433, 709, 729.

New York State Court of Chancery. "Kniskern and others vs. the Lutheran Churches of St. John's and St. Peter's, Philip Wieting, and others." In *Report of cases argued and determined in the Court of Chancery of the State of New York (1843–1847) before the Hon. Lewis H. Sanford, Assistant Vice-chancellor of the first circuit,* 2d ed., vol. 1, pp. 439-568. New York: Gould, Banks, 1846.

Archives of Cooperative Lutheranism
New York City

Empie, Paul. Clergyman, LCA agency executive. Interview 1 by Neil Mellblom and Helen M. Knubel, 7 February 1977. Lutheran Council in the USA. *Oral History Collection.*

Archives of Jesuit-Krauss Memorial Library
Lutheran School of Theology
Chicago, Illinois

Microfilm Corpus of American Lutheranism (MCAL), reels, 1, 6, 7.

Parish Archives

Nellis, Milo. *The Old Palatine Church, Together with a Description of the Gen. John Cochran House, also Articles on the Early Klock and Nellis Pioneers.* Saint Johnsville NY: Press of the Enterprise & News, 1930.

Trinity Evangelical Lutheran Church, West Sand Lake NY. Zion Lutheran Church, Second Lutheran Church. Typewritten History.

Trinity Lutheran Church, Stone Arabia, Town of Palatine Bridge, Montgomery County NY. Ledger vol. 1, part 1.

"Venture in Faith." Trinity Lutheran Church, West Sand Lake NY, 1953.

INTERVIEWS

Slater, Rev. James. Pastor, St. Paul's, Redwood NY, also Pastor, Four Corners Orleans Lutheran Church, a Franckean Synod church. July 1983.

Smith, Rev. Robert. Pastor, United Presbyterian Church of Schoharie NY (formerly St. Paul's Lutheran Church, built around 1795). July 1983.

PERIODICALS

Evangelical Review 1855–1860. Lutheran Theological Seminary Archives, Gettysburg. Also 1849–1865, Archives of the Milwaukee Public Library, Milwaukee WI.

Friend of Man. William Goodell, ed. Utica NY. 1 March 1837, 21 August 1839, 10 June 1840, 23 February 1841, 14 August 1841. New York State Library, Manuscripts and Special Collections.

Lutheran Herald. 1839–1842, 1844–1845. Lutheran Theological Seminary Archives, Gettysburg.

Lutheran Observer. 1831–1865. Lutheran Theological Seminary Archives, Gettysburg.

Missionary. 1848–1860. Lutheran Theological Seminary Archives, Gettysburg.

Schoharie County Historical Review. 20 (May 1956). Published by the Schoharie County Historical Society, Schoharie NY.

PRIMARY SOURCES

Books

Andreae, Johann Valentin. *Christianopolis: An Ideal State of the Seventeenth Century.* Translated by Felix Emil Held. New York: Oxford University Press, 1916.

Arndt, Johann. *True Christianity.* Classics of Western Spirituality. Preface by Heiko Oberman. Translated by Peter Erb. New York: Paulist Press, 1979.

Bachman, John. *The Doctrine of the Unity of the Human Race, Examined on Principles of Science.* Charleston SC: C. Canning, 1850.

Berkenmeyer, Wilhelm Christoph. *The Albany Protocol: W. C. Berkenmeyer's Chronicle of Lutheran Affairs in New York Colony, 1731–1750.* Edited by John P. Dern. Translated by Simon Hart, Sibranda Geetruid Hart-Runeman, and Harry J. Kreider. Cornwallville NY: Hope Farm Press, 1971.

The Book of Concord: Confessions of the Evangelical Lutheran Church. Translated and edited by Theodore G. Tappert.

Dox, H. L. *Memoir of Rev. Philip Wieting, a Pastor Forty Years in the Same Field.* Philadelphia: Lutheran Publication Society, 1870.

_____, ed. *A Reunion of Ministers and Churches. Held at Gardnersville, May 14-17, 1881.* Philadelphia: Lutheran Publication Society, 1881.

Finney, Charles G. *The Autobiography of Charles G. Finney.* Condensed and edited by Helen Wessel. Minneapolis: Bethany Fellowship, 1977.

_____. *Lectures on Revivals of Religion.* Edited by William G. McLoughlin. Cambridge: Harvard University Press, Belknap Press, 1960.

Francke, August H. *Memoirs.* Philadelphia: Committee of Publication of the American Sunday School Union, 1830.

_____. *Nicodemus; or, A Treatise against the Fear of Man. . . .* London: J. Downing, 1709.

_____. *Pietas Hallensis, a Demonstration of the Foot-Steps of a Divine Being Yet in the World: In an Historical Narration of the Orphan House, and Other Charitable Institutions, at Glaucha near Halle in Saxony.* London: J. Downing, 1705.

Luther, Martin. *Christian in Society (Part 1).* Vol. 44 of *Luther's Works.* Edited by James Atkinson. Philadelphia: Fortress Press, 1966.

_____. *Christian in Society (Part 2).* Vol. 45 of *Luther's Works.* Edited by Walther I. Brandt. Philadelphia: Muhlenberg Press, 1962.

_____. *Christian in Society (Part 3).* Vol. 46 of *Luther's Works.* Edited by Robert Schultz. Philadelphia: Fortress Press, 1967.

_____. *Christian in Society (Part 4).* Vol. 47 of *Luther's Works.* Edited by Franklin Sherman. Philadelphia: Fortress Press, 1959.

_____. *Lectures on Genesis.* Vol. 1 of *Luther's Works.* Edited by Jaroslav Pelikan. St. Louis: Concordia Publishing House, 1958.

_____. *Selected Political Writings.* Edited by J. M. Porter. Philadelphia: Fortress Press, 1974.

_____. *Selected Psalms (Part 2).* Vol. 13 of *Luther's Works.* Edited by Jaroslav Pelikan. St. Louis: Concordia Publishing House, 1956.

_____. *Table Talk.* Vol. 54 of *Luther's Works.* Edited by Theodore G. Tappert. Philadelphia: Fortress Press, 1967.

_____. *Word and Sacrament.* Vol. 35 of *Luther's Works.* Edited by E. Theodore Bachman. Philadelphia: Muhlenberg Press, 1960.

_____. *Works of Martin Luther.* Vols. 1-3. Philadelphia: Muhlenberg Press, 1930–1943.

Melanchthon, Philip. *Loci Communes 1555.* In *Melanchthon on Christian Doctrine.* Translated and edited by Clyde L. Manschreck. Introduction by Hans Engelland. New York: Oxford University Press, 1965.

_____. *Selected Writings.* Translated by Charles Leander Hill. Minneapolis: Augsburg Publishing House, 1962.

Muhlenberg, Henry Melchoir. *Journals.* 3 vols. Translated and edited by Theodore G. Tappert and John W. Doberstein. Philadelphia: Muhlenberg Press, 1942–1958.

_____. *The Notebook of a Colonial Clergyman.* Translated by Theodore G. Tappert and John W. Doberstein. Philadelphia: Muhlenberg Press, 1959.

Müntzer, Thomas. *Schriften und Briefe: Kritische Gesamtausgabe.* Vol. 33 of *Quellen und Forschungen zur Reformations-geschichte. . . .* Edited by Gunther Franz. Gütersloh: Verlagshaus G. Mohn, 1968.

Payne, Bishop Daniel Alexander. *Recollections of Seventy Years.* Compiled and arranged by Sarah C. Bierce Scarborough. Edited by E. S. Smith. Nashville: A. M. E. Sunday School Union, 1888. Reprint, New York: Arno Press and New York Times, 1968.

Schmucker, J. George. *The Prophetic History of the Christian Religion Explained; or A Brief Explanation of the Revelation of St. John.* Vol. 1. Baltimore: Schaeffer & Maund, 1817.

Schmucker, Samuel S. *The American Lutheran Church. Historically, Doctrinally, and Practically Delineated, in Several Occasional Discourses.* 2d ed. Springfield OH: D. Harbaugh, 1851. Reprint. New York: Arno Press, 1969.

_____. *American Lutheranism Vindicated. . . .* Baltimore: T. Newton Kurz, 1856.

_____. *The Christian Pulpit, the Rightful Guardian of Morals, in Political No Less Than in Private Life: A Discourse Delivered at Gettysburg, November 26, the Day Appointed by the Governor for Public Humiliation, Thanksgiving, and Prayer.* Gettysburg: H. C. Neinstedt, 1846.

_____. *The Church of the Redeemer.* Baltimore: T. Newton Kurz, 1867.

_____. *Elements of a Popular Theology, with Occasional References to the Doctrines of the Reformation Avowed before the Diet of Augsburg in 1530.* 1st ed., Andover: Gould & Newman, 1834; 2d ed., New York: Leavitt, Lord, 1834; 3d ed., Baltimore: Publication Rooms, 1842; 5th ed., Philadelphia: J. S. Miles, 1845; 6th ed., Philadelphia: E. W. Miller, 1848; 8th ed., Philadelphia: Miller & Burlock, 1957; 9th ed., to which is added an appendix, *The Formula for Government and Discipline of the American Lutheran Church.* Philadelphia: Smith, English, 1860.

_____. *Fraternal Appeal to the American Churches, with a Plan for Catholic Union on Apostolic Principles.* 1838. Reprint, by Frederick Wentz. Philadelphia: Fortress Press, 1965.

_____. *An Inaugural Address, Delivered before the Directors of the Theological Seminary of the General Synod of the Evangelical Lutheran Church.* Carlisle PA: J. Tizzard and J. Crever, 1826.

Lutheran Manual on Scriptural Principles. . . . Philadelphia: Lindsay & Blakiston, 1855.

Spener, Philipp Jakob. *Einfältige Erklärung der christlichen Lehr nach der Ordnung des kleinen Catechismi des teuren Manns Gottes Lutheri 1677.* Vol. 2, part 1, of *Philipp Jakob Spener Schriften.* Introduction by Werner Jentsch. Edited by Erich Beyreuther. Heidesheim: Georg Olms Verlag, 1982.

_____. *Pia Desideria.* 1675. Reprint, translated by Theodore G. Tappert. Philadelphia: Fortress Press, 1964.

_____. *The Spiritual Priesthood Briefly Described According to the Word of God in Seventy Questions and Answers.* 1677. Reprint, translated by A. G. Voigt. Philadelphia: Lutheran Publication Society, 1917.

_____. *A Summary of the Christian Faith.* Translated by Henry E. Jacobs. Philadelphia: General Council Publication House, 1905.

_____. *Theologische Bedencken.* Vols. 3-4. Halle: Waysenhaus, 1712.

Van Alstine, John. *Life and Dying Confession of John Van Alstine. Executed March 19, 1819, for the Murder of William Huddleston, Esq., Deputy Sheriff of the County of Schoharie with a Full Account of His Trial before the Honorable Ambrose Spener, in Schoharie, Feb. 17, 1819. Together with Mr. Hamilton's Speech, and Chief Justice Spener's Sentence.* Schoharie NY: Printed at the office of the Observer, 1819.

Van Alstine, Nicholas. *Historical Review of the Franckean Evangelical Lutheran Synod of New York.* Philadelphia: Lutheran Publishing Society, 1893.

Articles and Addresses

Bachman, John. "Reply to the Resolution of the Middle Conference." *Missionary* 2 (10 December 1857).

Krauth, Charles Philip. "The Lutheran Church in the United States." *Evangelical Review* 2 (July 1850): 1-35.

_____. "The Relation of Our Confessions to the Reformation and the Importance of Their Study, with an Outline of the Early History of the Augsburg Confession." *Evangelical Review* 1 (October 1849): 234-63.

Lawyer, John D. "A Scripture Guide to the Mode of Baptism: Being a Discourse Delivered by Request of the Evangelic Church at Argusville, N.Y., May 12, 1844." Albany NY: E. H. Pease, 1844.

Muhlenberg, Henry M. "Muhlenberg's Defense of Pietism." Translated by C. W. Schaeffer. *Lutheran Church Review* 12 (October 1893): 349-75.

Müntzer, Thomas. "Last Tract against Martin Luther." Translated with a Commentary by Hans J. Hillerbrand, *Mennonite Quarterly Review* 38 (1964): 20-36.

_____. "Sermon before the Princes." In *Spiritual and Anabaptist Writers*, Library of Christian Classics, vol. 25, edited by George H. Williams and Angel M. Mergal, 49-70. Philadelphia: Westminster Press, 1957.

Passavant, William A. "Free Speech." *Missionary* 2 (10 December 1857): 182.

Schaeffer, Charles F. "The Nature of the Fundamental Articles." *Evangelical Review* 3 (July 1851): 64-87.

_____. "Symbolic Theology." *Evangelical Review* 1 (April 1850): 457-83.

Schmucker, Samuel S. "Church Development on Apostolic Principles: An Essay." In *Miscellaneous Sermons, 1827-1893*. Gettysburg: H. C. Neinstedt, 1850.

_____. "Discourse in Commemoration of the Glorious Reformation of the Sixteenth Century, with a Reference to the Relation between the Principles of Popery and Our Republican Institutions." In *A Commentary on Saint Paul's Epistle to the Galatians*, by Martin Luther, 83-123. Philadelphia: Salmon S. Miles, 1840.

_____. Letter. *Colonization Herald*, 6 June 1838.

_____. *Memorial of Professor S. S. Schmucker, Relative to Binding Out Minor Colored Children: Read in the House of Representatives, March 7, 1839*. Harrisburg PA: McKinley & Lescure Printers, 1842.

——————. "Of Slavery: Propositions on the Subject of Slavery." Edited by Douglas Stange. *Concordia Historical Institute* 40 (July 1967): 82.

——————. "The Papal Hierarchy, Viewed in the Light of Prophecy and History, being a Discourse delivered in the English Lutheran Church, Gettysburg, February 2, 1845." In *Sermons and Papers against the Roman Catholic Church, 1833–1852.* Gettysburg: H. C. Neinstadt, 1845.

——————. "A Plea for the Sabbath School System." In *Sunday School Addresses and Reports, 1829–1834.* Gettysburg: Theological Seminary Press, 1830.

——————. "Vocation of the American Lutheran Church." *Evangelical Review* 2 (April 1851): 489-512.

SECONDARY SOURCES

Books

Aarflot, Andreas. *Hans Nielsen Hauge: His Life and Message.* Minneapolis: Augsburg Publishing House, 1979.

Abzug, Robert H. *Passionate Liberator: Theodore Dwight Weld and the Dilemma of Reform.* New York: Oxford University Press, 1980.

Aland, Kurt. *Four Reformers.* Translated by James L. Schaaf. Minneapolis: Augsburg Publishing House, 1979.

——————. *A History of Christianity.* Translated by James L. Schaaf. 2 vols. Philadelphia: Fortress Press, 1986.

Alexander, James W. *The Life of Archibald Alexander, D.D.* New York: Scribners, 1854.

Allbeck, Willard. D. *A Century of Lutherans in Ohio.* Yellow Springs OH: Antioch Press, 1966.

Althaus, Paul. *Ethics of Martin Luther.* Philadelphia: Fortress Press, 1965.

Ander, Oscar F. *T. N. Hasselquist.* Rock Island IL: Augustana Historical Society, 1931.

Anderson, Hugh George. *Lutheranism in the Southeastern States, 1860–1888.* The Hague: Mouton Press, 1969.

Anstadt, Paul. *Life and Times of Rev. Samuel S. Schmucker . . .* York PA: P. Anstadt & Sons, 1896.

Arden, G. Everett. *Four Northern Lights: Men Who Shaped Scandinavian Churches.* Minneapolis: Augsburg Publishing House, 1964.

Babcock, Kendric Charles. *The Scandinavian Element in the United States.* 1914. Reprint. Urbana: University of Illinois Press, 1967.

Bailey, David T. *Shadow on the Church*. Ithaca NY: Cornell University Press, 1985.

Bainton, Roland H. *Christian Attitudes toward War and Peace*. New York: Abingdon Press, 1960.

Baird, Henry H. *Life of the Rev. Robert Baird, D.D.* New York: A. D. F. Randolph, 1866.

Baird, Robert. *Religion in the United States of America*. 1844. Reprint. New York: Arno Press & New York Times, 1969.

Barnes, Gilbert Hobbs. *The Antislavery Impulse, 1830–1844*. Gloucester MA: Peter Smith, 1957.

Belfour, Edmund, trans. *Epitome of Rev. Dr. Erick Pontoppidan's Explanation of Martin Luther's Small Catechism "Feed My Lambs."* Chicago: John Anderson Publishing, 1904.

Bell, P. G. *A Portraiture of the Life of Samuel Sprecher*. Philadelphia: Lutheran Publication Society, 1907.

Bender, Harold, ed. *Recovery of the Anabaptist Vision*. Scottsdale PA: Herald Press, 1957.

Bergendoff, Conrad. *The Church of the Lutheran Reformation*. St. Louis: Concordia Publishing House, 1967.

Berkhof, H. *Christ and the Powers*. Translated by John Howard Yoder. Scottsdale PA: Herald Press, 1962.

Berkouwer, G. C. *The Return of Christ*. Grand Rapids MI: Wm. B. Eerdmans Publishing, 1972.

Blickle, Peter. *The Revolution of 1525: The German Peasant's War from a New Perspective*. Translated by Thomas Al Brady, Jr., and H. C. Erik Midelfort. Baltimore: Johns Hopkins University Press, 1981.

Bodo, John R. *The Protestant Clergy and Public Issues, 1812–1848*. Princeton NJ: Princeton University Press, 1954.

Bonhoeffer, Dietrich. *Letters and Papers from Prison*. Edited by Eberhard Bethge. New York: Macmillan, 1972.

Bonino, José Míquez. *Doing Theology in a Revolutionary Situation*. Philadelphia: Fortress Press, 1975.

_____. *Toward a Christian Political Ethic*. Philadelphia: Fortress Press, 1983.

Bronkema, Ralph. *The Essence of Puritanism*. Goes, Netherlands: Oosterbaan & LeCointre, 1929.

Brown, Dale W. *Understanding Pietism*. Grand Rapids MI: Wm. B. Eerdmans Publishing, 1978.

Brown, O. J. *Heresies*. Garden City NY: Doubleday, 1984.

Burk, John Christian Frederic. *A Memoir of the Life and Writings of John Albert Bengel (1687–1752)*. Translated by Robert F. Walker. London: William Ball, 1837.

Carney, W. H. Bruce. *History of the Allegheny Evangelical Lutheran Synod of Pennsylvania, Together with a Topical Handbook of the Evangelical Lutheran Church: Its Ancestry, Origin, and Development*. Vol. 1. Philadelphia: Lutheran Publication Society, 1918.

Clasen, Claus-Peter. *Anabaptism: A Social History, 1525–1618*. Ithaca NY: Cornell University Press, 1972.

_____. *The Palatinate in European History, 1559–1660*. Oxford: Basil Blackwell, 1963.

Cobb, Sanford H. *The Story of the Palatines: An Episode in Colonial History*. New York and London: B. Putnam's Sons, Knickerbocker Press, 1897.

Cohn, Norman. *The Pursuit of the Millennium: Revolutionary Messianism in the Middle Ages and Its Bearing on Modern Totalitarian Movements*. New York: Oxford University Press, 1970.

Cole, Charles C., Jr. *The Social Ideas of the Northern Evangelists, 1826–1860*. New York: Columbia University Press, 1954.

Cross, Whitney R. *The Burned-over District: The Social and Intellectual History of Enthusiastic Religion in Western New York, 1800–1850*. New York: Harper & Row, Harper Torchbooks, 1950.

Crossley, Robert N. *Luther and the Peasants' War*. New York: Exposition Press, 1974.

Davidson, James West. *The Logic of Millennial Thought: Eighteenth Century New England*. New Haven CT: Yale University Press, 1977.

Defoe, Daniel. *A Brief History of the Poor Palatine Refugees (1709)*. Introduction by John Robert Moore. 1709. Reprint. Los Angeles: Augustana Reprint Society, 1964.

Dickens, A. G., and Tonkin, John. *The Reformation in Historical Thought*. Cambridge: Harvard University Press, 1985.

Dillon, Merton L. *The Abolitionists: The Growth of a Dissenting Minority*. DeKalb IL: Northern Illinois University Press, 1974.

Drummond, Andrew. *German Protestantism since Luther*. London: Epworth Press, 1951.

Dumond, Dwight Lowell. *Antislavery: The Crusade for Freedom in America*. Ann Arbor MI: University of Michigan Press, 1961.

Ebeling, Gerhard. *Luther: An Introduction to His Thought*. Translated by R. A. Wilson. Philadelphia: Fortress Press, 1970.

Edwards, Mark U., Jr. *Luther and the False Brethren*. Palo Alto CA: Stanford University Press, 1977.

_____. *Luther's Last Battles: Politics and Polemics, 1531–1546*. Ithaca NY: Cornell University Press, 1983.

Engberg, Emmer, ed. *Centennial Essays: Augustana Lutheran Church, 1860-1960*. Rock Island IL: Augustana Press, 1960.

Erb, Peter C., ed. *Pietists: Selected Writings*. Preface by F. Ernest Stoeffler. New York: Paulist Press, 1983.

Evjen, John O. *The Life of J. H. W. Stuckenberg: Theologian, Philosopher, Sociologist*. Minneapolis: Lutheran Free Church Publishing, 1938.

Faust, Albert B. *The German Element in the United States*. 2 vols. Boston: Houghton Mifflin, 1909.

Ferm, Vergilius. *The Crisis in American Lutheran Theology: A Study of the Issue between American Lutheranism and Old Lutheranism*. Foreword by Luther Allan Weigle. New York: Century, 1927.

Filler, Louis. *The Crusade against Slavery, 1830–1860*. New American Nation Series. New York: Harper & Brothers Pub., 1960.

Finck, William J. *Lutheran Landmarks and Pioneers in America: A Series of Sketches of Colonial Times*. 4th ed. Introduction by Elmer F. Krauss. Philadelphia: United Lutheran Publication House, 1913.

Flew, R. Newton. *The Idea of Perfection in Christian Theology: An Historical Study of the Christian Ideal for the Present Life*. Oxford: Clarendon Press, 1934.

Forell, George. *Faith Active in Love: An Investigation of the Principles Underlying Luther's Social Ethics*. Minneapolis: Augsburg Publishing House, 1954.

Forgie, George B. *Patricide in the House Divided*. New York: W. W. Norton, 1979.

Foster, Lawrence. *Religion and Sexuality: Three American Communal Experiments of the Nineteenth Century*. New York: Oxford University Press, 1981.

Frick, William K. *Henry Melchior Muhlenberg, Patriarch of the Lutheran Church in America*. Philadelphia: Lutheran Publication Society, 1902.

Friedmann, Robert. *The Theology of Anabaptism*. Scottsdale PA: Herald Press, 1973.

Froom, LeRoy Edwin. *The Prophetic Faith of Our Fathers: The Historical Development of Prophetic Interpretation.* Vol. 4 of *New World Recovery and Consummation of Prophetic Interpretation.* Washington DC: Review & Herald, 1954.

Gerberding, G. H. *Life and Letters of W. A. Passavant.* Greenville PA: Young Lutheran, 1906.

Glatfelter, Charles H. *Pastors and People.* Breinigsville PA: Pennsylvania German Society, 2 vols. 1980–1981.

Gobbel, A. Roger; Matthews, Donald N.; and Matthews, Elaine C. *On the Glorious Hill: A Short History in Word and Picture of the Lutheran Theological Seminary at Gettysburg.* Lancaster PA: Pride Press, 1976.

Goen, C. C. *Broken Churches, Broken Nation.* Macon GA: Mercer University Press, 1985.

Groh, John E., and Smith, Robert H., ed. *The Lutheran Church in North American Life.* St. Louis: Clayton Publishing House, 1979.

Guerike, Henry Earnest Ferdinand. *The Life of Augustus Hermann Francke.* Translated by Samuel Jackson. Introduction by E. Bickersteth. London: R. B. Seely & W. Burnside, 1837.

Gummere, Richard M. *Seven Wise Men of Colonial America.* Cambridge: Harvard University Press, 1967.

Gutierrez, Gustavo. *A Theology of Liberation.* Maryknoll NY: York: Orbis Books, 1973.

Halbrooks, G. Thomas, ed. *Pietism.* Nashville: Broadman Press, Christian Classics, 1981.

Hamilton, J. Taylor, and Hamilton, Kenneth G. *History of the Moravian Church: The Renewed Unitas Fratrum, 1722–1957.* Bethlehem PA: Moravian Church in America, Interprovincial Board of Christian Education, 1967.

Hansen, Marcus Lee. *The Atlantic Migration, 1607–1860.* Cambridge: Harvard University Press, 1945.

Hauge, Hans Nielsen. *Autobiographical Writings of Hans Nielsen Hauge.* Translated by Joel M. Njus. Minneapolis: Augsburg Publishing House, 1954.

Hay, Charles, ed. *Memoirs of Rev. Jacob Goering, Rev. George Lochman, D.D., and Rev. Benjamin Kurtz, D.D., L.L.D.* Philadelphia: Lutheran Publication Society, 1887.

Hazelius, Ernest L. *History of the American Lutheran Church, from Its Commencement in the Year of Our Lord 1685 to the Year 1842.* Zanesville OH: Edwin C. Church, 1846.

Heathcote, Charles William. *The Lutheran Church and the Civil War.* Burlington IA: Lutheran Literary Board, 1919.

Hefner, Philip J., ed. *The Future of the American Church.* Philadelphia: Fortress Press, 1968.

Hertz, Karl H., ed. *Two Kingdoms and One World: A Sourcebook in Christian Social Ethics.* Minneapolis: Augsburg Publishing House, 1976.

Heymann, Frederick C. *John Zizka and the Hussite Revolution.* Princeton NJ: Princeton University Press, 1955.

Hildebrandt, Franz. *Melanchthon: Alien or Ally?* London: Cambridge University Press, 1946.

Hinrichs, Carl. *Luther und Müntzer.* Berlin: Walter de Gruyter, 1952.

A History of the Lutheran Church In South Carolina. Prepared by the History of Synod Committee. South Carolina Synod of the Lutheran Church in America, 1971.

Hofstadter, Richard. *America at 1750: A Social Portrait.* New York: Alfred Knopf, 1971.

Jackson, Gregory Lee. *Prophetic Voice for the Kingdom.* Chicago: Augustana Historical Society, 1986.

Jacobs, Henry Eyster. *A History of the Evangelical Lutheran Church in the United States.* New York: Christian Literature, 1893.

Janson, Florence Edith. *The Background of Swedish Immigration, 1840–1930.* Chicago: University of Chicago Press, 1931. Reprint. New York: Arno Press, and New York Times, 1970.

Jensson, J. C. *American Lutheran Biographies. . . .* Milwaukee: Hautkamp & Son, 1890.

Johnson, Emeroy. *Eric Norelius: Pioneer Midwest Pastor and Churchman.* Rock Island IL: Augustana Book Concern, 1954.

Jones, George Fenwick. *The Saltzburger Saga: Religious Exiles and Other Germans along the Savannah.* Athens GA: University of Georgia Press, 1984.

Jones, Rufus M. *Spiritual Reformers in the Sixteenth and Seventeenth Centuries.* London: Macmillan, 1914.

Kammen, Michael. *Colonial New York: A History.* New York: Charles Scribner's Sons, 1975.

Knittle, Walter Allen. *Early Eighteenth Century Palatine Emigration: A British Redemptioner Project to Manufacture Naval Stores.* Philadelphia: Darrance, 1937.

Krauth, Charles Porterfield. *The Conservative Reformation and Its Theology.* 1871. Reprint. Minneapolis: Augsburg Publishing House, 1963.

Kreider, Harry J. *History of the United Lutheran Synod of New York and New England.* Vol. 1, *1786–1860.* Philadelphia: Muhlenberg Press, 1954.

_____. *Lutheranism in Colonial New York.* Ann Arbor MI: Edwards Brothers, 1942. Reprint. New York: Arno Press, 1972.

Kromminga, D. H. *The Millennium in the Church: Studies in the History of Christian Chiliasm.* Grand Rapids MI: Wm. B. Eerdmans Publishing, 1945.

Kuhns, Oscar. *The German and Swiss Settlements of Colonial Pennsylvania.* New York: Abingdon Pess, 1900.

Latourette, Kenneth Scott. *Three Centuries of Advance, 1500 A.D. to 1800 A.D.* vol. 3 of *A History of the Expansion of Christianity.* Grand Rapids MI: Zondervan Publishing House, 1970.

Lazareth, William H. *A Theology of Politics.* New York; Lutheran Church in America, Board of Social Ministry, 1960.

Lesick, Lawrence Thomas. *The Lane Rebels: Evangelicalism and Antislavery in Antebellum America.* Studies in Evangelicalism, vol. 2. Metuchen NJ: Scarecrow Press, 1980.

Lindberg, Carter. *The Third Reformation? Charismatic Movements and the Lutheran Tradition.* Macon GA: Mercer University Press, 1983.

Loetscher, Lefferts A. *Facing the Enlightenment and Pietism: Archibald Alexander and the Founding of Princeton Theological Seminary.* Westport CT: Greenwood Press, 1983.

Lovelace, Richard F. *The American Pietism of Cotton Mather: Origins of American Evangelicalism.* Grand Rapids MI: Christian University Press, 1979.

Lustig, Mary Lou. *Robert Hunter, 1666–1734: New York's Augustan Statesman.* Syracuse NY: Syracuse University Press, 1983.

McLoughlin, William G. *Revivals, Awakenings, and Reform.* Chicago: University of Chicago Press, 1978.

McManus, Edgar J. *A History of Negro Slavery in New York.* Foreword by Richard B. Morris. Syracuse NY: Syracuse University Press, 1966.

McSorley, Harry J. *Luther: Right or Wrong? An Ecumenical-Theological Study of Luther's Major Work, "The Bondage of the Will."* New York: Newman Press; Minneapolis: Augsburg Publishing House, 1969.

Manierre, William R., II, ed. *The Diary of Cotton Mather D.D., F.R.S., for the Year 1712.* Charlottesville: University Press of Virginia, 1967.

Mann, William J. *Life and Times of Henry Melchior Muhlenberg.* 2d ed. Philadelphia: General Council Publication House, 1911.

Mannheim, Karl. *Ideology and Utopia.* London: Harcourt Brace, 1949.

Manschreck, Clyde Leonard. *Melanchthon the Quiet Reformer.* New York: Abingdon Press, 1958.

Marsden, George C. *Fundamentalism and American Culture: The Shaping of Twentieth-Century Evangelicalism, 1870–1925.* New York: Oxford University Press, 1980.

Martin, James P. *The Last Judgment in Protestant Theology (from Orthodoxy to Ritschl).* Grand Rapids MI: W.B. Eerdmans Publishing, 1963.

Marty, Martin. *A Short History of Christianity.* Philadelphia: Fortress Press, 1959.

Mather, Cotton. *Bonifacius: An Essay upon the Good.* Edited by David Levin. Cambridge: Harvard University Press, Belknap Press, 1966

_____*Diary of Cotton Mather.* Vol. 2, 1709–1724. American Classics. New York: Frederick Ungar, n.d.

Mattice, P.B., ed. *The Palatines of New York State: A Complete Compilation of the History of the Palatines Who First Came to New York State in 1708–1722.* Johnstown NY: Palatine Society of the United Evangelical Lutheran Church of New York and New England, 1953.

Mattson, A.D. *The Social Responsibility of Christians.* Philadelphia: Muhlenberg Press, 1960.

May, Henry. *The Enlightenment in America.* New York: Oxford University Press, 1976.

Mehl, Roger, *Catholic Ethics and Protestant Ethics (Luther and Calvin).* Translated by James H. Farley. Philadelphia: Westminister Press, 1971.

Mol, J.J. *The Breaking of Traditions: Theological Convictions in Colonial America.* Berkley CA: Glendessary Press, 1968.

Moorhead, James H. *American Apocalypse: Yankee Protestants and the Civil War, 1860–1869.* New Haven CT: Yale University Press, 1978.

Morgan, Jacob L.; Brown, Bachman S., Jr.; and Hall, John, eds. *History of the Lutheran Church in North Carolina.* United Evangelical Lutheran Synod of North Carolina, 1953.

Morris, John G. *Fifty Years in the Lutheran Ministry.* Baltimore: Printed for the author by James Young, 1878.

_____. *The Life of John Arndt.* Baltimore: T. Newton Kurtz, 1853.

Mumford, Lewis. *The Story of Utopias.* Boni and Liverright, 1922. Reissued, with a new Introduction by the author. New York: Viking Press, 1962.

Nagler, Authur Wilford. *Pietism and Methodism; or, The Significance of German Pietism in the Origin and Early Development of Methodism.* Nashville: Publishing House M.E. Church, South, 1918.

Neslon, E. Clifford, ed. *The Lutherans in North America.* Philadelphia: Fortress Press, 1975; rev. ed., 1980.

Nelson, E. Clifford, and Fevol, Eugene L. *The Lutheran Church among Norwegian-Americans.* Minneapolis: Augsburg Publishing House, 1960.

Neve, J. L. *A Brief History of the Lutheran Church in America.* Burlington IA: German Literary Board, 1916.

Nicum, John. *The Doctrinal Development of the Evangelical Lutheran Ministerium of the State of New York.* New York: By the author, 1887.

Nodtvedt, Magnus. *Rebirth of Norway's Peasantry Folk Leader Hans Nielsen Hauge.* Tacoma WA: Pacific Lutheran Press, 1965.

Pascal, Roy R. *The Social Basis of the German Reformation: Martin Luther and His Times.* London: Watts, 1933.

Perry, Lewis, and Fellman, Michael, eds. *Antislavery Reconsidered: New Perspectives on the Abolitionists.* Baton Rouge: Louisiana University Press, 1979.

Pfatteicher, Helen E. *The Facts about the Muhlenbergs.* Philadelphia: Muhlenberg Press, 1942.

Pinson, Koppel S. *Pietism as a Factor in the Rise of German Nationalism.* New York: Columbia University Press, 1934.

Qualben, Lars P. *The Lutheran Church in Colonial America.* New York: Thomas Nelson & Sons, 1940.

Redding, Saunders Jay. *The Lonesome Road: The Story of the Negro's Part in America.* Mainstream of America Series. Garden City NY: Doubleday, 1958.

Richard, James William. *The Old Lutheran Doctrine of Free-Will.* N.p., n.d.

_____. *Philip Melanchthon: The Protestant Preceptor of Germany, 1497–1560.* New York: G. F. Putnam's Sons, Knickerbocker Press, 1898.

Richard, Merle E. *Philip Jacob Spener and His Work; August Hermann Francke and His Work.* Philadelphia: Lutheran Publication Society, 1897.

Richards, Leonard L. *Gentlemen of Property and Standing: Anti-Abolition Mobs in Jacksonian America.* New York: Oxford University Press, 1970.

Riforgiato, Leonard R. *Missionary of Moderation.* Lewisburg PA: Bucknell University Press, 1980.

Rohne, J. Magnus. *Norwegian American Lutheranism up to 1872.* New York: Macmillian, 1926.

Ronnegard, Sam. *Prairie Shepherd Lars Paul Esbjorn, and the Beginnings of the Augustana Lutheran Church.* Translated by G. Everett Arden. Rock Island IL: Augustana Book Concern, 1952.

Roscoe, William E. *History of Schoharie County, New York, with Illustrations and Biographical Sketches of Some of Its Prominent Men and Pioneers.* Syracuse NY: D. Mason, 1882.

Rosenius, C. O. *The Believer Free from the Law.* Translated by Adolf Hult. Rock Island IL: Augustana Book Concern, n. d.

Rouse, Ruth, and Neill, Stephan Charles, eds. *A History of the Ecumenical Movement, 1517–1948.* 1958. Philadelphia: Westminster Press, 1968 reprint.

Rowe, David D. *Thunder and Trumpets: Millerites and Dissenting Religion in Upstate New York, 1800–1850.* Chico CA: Scholars Press, 1947.

Rupp, Gordon. *Patterns of Reformation.* Philadelphia: Fortress Press, 1969. Contains a translation of "The Prague Manifesto," by Thomas Müntzer, pp. 175-78.

Sachse, Julius Friedrich. *The German Pietists of Provincial Pennsylvania.* 1895. Reprint. New York: AMS Press, 1970.

_____. *Justus Falckner, Mystic and Scholar.* Philadelphia: Printed for the author by New Era Printing, 1903.

Sandeen, Ernest R. *The Roots of Fundamentalism: British and American Millenarianism, 1800–1930.* Chicago: University of Chicago Press, 1970.

Sattler, Gary R. *God's Glory, Neighbor's Good.* Chicago: Covenant Press, 1982.

Schaff, Philip. *America.* New York: C. Scribner, 1855. Reprint, edited by Perry Miller. Cambridge: Harvard University Press, 1961.

Schmucker, Luke. *The Schmucker Family and the Lutheran Church in America.* N. p., 1937.

Schneider, Carl E. *The German Church on the American Frontier.* St. Louis: Eden Publishing House, 1939.

Seiss, Joseph A. *The Last Times and the Great Consummation: An Earnest Discussion of Momentous Themes.* Baltimore: T. Newton Kurz, 1856. Reprint. Philadelphia: Smith, English, 1867.

Shaw, Joseph M. *Pulpit Under the Sky: A Life of Hans Nielsen Hauge.* Minneapolis: Augsburg Publishing House, 1955. Reprint. Westport CT: Greenwood Press, 1979.

Silverman, Kenneth. *The Life and Times of Cotton Mather.* New York: Harper & Row, 1984.

_____. *Selected Letters of Cotton Mather.* Baton Rouge: Louisiana State University Press, 1971.

Simms, Jeptha R. *History of Schoharie County and Border Wars of New York.* Albany NY: Munsell & Tanner, 1845.

Singleton, George A. *The Romance of African Methodism: A Study of the African Methodist Episcopal Church.* New York: Exposition Press, 1952.

Smith, Timothy. *Revivalism and Social Reform*. Nashville: Abingdon Press, 1957.

Sorin, Gerald. *Abolitionism: A New Perspective*. Foreword by James P. Shenton. New York: Praeger Publishers, 1972.

——————. *The New York Abolitionists: A Case Study of Political Radicalism*. Contributions in American History Series, vol. 11. Westport CT: Greenwood Pub. Corp., 1971.

Spaude, Paul W. *The Lutheran Church under American Influence*. Burlington IA: Lutheran Literary Board, 1943.

Sprague, William B. *Annals of the American Pulpit*. Vol. 9. New York: Robert Carter & Bros., 1869.

Stange, Douglas C. *Radicalism for Humanity*. St. Louis: Oliver Slave, 1970.

Staudenraus, P. J. *The African Colonization Movement, 1816–1865*. New York: Columbia University Press, 1961.

Stayer, James. *Anabaptists and the Sword*. Lawrence KS: Coronado Press, 1972.

Stayer, James, and Packull, Werner O., ed. and trans. *The Anabaptists and Thomas Müntzer*. Dubuque IA: Kendall/Hunt Publishing, 1980.

Stein, K. James. *Philipp Jakob Spener, Pietist Patriarch*. Chicago: Covenant Press, 1986.

Stephenson, George M. *The Religious Aspects of Swedish Immigration*. Minneapolis: University of Minnesota, 1932. Reprint. New York: Arno Press, and New York Times, 1969.

Stoeffler, F. Ernest. *German Pietism during the Eighteenth Century*. Leiden: E. J. Brill, 1973.

——————. *The Rise of Evangelical Pietism*. Leiden: E. J. Brill, 1965.

Storr, Gottlof Christian, and Flatt, Karl Christian. *An Elementary Course of Biblical Theology*. 2 vols. Translated with additions by Samuel Simon Schmucker. Andover MA: Flagg and Gould, 1826.

Strobel, P. A. *Memorial Volume to Commemorate the Semi-Centennial Anniversary of the Hartwick Lutheran Synod of the State of New York . . .* Philadelphia: Lutheran Publication Society, 1881.

Strozier, Charles B. *Lincoln's Quest for Union: Public and Private Meanings*. New York: Basic Books, 1982.

Stuckenberg, J. H. W. *Christian Sociology*. 1880. Reprint. London: R. D. Dickinson, 1881.

——————. *History of the Augsburg Confession*. Philadelphia: Lutheran Publication Society, 1897.

Stump, Joseph. *The Christian Faith: A System of Christian Dogmatics.* Philadelphia: Muhlenberg Press, 1942.

Sweet, Leonard I., ed. *The Evangelical Tradition in America.* Macon GA: Mercer University Press, 1984.

Thompson, W. D. J. *The Political Thought of Martin Luther.* Edited by Philip Broadhead. Preface by A. G. Dickens. Sussex: Harvester Press, 1984.

Torrance, T. F. *Kingdom and Church: A Study in the Theology of the Reformation.* Edinburgh: Oliver & Boyd, 1956.

Troeltsch, Ernest. *The Social Teaching of the Christian Churches.* Translated by Olive Wyon. London: George Allen & Unwin, 1931; 4th ed., 1956.

Tuveson, Ernest Lee. *Millennium and Utopia: A Study in the Background of the Idea of Progress.* Berkeley: University of California Press, 1949.

_____. *Redeemer Nation: The Idea of America's Millennial Role.* Chicago: University of Chicago Press, 1968.

Vann, James Allen. *The Making of a State: Württemberg, 1593–1793.* Ithaca NY: Cornell University Press, 1984.

Visser, Derk, ed. *Controversy and Conciliation: The Reformation and the Palatinate, 1559–1583.* Allison Park PA: Pickwick Publications, 1986.

Walker, Mack. *Germany and the Emigration, 1816–1885.* Cambridge: Harvard University Press, 1964.

Wallace, Paul A. W. *The Muhlenbergs of Pennsylvania.* Philadelphia: University of Pennsylvania Press, 1950.

Warneck, Gustav. *Outline of a History of Protestant Missions from the Reformation to the Present Time.* Authorized translation from the 7th German edition by George Robson. New York: Fleming H. Revell, 1903.

Weiser, Frederick S., ed. *Johan Friederich Weisers Buch Containing the Autobiography of John Conrad Weiser, 1696–1760.* Hanover PA: John Conrad Weiser Family Association, 1976.

Wenner, George U. *The Lutherans of New York: Their Story and Their Problems.* New York: Petersfield Press, 1918.

Wentz, Abdel Ross. *A Basic History of Lutheranism in America.* Philadelphia: Muhlenberg Press, 1955.

_____. *History of Gettysburg Theological Seminary, 1826–1926.* 2 vols. Philadelphia: United Lutheran Publication House, 1927. Reprint. Harrisburg PA: Evangelical Press, 1965.

_____. *Pioneer in Christian Unity, Samuel Simon Schmucker.* Philadelphia: Fortress Press, 1967.

Wildenhahn, A. *Pictures from Life. Philipp Jacob Spener. A Historical Life Picture.* Translated by G. A. Wenzel. Edited by J. K. Shryock. Easton PA: M. J. Riegel, 1881.

Williams, George H. *The Radical Reformation.* Philadelphia: Westminster Press, 1962.

Williams, George Huntson, and Mergal, Angel M., eds. *Spiritual and Anabaptist Writers.* Library of Christian Classics, vol. 25. Philadelphia: Westminster Press, 1957.

Wolf, Edmund Jacob. *The Lutherans in America: A Story of Struggle, Progress, Influence, and Marvelous Growth.* New York: J. A. Hill, 1890.

Wyatt-Brown, Bertram. *Lewis Tappan and the Evangelical War against Slavery.* Cleveland: Press of Case Western Reserve University, 1969.

Yoder, Don, ed. *Rhineland Emigrants.* Baltimore: Genealogical Publishing, 1985.

Zuck, Lowell H., ed. *Christianity and Revolution: Radical Christian Testimonies, 1525–1650.* Philadelphia: Temple University Press, 1975.

Articles

Ahlstrom, Sydney E. "Facing the New World: Augustana and the American Challenge." In *Centennial Essays: Augustana Lutheran Church, 1860–1960,* edited by Emmer Engberg, 1-27. Rock Island IL: Augustana Press, 1960.

_____. "The Lutheran Church and American Culture: A Tercentary Retrospect." *Lutheran Quarterly* 9 (1959): 321-42.

Bachmann, E. Theodore. "Samuel Simon Schmucker (1799-1873), Lutheran Educator." In *Sons of the Prophets: Leaders in Protestantism from Princeton Seminary,* edited by Hugh Thomson Kerr, 39-68. Princeton NJ: Princeton University Press, 1963.

Bailey, Richard. "The Sixteenth Century's Apocalyptic Heritage and Thomas Müntzer." *Mennonite Quarterly Review* 57 (January 1983): 27-44.

Balge, Richard D. "Pietism's Teaching on Church and Ministry As Evidenced in Its Pastoral Practice." *Wisconsin Lutheran Quarterly* 82 (Fall 1985): 248-62.

Bentley, William H. "Bible Believers in the Black Community." In *The Evangelicals: What They Believe, Who They Are, Where They Are Changing,* edited by David F. Wells and John D. Woodbridge, 108-21. Nashville: Abingdon Press, 1975.

Benz, Ernst. "Ecumenical Relations between Boston Puritanism and German Pietism: Cotton Mather and August Hermann Francke." *Harvard Theological Review* 54 (1961): 159-93.

_____. "Pietist and Puritan Sources of Early Protestant World Missions." *Church History* 20 (June 1951): 28-55.

Billington, Louis. "Popular Religion and Social Reform: A Study of Revivalism and Teetotalism, 1830–1850." *Journal of Religious History* 10 (June 1979): 266-93.

Bornkamm, Heinrich. "An Exposition of Luther's Doctrine of the Two Kingdoms." In *Reformation and Authority: The Meaning of the Peasant's Revolt*, edited by Kyle C. Sessions, 40-46. Lexington MA: Heath, 1968.

Bowers, Mary S. "The Life and Times of Rev. Philip Wieting." *Schoharie County Historical Review* 20 (May 1956): 3-7.

Brady, James A. Review of *Freidrich der Weise, Kurfürst von Sachsen, 1463–1525*, by Ingetraut Ludolphy. *Sixteenth Century Journal* 17 (Summer 1986): 251-52.

Brauer, Jerald C. "His Church and His World." In *The Scope of Grace*, edited by Philip Hefner, 259-77. Philadelphia: Fortress Press, 1964.

Brown, Dale. "Anabaptism and Pietism: Theological Definitions in Historical Perspective." *Covenant Quarterly* 28 (1970): 117-27.

"Church Feeling in the Lutheran Church." Editorial signed "Y.S.R." *Evangelical Review* 2 (January 1851): 390-401.

Coalter, Milton J., Jr. "The Radical Pietism of Count Nicholas Zinzendorf as a Conservative Influence on the Awakener Gilbert Tennent." *Church History* 49 (March 1980): 35-46.

Cobb, Sanford H. "The Palatine or German Immigration to New York and Pennsylvania," 5ff. Paper read before the Wyoming Historical and Geological Society. Printed for the society, Wilkes-Barre PA, 1897.

Cobbler, Michael Lee. "What Price Inclusion?" *Mt. Airy Parish Practice Notebook* 19 (Summer 1982): 1-16.

"The Confession of the Evangelical Lutheran Church." Article 2 *Evangelical Review* 5 (October 1853): 189-213.

Conrad, F. W. "Ministers of the Gospel, the Moral Watchmen of Nations." *Evangelical Quarterly Review* 16 (1865): 366-93.

Davis, David Brion. "The Emergence of Immediatism in British and American Antislavery Thought." *Mississippi Valley Historical Review* 49 (September 1962): 217-18.

Deeter, Allen C. "Pietism, Moralism, and Social Concern." *Covenant Quarterly* 33 (May 1975): 19-39.

Drummond, Andrew W. "The Divine and Mortal Worlds of Thomas Müntzer." *Archiv für Reformationsgeschichte* 71 (1980): 99-111.

Duke, James O. "Pietism versus Establishment: The Halle Phase." *Covenant Quarterly* 36 (November 1978): 3-16.

Editorial. *Evangelical Review* 7 (October 1855): 234-44.

Ehrehart, C. J. "Emmaus Orphan House." *Evangelical Review* 12 (April 1861): 586-87.

Fevold, Eugene L. "The Development of Norwegian-American Lutheranism in the Upper Midwest." In *The Lutheran Historical Conference: Essays and Reports, 1984*, 99-109. St. Louis: Lutheran Historical Conference.

Flesner, Dorris A. "The Beginning of English Lutheranism in the Upper Midwest." In *The Lutheran Historical Conference: Essays and Reports, 1984*, 43-69. St. Louis Lutheran Historical Conference.

Fortenbaugh, Robert. "American Lutheran Synods and Slavery, 1830-1860." *Journal of Religion* 13 (1933): 72-92.

_____. "The Representative Lutheran Periodical Press and Slavery, 1831–1860." *Lutheran Church Quarterly* 8 (1935): 151-71.

Fraenkel, Peter. "Ten Questions concerning Melanchthon, the Fathers, and the Eucharist." In *Luther and Melanchthon*, edited by Vilmos Vajta. Göttingen: Vandenhoeck & Ruprecht, 1961.

Francke, Kuno. "Cotton Mather and August Herman Francke." In *Studies and Notes in Philology and Literature*, vol. 5. Boston: Ginn, 1896.

Frederich, Edward C. "The Legacy of Pietism." *Wisconsin Lutheran Quarterly* 82 (Winter 1985): 3-4.

_____. "Lutheran Pietism Comes to America." *Wisconsin Lutheran Quarterly* 81 (Fall 1985): 263-72.

Friedman, Lawrence J. "Confidence and Pertinacity in Evangelical Abolitionism: Lewis Tappan's Circle." *American Quarterly* 31 (Spring 1979): 81-106.

Friesen, Abraham. "Thomas Müntzer and the Old Testament." *Mennonite Quarterly Review* 47 (1973): 5-19.

Gerdes, Egon. "Pietism: Classical and Modern." *Concordia Theological Monthly* 39 (April 1968): 257-68.

"Gettysburg Seminary Baccalaureate Address." *Evangelical Review* 11 (October 1859): 284-89.

Ginzberg, Lori D. " 'Moral Suasion Is Moral Balderdash': Women, Politics, and Social Activism in the 1850's." *Journal of American History* 73 (December 1986): 601-21.

Goen, G. C. "Broken Churches, Broken Nation: Regional Religion and North-South Alienation in Antebellum America." *Church History* 52 (March 1983): 29-35.

Greschat, Martin. "Die 'Hoffnung besserer Zeiten' für die Kirche." In *Zur neueren Pietismusforschung*, vol. 440, ed. Martin Greschat, 224-39. Darmstadt: Wissenschaftliche Buchgesellschaft, 1977.

Hall, George F. "Luther's Eschatology." *Augustana Quarterly* 23 (1944): 13-19.

Harless, Dr. "Christianity and Politics." Translated by G. A. Wenzel. *Evangelical Review* 14 (January 1863): 243-58.

Hefner, Philip. "The Real Challenge of the Nineteenth Century." *Dialog* 22 (Winter 1983): 35-41.

Hertz, Karl H. Letter to the Editor. *Lutheran*, 19 September 1984, 33.

Hirsch, Emmanuel. "Schwenckfeld und Luther." In *Lutherstudien*, 2, edited by S. Kortemeier, 35-67. Gütersloh: Bertelsmann, 1954.

Hoffman, J. N. "The Symbols." *Evangelical Review* 2 (January 1851): 402-409.

Hoskins, J. P. "German Influence on Religious Life and Thought in America during the Colonial Period." *Princeton Theological Review* 5 (1907): 225-27.

"Introductory: The Objects and Position of the Evangelical Review." *Evangelical Review* 1 (July 1849): 16-18.

Jacobs, Henry E. "The Confessional Problem in the Lutheran Church of America in 1742." *Lutheran Church Review* 31 (April 1912): 245-52.

_____. "The Confessional Reaction in the General Synod in the Nineteenth Century." *Lutheran Church Review* 31 (1912): 154-56.

Johnson, Jeff G. "Black Lutherans in the New World." *Cresset* 47 (February 1984): 8-13.

Jordahl, Leigh D. "Schmucker and Walther: A Study of Christian Response to American Culture." In *The Future of the American Church*, edited by Philip J. Hefner, 71-90. Philadelphia: Fortress Press, 1968.

Kiwiet, Jan J. "The Theology of Hans Denck." *Mennonite Quarterly Review* 32 (1958): 3-27.

Klassen, Herbert. "The Life and Teachings of Hans Hut." *Mennonite Quarterly Review* 33 (July 1959): 171-205.

Klein, Crista R. "General Synod Shaped by America." *Lutheran Standard* 6 (February 1987): 13.

Kohl, Manfred W. "Pietism as a Movement of Revival." *Covenant Quarterly* 32 (August 1975): 3-23.

Kreider, Harry J. "Negro Lutheran Work in New York." *Lutheran Church Quarterly* 20 (July 1947): 261-71.

_____. "New York Synod Convention in Wisconsin, 1860." *Lutheran Church Quarterly* 19 (October 1946): 408-11.

Kuenning, Paul P. "Luther and Müntzer: Contrasting Theologies in Regard to Secular Authority within the Context of the German Peasant Revolt." *Journal of Church and State* 29 (Spring 1987): 305-21.

_____. "Thomas Müntzer: Theologian and Rebel with a Cause." *Covenant Quarterly* 44 (November 1986): 3-23.

Lane, Belden C. "Miller and the Eldership: A Knickerbocker Goes to Nassau." *Princeton Seminary Bulletin*, n.s. 6 (1985): 211-15.

Lindberg, Carter. "A Response to Hans-Jürgen Goertz on History and Theology." *Mennonite Quarterly Review* 53 (July 1979): 189-92.

Mackay, John A. "Archibald Alexander." In *Sons of the Prophets*, edited by Hugh Thomson Kerr, 1-21. Princeton NJ: Princeton University Press, 1963.

McLoughlin, R. Emment. "Spiritualism and the Bible: The Case of Caspar Schwenckfeld." *Mennonite Quarterly Review* 53 (October 1979): 282-98.

McLoughlin, William G. "Pietism and the American Character." *American Quarterly* 17 (Summer 1965): 163-86.

Mann, William J. "Lutherans in America before Muhlenberg." *Lutheran Church Review* 6 (1887): 93-114.

Mattson, Karl E. "The Theology of the Augustana Lutheran Church." In *Centennial Essays: Augustana Lutheran Church, 1860-1960*, edited by Emmer Engberg, 27-42. Rock Island IL: Augustana Press, 1960.

Mehl, Robert. "The Basis of Christian Social Ethics." In *Christian Social Ethics in a Changing World: An Ecumenical Theological Inquiry*, edited by John C. Bennett, 44-58. New York: Association Press, 1966.

Mellick, Andrew D., Jr. "German Emigration to the American Colonies, Its Cause, and the Distribution of the Emigrants." *Pennsylvania Magazine of History and Biography* 10 (July 1886): 241-50; (October 1886): 375-91.

Muhlenberg, F. A. "Educational Efforts of the Pennsylvania Synod." *Evangelical Review* 10 (April 1859): 530-63.

Murphy, Larry. "Apocalypse and Millennium in America." *Explor* 4 (Spring 1978): 58-65.

Noon, Thomas R. "Daniel Payne and the Lutherans." *Concordia Historical Institute Quarterly* 53 (Summer 1980): 51-69.

Nothstein, O. "The History of Lutheranism in Illinois." *Augustana Quarterly* 27 (July 1948): 238-41.

Packull, Werner. "Gottfried Seebass on Hans Hut: A Discussion." *Mennonite Quarterly Review* 49 (January 1975): 57-67.

"Patriarchs of the Lutheran Church from Halle." *Evangelical Review* 15 (April 1864): 159-90.

"The Pietistic Controversy." *Quarterly Review of the Evangelical Lutheran Church* (April 1874): 278-301.

"The Present Position of the Lutheran Church." *Evangelical Review* 11 (July 1859): 11-43.

Prout, William Cardwell. "Spener and the Theology of Pietism." *Mennonite Quarterly Review* 28 (1954): 46-49.

Rauschenbusch, Walter, trans. "Letter of Conrad Grebel and Friends to Thomas Müntzer." *American Journal of Theology* 9 (January 1905): 94-96.

"Reminiscences of Deceased Lutheran Ministers: Ernest Lewis Hazelius, D.D." *Evangelical Review* 4 (January 1856): 385-86.

"Report on General Synod, Seventeenth Session, June 14, 1855, Dayton, Ohio." *Evangelical Review* 7 (July 1855): 129-30.

Richard, J. W. "The Confessional History of the General Synod." *Lutheran Quarterly* 25 (October 1895): 458-90.

Ritschl, Albrecht. "Prolegomena to the History of Pietism." In *Three Essays*, translated by Philip Hefner, 51-147. Philadelphia: Fortress Press, 1972.

Ritter, John N. "Muhlenberg's Anticipation of Psychosomatic Medicine." *Lutheran Church Quarterly* 19 (April 1946): 181-88.

Ronnegard, Sam. "The Religious Movements in Northern Sweden a Hundred Years Ago and the Augustana Synod." *Augustana Quarterly* 27 (July 1948): 224-27, 230-32.

Sachse, Julius F. "The Influence of Halle Pietism in the Provincial Development of Pennsylvania." *Lutheran Quarterly* 31 (April 1901): 170-76.

Schlabach, Theron F. "Mennonites and Pietism in America, 1740–1880: Some Thoughts on the Friedmann Thesis." *Mennonite Quarterly Review* 57 (July 1983): 222-40.

Schmidt, Martin. "Ecumenical Activity on the Continent of Europe in the 17th and 18th Centuries." In *A History of the Ecumenical Movement, 1517–1948*, edited by Ruth Rouse and Stephen Charles Neill, 99-105. Reprint. Philadelphia: Westminster Press, 1968.

_____. "Spener und Luther." *Luther Jahrbuch* 24 (1957): 102-29. Berlin: Lutherische Verlaghaus.

Schuchard, C. G. "A Critical Estimate of Henry Melchior Muhlenberg in the Development of the American Lutheran Church." *Lutheran Church Review* 46 (1927): 373-90.

Schwab, J. C. "German Antecedents and Elements in the Making of Henry Melchior Muhlenberg." *Lutheran Church Review* 31 (1912): 82-87.

Sernett, Milton C. "Lutheran Abolitionism in New York State: A Problem in Historical Explication." In *Essays and Reports, 1982,* 16-37. St. Louis: Lutheran Historical Conference, 1984.

Seyffarth, Gustav. "Chiliasm, Critically Examined according to the Statements of the New and Old Testaments, with Reference to the Most Recent Theory of the Millennium." *Evangelical Review* 12 (January 1861): 341-400.

Sherman, Franklin. "The Vital Center: Toward a Chalcedonian Social Ethic." In *The Scope of Grace,* edited by Philip Hefner, 231-56. Philadelphia: Fortress Press, 1964.

Skarsten, Trygve R. "The Doctrine of Justification in Classical Lutheran Pietism: A Revisionist Perspective." *Trinity Seminary Review* 2 (Fall 1981): 20-29.

Smith, Gerrit. "Reply to Rev. Dr. Samuel S. Schmucker." *Pennsylvania Freeman,* 19 June 1838.

Solberg, Winton U. "Science and Religion in Early America: Cotton Mather's *Christian Philosopher.*" *Church History* 56 (March 1987): 73-92.

Sparks, C. E. "The Development of the General Synod of the Lutheran Church in America." *Lutheran Quarterly* 36 (October 1906): 582-84.

Springer, Francis. "Lutheranism in the United States." *Evangelical Review* 11 (July 1859): 99; 106-109.

_____. "Our General Synod." *Evangelical Review* 11 (July 1859): 129-30.

Staiger, C. Bruce. "Abolitionism and the Presbyterian Schism of 1837–1838." *Mississippi Valley Historical Review* 36 (December 1949): 391-414.

Stange, Douglas. "Bishop Daniel A. Payne and the Lutheran Church." *Lutheran Church Quarterly* 16 (1964): 354-59.

_____. "The 125th Anniversary of Fraternal Appeal." *Concordia Historical Institute Quarterly* 40 (1967): 43.

Stayer, James. "The Swiss Brethren: An Exercise in Historical Definition." *Church History* 47 (1978): 191-93.

_____. "Thomas Müntzer's Theology of Revolution in Recent Non-Marxist Interpretation." *Mennonite Quarterly Review* 43 (April 1969): 142-52.

Stein, K. James. "Philipp Jakob Spener's Hope for Better Times for the Church: Contribution in Controversy." *Covenant Quarterly* 37 (August 1979): 3-20.

Sternberg, L. "Revivals." *Evangelical Quarterly Review* 15 (1864): 273-92.

Stoeffler, F. Ernest. "Can These Bones live?" *Christian History* 5 (1986): 9-12.

Stoever, Martin L. "Reminiscences of Lutheran Clergymen." *Evangelical Review* 6 (October 1854): 261-68; 7 (April 1855): 538-44; (October 1855): 152-73.

Sweet, W. W. "The Churches as Moral Courts of the Frontier." *Church History* 2 (1933): 3-21.

Syrdal, Rolf A. "Hauge's (1846) Lay Evangelism Builds a Missionary Church: What Is the Proper Role of Lay Activity?" In *Church Roots: Stories of Nine Immigrant Groups That Became the American Lutheran Church*, edited by Charles P. Lutz, 60-81. Minneapolis: Augsburg Publishing House, 1985.

Tappert, Theodore G. "The Muhlenberg Tradition in the Nineteenth Century." *Lutheran Church Quarterly* 15 (1942): 394-403.

Thompson, Bard. "The Palatinate Church Order of 1563." *Church History* 23 (December 1954): 339-51.

Volf, Miroslav. "Interview with Jürgen Moltmann." *Christian Century* 100 (16 March 1983): 248.

Weborg, Charles John. "Pietism: The Fire of God Which Flames in the Heart of Germany." In *Protestant Spiritual Traditions*, edited by Frank C. Senn, 183-216. New York: Paulist Press, 1986.

Weigelt, H. "Interpretations of Pietism in the Research of Contemporary German Church Historians." *Church History* 39 (June 1970): 236-41.

Weiser, R. "A Want in the Lutheran Church Met by the Founding of the Missionary Institute." *Evangelical Quarterly Review* 10 (1858–1859): 332-47.

Weng, Armin George. "The Language Problem in the Lutheran Church in Pennsylvania, 1742-1820." *Church History* 5 (1936): 359-75.

Wentz, Abdel Ross. "Relations between the Lutheran and Reformed Churches in the Eighteenth and Nineteenth Centuries." *Lutheran Church Quarterly* 6 (1933): 301-27.

_____. "The Work of Samuel Simon Schmucker." *Lutheran Quarterly* 57 (January 1927): 68-85.

Wynn, W. H. "Dr. Samuel Sprecher, Philosopher, College President, and Man of God: An Appreciation." *Lutheran Quarterly* 36 (April 1906): 281-93.

Ziegler, Henry. "Politics and the Pulpit." *Evangelical Review* 16 (April 1865): 245-58.

UNPUBLISHED SOURCES

Anderson, Hugh George. "A Social History of Lutheranism in the Southeastern States (1860–1886)." Ph.D. diss., University of Pennsylvania, 1962.

Beck, Nestor. "Faith and Works: A Study of Articles IV-VI and XX of the Augsburg Confession (1530)." Ph.D. diss., Concordia Lutheran Seminary, 1973.

Bost, Raymond. "The Rev. John Bachman and the Development of Southern Lutheranism." Ph.D. diss., Yale University, 1963.

Brown, Dale Weaver. "The Problem of Subjectivism in Pietism: A Redefinition with Special Reference to the Theology of Philipp Jakob Spener and August Hermann Francke." Ph.D. diss., Garrett Theological Seminary and Northwestern University, 1962.

Conner, George. "The Influence of German Pietism on American Religious Thought and Practice." Master's thesis, McCormick Theological Seminary, 1947.

Haney, James Lawton. "The Religious Heritage and Education of Samuel Simon Schmucker: A Study in the Rise of 'American Lutheranism.' " Ph.D. diss., Yale University, 1968.

Lentz, Harold. "History of the Social Gospel in the General Synod of the Lutheran Church in America." Ph.D. diss., Yale University, 1943.

Maulshagen, Carl. "American Lutheranism Surrenders to Forces of Conservatism." Ph.D. diss., University of Minnesota, 1936.

Monseth, Francis W. "Millennialism in American Lutheranism in the Light of Augsburg Confession, Article XVII." Th.D. dissertation, Concordia Lutheran Seminary, 1986.

Nelson, Harvey L. "A Critical Study of Henry Melchior Muhlenberg's Means of Maintaining His Lutheranism." Ph.D. diss., Drew University, 1980.

Schrag, Felix James. "Pietism in Colonial America." Ph.D. diss., University of Chicago, 1948.

Svendsbye, Lloyd. "The History of a Developing Social Responsibility among Lutherans in America from 1930 to 1960, with Reference to the American Lutheran Church, the Augustana Lutheran Church, and the United Lutheran Church in America." Th.D. diss., Union Theological Seminary, 1966.

Underdahl, Eldon J. "The Social Thought of J. H. W. Stuckenberg, a Late Nineteenth Century Social Scientist." Master's thesis, Lutheran Theological Seminary, Minneapolis, 1969.

Weborg, Charles John. "The Eschatological Ethics of Johann Albrecht Bengel: Personal and Ecclesial Piety and the Literature of Edification in the Letters to the Seven Churches in Revelation 2 and 3." Ph.D. diss., Garrett Theological Seminary and Northwestern University, 1983.

INDEX

 *The Rise and Fall of American Lutheran Pietism*

Typography designed by Margaret Jordan Brown
Composition by Mercer University Press Composition Department
Dust jacket and binding designed by Alesa Jones

Production Specifications:
text paper—50 lb. Glatfelter's Natural, smooth finish
    endpapers—Rainbow Antique Cerulean
    covers (on .88 boards)—Holliston Roxite B-grade cloth #53525, linen
        finish
    dust jacket—80 lb. C-1-S, printed PMS 293 (blue), PMS 120 (yellow), and
        film laminated

Printing (offset lithography) and binding by Braun-Brumfield, Inc., Ann Arbor MI